A JOURNEY INTO PLATONIC POLITICS

Plato's *Laws*

Albert Keith Whitaker

University Press of America,® Inc.
Lanham · Boulder · New York · Toronto · Oxford

Copyright © 2004 by
University Press of America,® Inc.
4501 Forbes Boulevard
Suite 200
Lanham, Maryland 20706
UPA Acquisitions Department (301) 459-3366

PO Box 317
Oxford
OX2 9RU, UK

Library of Congress Control Number: 2003111404
ISBN 0-7618-2689-0 (paperback : alk. ppr.)

Contents

Acknowledgments

Any lengthy expedition requires much preparation, encouragement, and support, and mine through the *Laws* is no exception. I owe thanks to Dr. Leon R. Kass, MD who first showed me the way to the *Laws* and who, with his gentle yet incisive questions, helped guide my initial explorations. My gratitude also extends to the Jacob Javits Fellowship Program and the Olin Center for the Study of Democracy at the University of Chicago, which funded my graduate study of Plato's work. The production of this guide to the *Laws* would have been impossible without the bountiful support of the National Association of Scholars and John M. Olin Foundation's Junior Faculty Fellowship. I am also grateful to the Dean of Arts and Sciences at Boston College for an undergraduate research fellowship, and to Craig Fessenden, my research fellow, who read and commented on a previous draft of this work. Finally, I am most thankful to the students with whom, in the Fall of 2000, I spent 15 weeks discussing the *Laws*, and who offered many inspired responses to this material. This book is written, first and foremost, for students, and I have always kept them in mind.

Introduction

Nathaniel Hawthorne tells the story of a man named Peter Goldthwaite who got it into his head that one of his ancestors had secreted a treasure of gold coins in the walls of his familial mansion. This dream of ancestral wealth kept Peter from pursuing any useful occupation; eventually it even drove him to ripping out the walls of his spacious home in order to discover his imaginary inheritance. In the process, since he had no way of keeping his hearth warm or his stove lit, Peter gladly burned up the debris from his excavations, always assuming that his eventual discovery would more than cover the costs of a new home. In this way, as Hawthorne observes, Peter's house slowly went up in smoke through its own chimney.

There is a way of philosophizing, of pursuing wisdom, which closely resembles Peter Goldthwaite's misguided quest. Peter considered himself, as crazy people often do, the very soul of rationality—a presumption not unknown among would-be philosophers. The prize that some of these thinkers pursue, analogous to Peter Goldthwaite's treasure, is the "logos of life," the reasoned account of living, the explanation—formed on the basis of reason alone—why this life (the philosophic life) is the very best life for a human being to live.

There is no shortage of opinions about how human beings should live; maybe there are even "one thousand and one," as one philosopher put it. But where is the reasoned account, the scientific defense of the one right way to live? It is, these thinkers say, boarded up and plastered over by those pervasive opinions. Tear down the opinions, smash them with reason's sledgehammer, burn them up in the furnace of the intellect, and— if one has the nerves for it—one will find the truth. But these opinions are the traditions, the allegiances, and the standards which give all other human beings their intellectual and moral home. No matter, respond the cerebral cousins of Peter Goldthwaite: up the flue they go.

Unfortunately, such activity, pursued under the banner of "reason," soon leaves one standing in a moral ruin. The attempt, in vogue since the days of Descartes, to shine a light through the shadows of opinion, assumption, belief, or faith has not improved our vision; it leads rather to blindness. One does not come to understand life by eagerly trying to refute all beliefs about justice or love or God; instead, such an attempt threatens life, and hence understanding. And this is not a speculative hypothesis. As unwanted is the tyranny of unreason, the tyranny of reason provides no escape. Reason's attempt to make itself sovereign, to ground itself, to provide, to prove—through "critique" of one sort or another—the rightness of some particular way of life or way of politics has, directly or indirectly, spawned every radical political movement, every attempt to modernize or naturalize or globalize the human race, all the would be "solutions"—final or otherwise—to age-old "problems," in short, every sort of "Idealism" (and "Realism") that has tortured humanity over the last two hundred years. Reason's rule amounts to unreason unbounded.

But how can studying Plato's *Laws* provide any sort of response, even a very modest one, to this unhappy situation? The *Laws* depicts a conversation between a stranger from Athens—apparently a philosopher—and two politicians, one from Crete and the other from Sparta. All three are old men. Their conversation is about politics, indeed, about a new city that the Cretan legislator must soon found (see 702b-c). While they talk, they travel up the side of Mount Ida to the cave and temple of Zeus, seeking, it seems, the god's blessing on this political endeavor. In short, their words and deeds seem worlds away from those of the 21st century West. They pursue politics under divine oversight and perhaps even divine guidance. They propose laws that would punish impiety, that would make marriage mandatory, that would allow slavery, and that would put strict limits upon the making and spending of money.

So, why join these illiberal old Greeks in their journey and hover, listening, at the edge of their conversation? Certainly we have no need of another example of an "expert" trying to subject politics to the rule of his "reason." Nor need we look to the *Laws* as a whole as a "blueprint" for founding a new political system, even though many readers—Aristotle (4th century BC), Plotinus (3rd century AD), Plethon (15th century), even most scholars at the present—have taken it as such. But both of these characterizations exaggerate and distort the substance of the book. As will be seen, the characters of the *Laws* do anything but tear down their moral and intellectual home. Rather, they take a house that is in some state of disrepair and do the best that they can—recognizing reason as a tool of limited power—to improve it and dress it to advantage. They provide an example, then, of sober, restrained reasoning about political and individual life.

Thus one should not take up the *Laws* as a plan for a new society nor as a means to critique one's own nation and its customs. Indeed, the *Laws* benefits most those readers who are comfortable in their love for and allegiance to the standards and institutions of their time and place. Perhaps this claim sounds surprising. But it should surprise only those who believe that love and loyalty are deep set obstacles to thought and reflection. In contrast, such attachments, and not their facile critique, are precisely what leads us to take a healthy interest in and reflect fruitfully upon other people's ways. The characters of the *Laws* recognize this truth as well. They recommend that the highest body of the new city, a council of thinkers and legislators, young and old, should regularly send spies to other nations, to search out the "beauties" in their foreign habits, beauties that might—or might not—be able to be transplanted back to the council's city (951b-953c).

The following study of the *Laws* attempts to do something of the same thing, to treat Plato's dialogue as, in effect, a foreign country, through which readers are led as if they were on a mission for our own Nocturnal Council. Just as such a mission could not detail every facet of the foreign land and the life of its people, so too this book does not claim to expound the meaning of every statement in the *Laws*. It is not a thorough commentary on the text; it aims at the "beauties," or at least at the most salient points, of the dialogue's twelve books, all in an attempt to hold up the sober and restrained political reasoning of the *Laws* as a worthy example. This work also largely omits intrusive references to that of other scholars, not because these travellers do not offer insights of their own, but because such references might obstruct the view of first-time visitors to the *Laws*, especially that of students.[1] Finally, such a mission should explain to readers why they will find in this book prominent references to modern controversies and institutions as well as extensive comparisons of the *Laws'* institutions with those of modern nations. The ambassadors from the Nocturnal Council would presumably never forget where they came from.

It would be silly to deny, of course, that part of the joy of such a mission is to get away, for a time, from one's familiar haunts, to shake off, for a while, the dust of old habits, to take a glimpse of the world through a completely foreign medium. (Still, such enjoyment always depends upon the presumption that, at some point, one will return.) However, an enduring and serious study seeks roots deeper than momentary pleasure, great as it may be. It is at least in part because one loves one's own nation, with all its excellence and its limitations, that one studies others' customs. It is at least in part because one love's one's own home—even if it has drafty doors and noisy plumbing—that one enjoys walking down the street and peeking into others' windows.

It is not through reason that we get hold of the greatest truths or realities in our lives. Someone may, if he has the taste for it, apply his intellect to these truths, with the result of shedding more or less light upon them (depending upon his nature—and theirs). But it makes as much sense for someone to claim to 'ground' or to 'establish' or to 'prove' these truths through the use of reason alone, as it would for a hungry man to try to feed himself by jumping down his own throat, or as it did for Peter Goldthwaite to build himself a lasting home by stuffing his present one, plank by plank, up its own chimney. If he is suited for it, one does no harm by accepting reason's arm and by touring other men's lands and domiciles; the harm comes when he imagines that it is best to become reason's vagabond, and to forget (or repudiate) himself and his home.

Note

[1] Also for the benefit of students (and their teachers) this book includes a number of appendices. These offer study questions and selected outside readings geared to each book of the *Laws*, as well as a "map" of the dialogue as a whole.

Chapter One:
The End of the Road

God

This chapter begins with the same word with which the *Laws* begins: God. In front of the characters of this dialogue lies a mountain road leading from a city to a mountainous holy place. In front of us, the readers of the dialogue, lies the word "God." From the very beginning Plato artfully tries to put his readers into the shoes, so to speak, of his characters. For both them and us, the journey into Platonic politics begins with "God," and it remains unintelligible unless we always keep in mind the presence of the divine.

The Cave

As in any drama, the characters of this dialogue emerge as part of a scene. In this case, dawn is just breaking over the Aegean Sea and beginning to illuminate Knossos, the greatest city in Crete, an island half-way between the youthful city-states of Greece and the ancient kingdom of Egypt. On the dusty road from the city to the plains below Mount Ida two figures can be seen slowly climbing the path. One has the long hair, black staff, and drab clothing characteristic of a Spartan. The other is clearly a Cretan, a smaller, darker, shrewd looking fellow. Both are quite elderly. Then, from the Cypresses beside the road, a foreign voice hails the two, the voice of a stranger from Athens. He approaches, old as well, but with a much sprightlier step than the other two; his darting eyes are set comically towards the side of his balding head, from the middle of which pokes a snub nose. The three old men greet each other and continue on the road, a road that leads up the mountain and ultimately to the cave of Zeus.[1]

Let us, for a moment, leave these elderly travellers behind and fly ahead to the object of their journey—over the fields of grape and olive, past the thick groves of cypresses and even oak trees, above the dry and rocky foothills of Ida, over the graceful highland plateau of Nida with its shepherds and their flocks, and finally, beneath the summit, but nearly five thousand feet above sea-level, to the cave of Idaean Zeus.

Our fellow travellers set out at dawn, with the sun rising to their left. This same sun, it was believed, holy Mount Ida could spy even before its rising, and its appearance from the East floods the mouth of the sacred cave with light.[2] By Morrow's calculation, it would take the three old men at least ten or eleven hours to reach the lofty site (27n.45). Even on the summer solstice—which affords Crete about 14 hours of daylight—their arrival would find shadows long fallen over the cave (see 683c).

What would they see? Before the cave itself stands a lofty tree—a poplar or perhaps a willow—likely decked with votive offerings, perhaps small bronze shields or hanging terracotta devices (Willetts 242n.77, 144). Not far from the tree stands a large fallen slab, used for centuries as an altar. Stuffed into the sides of the altar or laid on top of it are offerings from an agricultural people, fruits and grains and curiously shaped dolls and figures.

The cave's massive entrance yawns behind, an eyeless mouth in the bleak rock wall of Ida, one measuring nearly 100 feet wide and 30 feet high. Whether in the dawn or by torch light, this mouth glitters with the richness of more substantial offerings, gold, silver, and bronze, deposited there by other pilgrims. Stepping inside, the visitor enters a massive chamber, sloping downward like a theater. On all sides sparkle the decorations of one of the most important religious sites in Greece: "vases and utensils, figurines and rings, sealstones and pieces of jewelry," as well as beaten-bronze shields and weapons (Kofou 159 and 189). Over an 100 feet into the depths of the cave, and to the right, opens another large chamber, which, in the dusky light, reveals a number of altar-places, black with ashes and burnt bones, decorated with the skulls of the ubiquitous Cretan bull (see Willetts 144). Finally, at the very back of the main chamber, an aged ladder climbs nearly 25 feet from the floor to a smaller, nearly hidden cave. In this most secret place, only ten feet wide, occur rites of initiation and propitiation; stalagmites there have been fashioned by forgotten hands into grotesque human shapes; and at the very back of the secret chamber lie more bones of oxen offered to the speluncular deity (Kofou 189).

The Sun

Who is this god? An answer to that question can be obtained by considering more closely the second prominent feature of the dramatic scene that Plato has constructed: not only its place, but its time.

As mentioned, the characters set out for the cave of Idaean Zeus on the summer solstice, the day when the sun reaches its height in the sky and affords the earth the longest period of sunshine. But for the Greeks this day is not considered a "solstice," that is, a day that "the sun stands still." Rather, as Megillus puts it (683c5), it is the "God turning" (*theou trepomenou*), the day the sun turns from its higher, summery elevations and begins slowly to sink towards lower and shorter winter days. The emphasis falls upon the motion of this God, especially its cyclical motion.

It is not known whether the cult of Idaean Zeus enjoyed any special celebration on the summer solstice. But there exists a connection between the motion of the sun-God and the life of this cave-God. The yearly rise and fall of the sun, from winter's darkness to summer's brilliance and back again, is obvious to all observers. The cult of Idaean Zeus taught a similar story about its revered deity.

The Zeus of Mount Ida's cave was the famous "Cretan-born Zeus," *Zeus Kretagenes*. According to the most famous account, that of Hesiod's *Theogony* (453 ff.), this Zeus, the son of Kronos, was born from his mother Rhea in secret, in a cave somewhere on Crete's Mount Dikte, in order to escape being devoured by his father. After his birth, he was carried by his sacred followers, the Kouretes, to the cave on Mount Ida. There he grew up in hiding. Nymphs fed him. A goddess gave him a golden ball to play with and a golden cradle in which to sleep (see Willetts 242).

But this is only the ascending part of the story. According to the ancient sources, this Idaean Zeus is born and grows up to maturity every year; and every year he also dies—or, perhaps, is slain by his followers (Willetts 240-241). He is mortal and immortal, always dying and always returning to life (Kofou 159). Crete is his birth-place, but Ida is also his "tomb." [3] The philosopher Pythagoras is even said to have written an epitaph for him there: "Here Zan lies dead, whom they call Zeus" (Willetts 242). This "dying God," who in ritual may have held the form of a bull that is torn apart and devoured by his followers, takes the place of the deity known in the rest of Greece as Dionysos (Willetts 202).

Like the sun, then, this Zeus lives a life of "turnings." He falls from his zenith into death. But, not abandoning his followers and their land, he rises from the dead and thus resurrects them too, with hopes of life and bounty ahead. This religious context, then, meshes perfectly with Plato's choice to set the dialogue on or near the summer solstice. This choice does not mean to foreshadow gloomy prospects for these old men—that their political project (and their lives) will sink into darkness just as the sun does. Rather, Plato's choice of the time and place of this dialogue should cause us to understand that the political project of the

Laws takes place under the aegis of gods—Zeus and the Sun—who promise the inevitability of decline and death, but who also herald the possibility of rejuvenation and rebirth.

Images

The cave and the sun stand as two of the most important dramatic features in Plato's *Laws*. One might call them, together, the terrestrial and celestial frame of the work. But by their prominence they also point the reader away from the *Laws* and towards Plato's most famous dialogue, the *Republic*, in which artful images of the sun and a cave play a central role. This connection between the two works seems hardly accidental, and is worth momentary consideration as we attempt to orient ourselves in the *Laws*.

In the *Republic*, Socrates introduces the sun as "the child of the Good," the first of three images meant to illuminate, partially, his "idea of the Good" (see 506d-e and 508a). Just as the sun not only illuminates but also supports the growth and nourishment of the visible world, Socrates explains, so too the Good renders the intelligible realm both intelligible and existent (509a-b).

The sun also stands at the center of the second image Socrates employs here (the "divided line," 509d), and at the height of his third image, that of the cave. The image employing the cave Socrates offers as "an image of our nature in its education [*paideia*] and its lack of education" (514a1-2). The condition of lack of education is represented by the inmates of the cave, who are bound to seats facing away from its entrance, and who engage in contests of naming the shadows cast, by puppeteers using firelight, on the back wall of the cave (514a-b, 515b). Education, in contrast, takes place when one of the prisoners is released from his bonds, dragged up the path to the cave's entrance, acclimates himself to the outside, and begins to study the world not of shadows but of true beings as they are illuminated by the sun—eventually even studying the sun itself (515c-516c).

What lessons can these famous images hold for the *Laws*? One might, quite naturally, contrast the journey of the characters in this dialogue with that of the would-be philosopher of the *Republic*'s cave. On this day of greatest sunshine and solar illumination, Kleinias, Megillus, and the Athenian stranger seek "the shade of lofty trees" in order to give them respite from the sun, while they undertake their long journey to a cave, a place where the sun's rays cannot penetrate (625b4, b2). In contrast, in the *Republic*, the would-be philosopher is dragged out of the shadows, out of the depths, and into the light. Thus the journey of the *Laws* could be said to oppose the movement of the *Republic*—the flight from light to darkness compared to the flight from darkness to light. Put differently, in one, philosophy barely if ever appears; in the other philosophy, in the person of Socrates, cannot be ignored.[4]

But such a comparison, which takes the *Republic*'s image of the cave as the interpretive authority and then sets up a simple contrast, does not do just to the complex nature of the sun and the cave in the *Laws*. Here the cave and the sun do not stand in simple opposition but rather share many features. Both possess divinity. Both of these divinities offer life. And both, in a way, offer illumination—the sun by its light and the cave, as will be seen, through the inspiration of legislation.

Both also involve a "turning"—and it is with this observation that we can begin to reinterpret the *Republic*'s image and its relation to the *Laws*. The sun, in the *Laws*, is not a static entity, an immovable source of being in the sky; this sun rises and falls and turns throughout the year. Likewise, as seen, the god of the cave in the *Laws* is no rigid fixture of a shadowy world; he too rises, falls, and rises again. In this respect, both deities from the *Laws*—the sun and Idaean Zeus—resemble not the sun and the cave of the *Republic*, but the would-be philosopher from that dialogue, whose education, Socrates explains, amounts to a "turning" or a "leading round" (*periagoge*) (518d4). In addition, this turning is not a solitary event. As Socrates makes clear, no philosopher may simply remain in the upper realm, but he must also return to the cave, to take part in ruling the people there (520b-e). His motion resembles the true motion of the sun: not unidirectional but cyclical.

To be sure, in the *Republic* Socrates speaks of the philosopher as being "compelled" to return to the cave (see 519c-e). But, given that the *Republic* is a dialogue, a drama, and not a disembodied treatise, there is reason to believe that Socrates tailors his discussion here to the needs of his interlocutors, especially to Glaucon, whose eagerness to engage in politics before he is ready Socrates has already tried to check (see 347a-e). In many other ways, as well, does the Platonic corpus disputes this overly simplistic picture of the philosopher being forced to return to a consideration of politics. After all, we see in the *Laws* an Athenian stranger who seems very much a Socratic philosopher, and who willingly and at great length engages in a discussion of politics with eminently practical non-philosophers. Further, even if we ignore Plato's letters and his actions in Syracuse, the careful and long consideration of political things as such that must have informed the mind of the *Laws*' author reveals an interest in politics which transcends the merely necessary or the merely introductory.[5] Finally, while Socrates in his *Apology* points out that he has avoided holding any ruling office, he explains that he has done so because he could have done little good for his home city as a ruler and that he instead has used his life to serve justice by counselling his fellow-citizens in private. In any event, the *Apology* in particular and the Socratic dialogues as a whole make clear that Socrates took a special interest in conversing with young men of specifically political promise.

In short, the dramatic scene of the *Laws* helps to deepen the proper understanding of these famous images from the *Republic*, and hence of Platonic political philosophy in general. The "cave" is not merely a pit of error, to be escaped, but a locus of life-giving divinity, not transparent to the eye or mind, of course, but nonetheless a source of attraction and inspiration. The "sun" is not merely an unswerving beacon, but rather in its motion a symbol for the life of the philosopher, moving back and forth in a middle region between constant illumination and complete darkness. The philosophic "turn," then, does not exchange one rigid point of view for another, its opposite, but rather introduces the student to a life of holding together the different but complementary ends of human activity—politics and contemplation, theory and practice.

Man and God in Crete

Every drama has its scene, but it also has its characters. As a drama, each Platonic dialogue can thus be understood from many different points of view. One can try to understand what Plato, the author, was thinking in writing it, what he was trying to convey to readers. To do this, one also can and must try to understand what the participants of the conversation are thinking while speaking. After all, their opinions are the engines that move the words and actions of the drama. We must take a look now at the characters of the dialogue and what they think about its first word—"God."

What does this imposing word mean to them? This is the question with which we, the readers, begin. We thus imitate the dialogue once more, as it also begins with a question: "A god, O strangers, or some human being—which is the cause of your laws?" The Athenian asks this question of the other two, and they, Kleinias the Cretan and Megillus the Spartan, are quite straightforward in revealing what they think in response. Kleinias responds along these lines: the cause of our laws is a god. That god is Zeus. That is, at least, the most just thing to say. But in Sparta they tell a somewhat different story. They also say that the cause of their laws is a god, but the believe that the god is Apollo (624a). The dialogue's initial question finds an initial answer, or two answers.

Kleinias and Megillus' words—their affirmations that they believe that the cause of their laws is a god—are confirmed by the setting and the action of this little drama. As seen, the three of them are walking from the Cretan city of Knossos to the cave and temple of Zeus. But why are they going there? To answer this question, we must use our liberty as readers, remove ourselves from the drama, and jump ahead in the conversation.

At the end of Book Three of the *Laws* the Cretan, Kleinias, tells his fellows that he is a statesman, one chosen by his home city of Knossos to propose laws for a new colony that the Cretan cities are to found. He has very great latitude in legislating: he can simply give the new colony the current laws of Knossos or he can enact an entirely new law code (702b-c). Now, Zeus, the god whose devotees claim he was nursed in infancy in this cave atop Mount Ida, is the foremost god of the Cretans. The Cretans even claim that Zeus gave them their laws, through an intermediary, King Minos (624b).

So, Kleinias is a Cretan statesman who faces a great task of legislation; and he is journeying to the cave of Crete-born Zeus, the god who his people say gave their first King his first laws. The most obvious explanation for this journey, then, is that Kleinias is going to pray to this divine legislator, Zeus, for a blessing, and perhaps for inspiration. Kleinias reveals by his words and his deeds the importance of the god to his life. He, and perhaps the others too, believe that the god not only watches him but directs him. His words and deeds reveal the belief that one can and should appeal for divine direction in the most important matters, such as legislation. The god, for him, is the ultimate source of political guidance.

Kleinias' answer to the dialogue's initial question, however, underscores that the god does not direct only one or a few human beings but rather the entire political community; the god, he answers, is the cause of the law itself. Important consequences flow from this belief, consequences that observers from a modern democratic society may not immediately perceive.

First, this belief establishes a certain hierarchy, in time and in authority, of political things. In the beginning is the god. From the god proceeds the law. And this law then sets in order a community. The god and the law precede the community. Before there was Knossos there was Zeus and his law. Also, before there was Kleinias, a citizen of Knossos, there was Zeus and his law. The law and the god precede every member of the community, insofar as he is a member of this community.

Second, Kleinias' belief teaches that the city is not master of its own destiny. Knossos or Sparta did not make themselves. These cities came from gods, from powers far above themselves. And these powers may limit the cities through the laws and directions the gods bestow upon them.

Finally, his belief implies that similar restrictions rest upon the citizens of any such political community. Kleinias, as a citizen, did not choose that Knossos exist, that it have this law-code, or that it have Zeus as its founder. The greatest political act, the founding legislation, is out of his control. But more than that. Since this founding legislation was handed down by a god, it would be wrong, impious even, for him openly to question the goodness of this legislation.[6] Citizenship in such a city is characterized more by obedience or even reverence than autonomy.

This stance towards politics is quite different from the one widely taken today. Much of the present world is ruled by modern democracies or free societies, such as the United States. Modern democracy openly denies that its laws have a more-than-human source. It openly proclaims that the foundation of the law is human reason, human nature, or perhaps even human will. Therefore, in modern democracies considerable forces militate against citizens' revering the law as more-than-human, or sacred. Such citizens come to see themselves not as products of the law; rather, it is a product of them; they, as individuals, are prior.

Kleinias may have looked at himself, his life, as constituted and governed by some law higher than and prior to himself. Citizens of the modern democratic regime, in contrast, tend to see themselves, as individuals, as prior to any political community and any communal law. Kleinias implies that a god gathered together human beings, gave them a law, and thus created a new nation. The citizens of modern democracies imagine themselves, as individuals, coming together and then deciding what common rules to obey. For citizens of modern democracy, the citizen comes first; for Kleinias, the god comes first. For citizens of free societies, the primary political fact is individual freedom or individual "rights," which imply the superiority of the individual to the law. The individual and his rights are the limit upon the law. For Kleinias, the primary political fact is divine providence. The god is the only limit on the law.

The difference between Kleinias' view of politics and the prevalent contemporary view can be made a bit clearer by considering some famous sentiments expressed around the time of the first appearance of modern democracy, the time of the American Revolution. The first belongs to Edmund Burke, a conservative English political thinker, though generally a friend to the Americans. He agreed with Enlightenment thinkers that civic society rests upon a contract or partnership; but, he insisted, the state is "a partnership not only between those who are living, but between those who are living, those who are dead, and those who are to be born." This thought bears similarities to Kleinias and Megillus' view.[7] What community one belongs to, what law one obeys—these are not matters of individual choice. Instead, one is born into a community, one is born a citizen, one is born a servant to certain old-established laws. This is Burke's view. But it is worth comparing another famous sentence, this one penned by Thomas Jefferson in his "Summary View of the Rights of British-America." In it, Jefferson proclaims "a right which nature has given to all men, of departing from the country in which chance, not choice, has placed them, of going in quest of new habitations, and of there establishing new societies, under such laws and regulations as to them shall seem most likely to promote public happiness."[8] This is much closer to the view of politics that predominates today. What community one belongs to, what laws one obeys—these are matters of individual choice. If one does not like the community one was born into, one can change it or leave; no claims of piety or reverence need stand in the way.

Given such teachings, no doubt Kleinias and Megillus' beliefs would seem outlandish today—their beliefs that a god gathered together some human beings, gave them a law-code, and so formed a new nation. But is such belief completely foreign? Most people know the Bible much better than Plato's *Laws*. But the Hebrew Bible, especially the Torah, is largely the story of God's choosing the Israelites, his giving them their law, and his founding a new nation in them. The two roots of Western thought—Greece and Israel—are not so different, at least on this point.

But perhaps someone would reply that the Old Testament story is just as silly as Kleinias and Megillus' beliefs. "Different god, same nonsense." So we should consider this question: Is the modern democratic view—the view that the individual and his rights are superior to the law and to the political community—obviously more sensible?

The modern democratic view makes the individual politically primary or politically supreme. The modern democratic individual does not have to answer to anyone or anything besides himself and perhaps his conscience. If he has duties, they are duties he has chosen. They are not obligations imposed by any power higher than himself.

This is what prevalent political opinion teaches. But is it also what life teaches, that the individual is the politically supreme being? Is it not closer to common experience to say, instead, that people are born attached to other people—their families—and born attached to communities—their home-cities or their native lands—and that they are even born attached to certain faiths? Seen in this light, does not the modern democratic claim that the individual is politically supreme sound more like a wish than a true description of what is? If this is so, it is worth wondering which is more outlandish: Kleinias and Megillus' view of the political priority of divine law, or the modern liberal view of the priority of the individual.

Kleinias' words to the stranger about the cause of the law are brief but rich. They open to contemporary readers a world of belief that is obscured by present day opinions. At the center of Kleinias' belief is the god: the god is the cause of the laws. There is one more consequence of this belief that should be considered, in order to understand better what this word, "god," means to Kleinias and Megillus. Kleinias and Megillus are, as seen, going to the cave of Zeus, most likely to ask for a blessing and some guidance, since Kleinias must found a new city. Kleinias has some grounds to hope for this blessing and guidance, because he claims to believe that Zeus generously gave his very own city its earliest laws.

These elements of the drama reveal what Kleinias thinks about human need and divine generosity. Human beings, of course, have many needs. But the deepest need is the one that not only presses powerfully, such as erotic desire, or that is deadly if unmet, such as hunger or thirst, but which human beings also have no hope of fulfilling on their own. It is this need that, in Kleinias' view, the god fulfills. What does he give human beings? He gives law. Kleinias' words and deeds reveal that he believes that human beings are not self-sufficient in this regard. What people really need—and cannot provide on their own—is to live together with a common end. That common end is what the law—the Cretan or Spartan law, for example—reveals and commands. And the beneficent god gives the people this law. To put all this one more way: Kleinias appears to believe that humans lack the knowledge of how to live well together and of what to live for. The god's providence fills that lack. The god gives us what we truly need.

Again, one should not ignore how deeply different this view is from the one popular today. A democratic society such as America's teaches that governments are instituted among men (and by men) in order to protect their individual rights. This is the fourth "self-evident truth" of the Declaration of Independence. Again, each individual—with all his individual rights—is prior to the law.

Implicit in this view is the belief that each individual does not have to look to the law in order to find guidance in how to live. The citizens of a liberal regime look to the law for protection or security. They look to themselves, in private, for direction in how to live. The law does not guide but merely protects this self-chosen, self-directed, "pursuit of happiness." To put it most radically, a liberal regime teaches that each citizen, as an individual, has or can attain by himself a sufficient understanding of how to live. Unlike Kleinias, the modern democratic individual rejects the view that each human being, by himself, is radically needy or incomplete. Of course, people still need to work together in order to feed and clothe themselves. Citizens of modern democracy also need other people for companionship or love. But otherwise, and above all morally and intellectually, such citizens are taught to see themselves as completed wholes. In a word: the citizens of modern democracies come to have such low expectations of public life because they have such a high estimation of themselves as individuals and of their ability to guide themselves aright. This is a fundamental difference between the present and the past.

So, these are several elements of Kleinias and Megillus' characters, as drawn from the opening scene, and as concerning the word "god." They profess that gods are the founders of their political communities, prior to the law and far superior to any individual human beings or human will. Also, Kleinias and Megillus seem to believe that one of the greatest human needs is for direction in how to live well, and that the gods are the best source for such direction. In all these respects, they differ with the public teaching of modern democracy.

Divine Politics

The Athenian stranger begins the *Laws* with a question about Kleinias' and Megillus' cities, the question of the source of their laws. But their conversation only begins to gain momentum as the stranger asks Kleinias, the Cretan, what good things the Cretan divine law aims at. Kleinias offers various possibilities, but he says that primarily Zeus' law makes the Cretans victorious in war (625c-626b). The stranger then does something surprising for a stranger and a foreigner to do: he questions this Cretan statesman's suggestions about the good of the Cretan law. The stranger does not argue on the basis of some special knowledge of the Cretan law; rather, he argues on the basis of knowledge of what is good. The things that Kleinias thought were the good goals of the Cretan law do not appear to him to be so good.

As a result of this exchange Kleinias becomes puzzled and a good bit frustrated. Do the stranger's questions mean that he thinks the Cretan laws are no good (630d)? In response to this challenge, the stranger offers his first long speech (631b-632d). He gives this speech to indicate to Kleinias how his laws, the Cretan laws, should be praised—if in fact they are good laws. The main object of praise, according to the stranger, should be that the law makes those who use it happy. How might it do that? By providing the people with all the "good things" (631b6). The stranger then divides these goods into two classes: The human goods— health, beauty, strength and wealth, and the "divine goods"—prudence or intelligence, moderation, justice, and courage. If a city acquires the divine goods, the stranger asserts, it will also acquire the lesser, human goods. Thus the good law should be praised, above all, for leading people to the "divine goods." For the "divine goods" look authoritative.

The stranger also brings up divinity a bit later in this same book. As the stranger, Kleinias, and Megillus continue to discuss the now-questioned Cretan laws, the stranger suggests to them that above all they should consider education. Human beings need education, for, he proposes, they are nothing but "divine puppets," the playthings of the gods (644d). These puppets are jerked about by iron cords of hope and fear (644c), and left to themselves, their lives would be a mess. But they do have a savior—not "within" themselves but "above"—"the golden and sacred pull of calculation" (644e). Thus the gods offer human beings some way to save themselves. And this salvation is not simply personal. Cities, the stranger asserts, may take the lead of calculation from the gods or from human beings who have come to understand it, and enshrine this sacred principle in the form of law (644d and 645a).

These same passages explain why earlier the stranger asserts that any good law must aim at the "divine goods" of prudence, moderation, justice, and courage (631c-d). The goods appear to be the perfection of human character. But they are perfections revealed to us, it seems, by the divine lead of calculation.

Still, the stranger does emphasize that the human puppet must make its own effort to lay hold of that divine cord; it is a puppet, but a willful one. And so the stranger reveals his own character to be perhaps just as enterprising, or even more so, than that of the Cretan legislator, who has embarked to found a city. But the stranger's intentions reveal themselves only upon the most careful inspection.

The question of who the Athenian stranger is has a long and varied history. Aristotle and others following him have identified the stranger with Socrates, the principal interlocutor of most platonic dialogues.[9] Other students of the *Laws* see in the stranger a representative of the Fourth Century Academic philosopher *cum* legislator.[10] And a few less sympathetic readers take the stranger to be a narrow moralist or bullying, unsocratic dogmatist.[11] However, by far and away the majority of scholars believe that the stranger is a barely disguised "mouthpiece" for Plato himself.[12] Unfortunately, since Plato is an author almost as nebulous as Homer, this last identification may appear to explain the obscure through the more obscure.

The answer one proposes to this question, "Who is the stranger?" clearly has great weight for one's reading and understanding of the *Laws*. Those who see the stranger as a philosopher—whether a member of the

Academy or a stand-in for Socrates or Plato—are inclined to argue further that philosophy guides the progress of the *Laws* as a whole. (Two of the most influential exponents of this view are Shorey[13] and Morrow[14].) In contrast, those who deem the stranger unphilosophic or unsocratic tend to read the *Laws* itself as a "dogmatic" or even "theocratic" treatise.[15] (Versenyi may be perhaps the most strident propounder of this argument.[16]) In the view of this latter group of thinkers, though the exponent of this authoritative code—the Athenian stranger—is deeply unphilosophic, he may be nonetheless quite politically astute.[17]

What then does the stranger want? As noted, the stranger begins the conversation which is the *Laws* with a very strange question, "A god, O strangers, or some human being—which is the cause of your laws?" (624a1-2). It would certainly be odd for this question to serve as the exact beginning of *any* conversation. Was there no round of introductions (at least on the part of the two statesmen, Kleinias and Megillus)? No antecedent banter? Strange as it may be, it does not seem so.

This conclusion rests on the deduction that Megillus truly is a stranger to the stranger. Kleinias introduces Megillus simply as a "Lacedaimonian" (624a4). Thus in each of his three references to Megillus before 642c2 (633c8, 635e5 and 637b7) the Athenian stranger refers to Megillus as "Lacedaimonian Stranger"; only at 683b4, in practically his first interaction with Megillus since Megillus introduced his own name at 642c2, does the stranger refer to Megillus by name. It seems reasonable to conclude, then, that the stranger did not know Megillus before this conversation.

We should also note that the Athenian stranger starts the conversation with the two others and that the two others were a pair before the Athenian's interruption. Kleinias and Megillus' closeness can be deduced by the way the stranger directs his opening question to both of them (note the dual number at 624a1) and by the amicable way Kleinias includes Megillus in the conversation at 624a4 and 626c3. We should not, however, assume that Kleinias and Megillus were close friends. Kleinias' generic introduction of Megillus as "Lacedaimonian" could very well reflect his own ignorance of Megillus' name. Furthermore, at 702b4-c1, Kleinias reveals that, like the Athenian stranger, Megillus has just happened to "come along" at this opportune time.

Given the character of the initial exchange and the stranger's apparent unfamiliarity with Megillus, it is safe to propose that the dialogue begins exactly where we have it; there was no previous conversation between the three which we have missed. This conclusion makes the stranger's opening question all the more striking and odd.

But if the stranger can be shown to know who *Kleinias* is and what his mission is before intruding on his walk, would the stranger's opening question not make more sense? Kleinias certainly does not appear to know the stranger and indeed never learns his name in this conversation. (Kleinias deduces the stranger's nationality by his accent, since Kleinias calls him "Athenian stranger" only after several minutes of talking; see 626d3 and Megillus' reference to the Athenian's dialect at 642c5.) In contrast, though Kleinias never says his own name, never mentions where he is going, and only hints at his own nationality at the beginning of the conversation (by the references to Zeus at 624a4 and to "We Cretans" at 625a1), the Athenian, with no further information offered, calls him "Kleinias the Knossian" (629c3) and knows, without being told, that Kleinias is on his way to the cave and temple of Zeus (625b1-2). Perhaps he deduced Kleinias' nationality by Kleinias' own accent, or simply by the fact that they are walking on the outskirts of Knossos (see 625b1); maybe he knew Kleinias' destination by the road they are traversing (though this inference would seem quite a leap). But where did this visitor from Athens get Kleinias' name? Not from thin air. In short, the stranger knew who Kleinias is, where he is from, and where he is going before he, the stranger, decided to interrupt Kleinias' sojourn.

Following this lead, from later passages in the *Laws* we can conclude even more about the stranger's knowledge. At the end of Book Three Kleinias summarily describes the commission he and nine others have received from Knossos and most of Crete to lay down the laws for a new colony. In this brief description of his political mission Kleinias gives the stranger no hint of where the proposed colony is to be located (see 702c3-8). (The realm of possibility is wide: Greek cities of the classical period supported colonies from the eastern end of the Black Sea to the southern end of present-day Spain.) And the stranger appears to be completely ignorant of the planned location, since he asks Kleinias several basic questions about it at the opening of Book Four—questions, however, whose answers do not by themselves provide enough information to deduce the spot for sure (704a1-705c2). (For example, see Morrow 31, for a very informed but still tentative guess at the exact location in present-day Crete of the site of the proposed city.) The stranger also does not ask the proposed city's name, waving it aside as an issue that can be settled by borrowing a name from a local river, spring, or god (704a2-b1). Throughout the rest of the dialogue Kleinias does not breathe a word about the planned location of the new colony.

However, deep in their much later discussion about the arrangement of the physical structures of the city, the stranger suddenly refers to "local Magnesian deities" (848d3). Then at 860e6 he mentions "the city of the Magnesians" as the city they are legislating for. He speaks of Magnesia three more times (919d3, 946b6, 969a6) as the place of the proposed city; Kleinias never objects nor, more importantly, corrects him. Kleinias' revelation of his commission prompts the entire founding of the "city-in-speech" (702b4-e2). Kleinias thinks that luck alone has brought the three of them—he, Megillus, and the stranger—together (702b5). But Kleinias seems mistaken. The stranger knows who Kleinias is, where he is from, and where he is going before he interrupts him. The stranger also appears to have detailed knowledge of the political task which faces Kleinias, a task which Kleinias describes as, up till that point, "hidden"—even from his fellow Doric statesman Megillus (702c1). The stranger opens this whole conversation with a question about the source or cause of "laws." He gets Kleinias to bring his political agenda into the open both by displaying his (the stranger's) own deep understanding of political matters (in Books One through Three) and then by asking what can only be described as a leading question (702b1-3). Finally, even though Megillus gives some indications of being the more sophisticated of the two statesmen,[18] the stranger seems anxious to keep Kleinias as his main interlocutor; certainly he spends most of the dialogue talking with Kleinias. It seems not unreasonable, then, to conclude that the stranger has sought out a conversation with a serious political actor in order to affect profoundly his prosecution and his understanding of his political task.

But what does the stranger have in mind by injecting himself into the bustle of Cretan *grosse Politik*? The stranger's political involvement may have a firmly practical, though quite ambitious, motive. Consider his initial advice to Kleinias about how to distribute the city's property. He pronounces that the lawgiver must attend before all else to the fertility of the earth and the disposition of neighboring cities. That is, the city should occupy enough ground to feed a certain number of moderate men without needing imports, enough men to defend the city from possibly unjust neighbors or to bring aid to friendly neighbors who are attacked unjustly (737c6-d5). To interpret the stranger's words, the city's first concern is food and the defense of the source of that food.

However, although the stranger is quite careful here to speak only of defensive war, at 704c5-7 Kleinias told him that the proposed city is quite far from any neighbors. In geo-political terms, as one might say, perhaps the stranger has more enlarged goals than simply warding off neighborly attacks. Illuminating on this point are Aristotle's comments in the *Politics* Book Two that the stranger's hypothetical specification of 5040 male citizens would require "a territory as large as Babylon" (1265a11-18); that the geography of Crete stabilizes its political institutions (1272b16-17); and that Crete, by its location, seems "naturally intended for rule in Greece" and in the Mediterranean as a whole (1271b34). Perhaps Plato's stranger shows us how to beat Alcibiades or Pericles at their own game, namely, how to create a hegemonic yet well-governed world-power, and upon a peaceful foundation.

Openness

In the case of Kleinias and Megillus' characters, some benefit was found in comparing their views with those prevalent today. To do the same with the Athenian stranger requires taking a step back from these political speculations—themselves quite important to understanding the dialogue—and making one more interpretive pass at his rich opening comments.

The stranger begins, as we did too, with a question, not a statement. Again, his question: "A god, O Strangers, or some human being—which one is the cause of the laying down of your laws?" The stranger does not appear on the scene to trumpet his own views or to talk about his home city or himself. (Indeed, he is so reticent about himself that no one ever learns his name.) Instead, he asks questions. He is there, it seems, to learn. Whatever his ultimate political aspirations, at least at the beginning, he presents himself not as the teacher of these politicians but as their student (Strauss, *What is Political Philosophy?* 29-30).

But what is it he wants to learn about? He is not simply interested in gods. If he were, perhaps he would go talk to a priest; as, for example, Socrates does in Plato's *Euthyphro*. Instead, his primary interest is politics. More precisely, his primary interest concerns the ground of political life: What is the cause of the law? What is the source of political authority? His opening question offers two main possibilities. The cause or the source could be a single human being. Or that cause or source could be a god. So, at the beginning at least, he is interested in gods insofar as some people say that gods are the ground or source of political authority. He finds two such people right here.

This beginning indicates that the Athenian stranger has an extraordinarily open mind. He wants to learn about politics, about its ground or source. Where does he start his learning? He does not merely sit and think by himself. He inquires, instead, into what people say about these things, especially what politically serious people say. Some politically serious people say that the ground or source of political life is god, and the stranger is most interested in this claim. Of course, we should be careful not to confuse interest for agreement. The stranger does not say that he agrees with this view. He does not chime in and say, "Oh yes, I believe that Athena should be given the credit for the laws in my home city, Athens." And yet he clearly does think that something serious can be learned by discussing such claims.

This same point can be taken one step further. The stranger is interested in the claim that a god is the cause of a nation's laws. He does not say that he agrees with that view. But he does not say that he disbelieves it either. In fact, nowhere in the *Laws* does he make such a denial. Quite to the contrary, he repeatedly expresses the view that the gods will guide and support, in various ways, the new city they begin to discuss.[19] In short, he seems to be open to the possibility that gods give laws to certain human beings; he seems to be open to the possibility of divine law.

He therefore would also have to be open to the view that the best way to live is in obedience to divine law. And he must then be open to the opinion that human beings are radically needy—that they are radically ignorant of how to live well—and that they need divine direction in order to live well. What does this openness reveal about the stranger? Maybe, most simply, the stranger wants to see if these much-renowned divine laws can help him lead his own life any better. Though, as shown, the drama allows for the deduction of large designs, perhaps this is the safest starting point for understanding the stranger's intentions.

When considering Kleinias and Megillus, we first drew out their opinions and then compared them with more contemporary views. That comparison was pretty much a contrast. It is instructive to do the same with the stranger's view, although little of it is visible at this point. To some degree, the stranger's thought seems closer to modern thinking than that of Kleinias and Megillus. Kleinias and Megillus affirm that religion, god's word, should have or does have an authoritative role in political life. Modern democratic thought, in contrast, tends to separate religious beliefs—as religious beliefs—from fundamental political authority. The stranger also does not seem simply to promote religious rule—at least not at this point.

But, on the whole, the stranger's views of the possible role of religion in politics is still quite far from that of today. The difference, at this point, does not concern the political place of religious authority or the like. Rather, it can be seen in the difference between questions and statements.

The stranger, as said before, has an open mind when it comes to god and politics. He asks questions in order to learn about the source of law. In contrast, modern democracy claims to know that the ground or source of political authority is the free choice of individual human beings. Everyone has heard stories about gods acting as political authorities. But modern democratic thought treats those stories as stories; it proclaims the politically supremacy of the human individual. God may make a very good personal adviser, if an individual chooses to listen to Him, but the modern democratic individual strongly doubts that any good can come from believing that god's word should be the ultimate political authority. The stranger, in contrast, is open to that possibility. He does not reject it out of hand. He wants to learn about it. Maybe there is some good in it, some benefit that other ways of looking at politics lack? This is, ultimately, the stranger's openness—whether it charms or dismays us says more about us than about him.

Notes

[1] For the identification of this cave and sanctuary as that of Idaean Zeus, see Morrow 27-28. Willetts agrees that Ida is their goal, and supports Morrow's rejection of the cave of Psychro (on Mount Dikte), showing that worship in the latter cave ended in the geometric period (298, 215-216). Willetts also argues that Dictaean Zeus may not have had *any* precise site of worship in classical times and later (216n.105).

[2] For the association of the mountain with the sun, see Willetts 143n.23. On the orientation of the cave's mouth, see Kofou 162.

[3] Willetts also catalogues several other places in Crete which claimed the honor of being Zeus' tomb (219).

[4] For this dramatic comparison of the two dialogues, see Pangle 381-382 and Bloom, *Republic* xvi-xvii. Both expand upon the suggestions of Strauss (*Argument and Action* 14 and *What is Political Philosophy* 32, *et passim*).

[5] Strauss (*Argument and Action* 42) makes this comment on the fact that the *Laws'* conversation occupies one day: "Taking into account the *Laws* as a whole, we may observe that, since the day is very long, it is sufficient for elaborating a complete code of law; a complete code of law can be elaborated by a competent man in a single day of sufficient length." His imputation is clear: legislation, the summit of politics, is not, truly, such a momentous affair. A smart person can expound a decent law-code in one day. Strauss' swipe at the stranger's political activity strangely ignores the considerable thought about political affairs that must have gone into constructing this day-long conversation. As Strauss himself reminds readers of Plato elsewhere, each dialogue is a carefully constructed whole, in which all elements of chance have been eliminated by the author's poetic attention (*City and Man* 50 ff., especially 59-60). This denigration of politics rests on his judgment that "'political philosophy' means primarily not the philosophic treatment of politics, but the political, or popular, treatment of philosophy, or the political introduction to philosophy—the attempt to lead the qualified citizens, or rather their qualified sons, from the political life to the philosophical life" (*What is Political Philosophy* 93-94). This understanding of political philosophy itself rests upon the reading of the *Republic*'s "cave" described and contested above.

[6] Even the Athenian stranger says that the "finest law" of the Cretan code is the one that prohibits young people from criticizing the divine law (634d-e). By Book Ten the three agree to make expressions of impiety illegal in the proposed city.

[7] Importantly, Burke makes this argument about the state as part of a larger argument on behalf of the establishment of state religion (see *Reflections on the Revolution in France* paragraph 165).

[8] August, 1774, second paragraph. Of course, the American Declaration of Independence also contains similar language: "…whenever any Form of Government becomes destructive of these ends, it is the Right of the People to alter or to abolish it, and to institute new Government, laying its foundation on such principles and organizing its powers in such form, as to them shall seem most likely to effect their Safety and Happiness."

[9] Aristotle, *Politics* II.6, 1265b11. Strauss explicates and defends Aristotle's identification of the Stranger with Socrates in at least two places (*What is Political Philosophy* 33 and *Argument and Action of Plato's Laws* 2, but cf. page one of the same book). He is followed in this line of argument by Pangle 379 and 511n.2.

[10] The postulation of an Academic "think-tank" which supplied constitution-writers to contemporary states hinges upon an off-hand remark by Plutarch. It began to be advanced as an explanation for the *Laws* and the Athenian stranger first by Burnet 256 and Taylor 463-464, but has found its most thorough expression in Morrow 6-10, 573 and Saunders, "Plato's Later Political Thought" 482-484.

[11] Ast, who athetesized the dialogue, calls the stranger the mouthpiece of a narrow moralist (388). Versenyi 73-75 and Nightingale 294-300 both take the stranger to be a stand-in for an old, dogmatic, and even theocratic Plato, a Plato as far removed from his familiar Socratic roots as could be.

[12] This would be a very long list and would include most of the scholars mentioned in the next two notes. To identify the stranger with Plato is hardly a modern phenomenon, however. Diogenes Laertius calls the stranger "Plato or some nameless creation" (*Lives of the Eminent Philosophers* III.52) and the Scholiast to *Laws* Book One also takes the stranger to be a stand-in for Plato.

[13] Shorey, *Unity of Plato's Thought* 86-87; "Plato's *Laws* and the Unity of Plato's Thought" passim; *What Plato Said* 356-357 and 407. Taylor also charges that the argument that Plato, in his later life and work, turned from science to religion, is "a complete misinterpretation of the concluding section of the *Laws*," the section dealing with the Nocturnal Council (497). Dies seems to think that the "religious" parts of the *Laws* simply fill out the beliefs prescribed in *Republic* Book Two (lxx-lxxi).

[14] Morrow 576-591. Vlastos makes much of one of Morrow's arguments—that as an older man Plato came to the conclusion that no human beings (even philosophers) could govern well without laws—arguing that Plato's late realization of the corruptibility of philosopher-rulers causes a change in his theorizing and leads Plato towards the more "democratic" reforms of the *Laws* (36). Shiell 389-390 and Guthrie 382 have a similar view of the matter, though cf. Guthrie 322-323. More generally, Morrow argues that in both the *Republic* and

the *Laws* philosophy and law work in cooperation. Kahn and Levinson, in their reviews of Morrow's book, affirm this supposed cooperation even more strongly than Morrow does (*Journal of the History of Ideas* 419-421, 423 and *Classical Philology* 136-137). On a similar note Saunders, *Plato's Laws* 34, argues that Plato assumes that politics is an exact science grounded in "absolute" moral ideas, a characterization which leads him, like Stalley, to castigate Plato for being "illiberal" or "totalitarian" (ibid. and "Plato's Later Political Thought" 477).

[15] For the classic statement of this view, see Grote 277. See also Bury xiv, who calls the city of the *Laws* a "theocracy" (a characterization also used by Klosko 198, and 231, where he describes the *Laws* as "in many ways a religious work"). Barker, though he certainly claims that Plato remained an "earnest" rationalist (and would-be-tyrant) to the end, also claims that Plato added a "religious side" to his legislation in the *Laws* (381-382). Sabine goes even further: though he opines that Plato's "ideal" in the *Laws* is still the rule of philosopher-kings, he denies that they compose the ruling Nocturnal Council, asserting instead that the Council's "wisdom" is imbued with a "religious nature" (78 and 91).

[16] Versenyi strongly attacks Morrow's position that both philosophy and law rule in the *Laws* (67-80). Of the many reviews of Morrow's book, only those of Crombie (104-107); Grube (283); and Sinclair (440), come anywhere close to Versenyi in confronting Morrow with the incompatibility of philosophy and law as principles of political rule. Saunders, in his review of *Plato's Cretan City*, approaches the problem from the other (textual) direction and upsets Morrow's claim that law puts any restraint on the philosopher-kings of Callipolis (182).

[17] On this latter point, see the argument of Mary Nichols 239-240, who argues that the Stranger is unphilosophical or perhaps pre-Socratic although quite politically interested and able.

[18] See 680c6-d3 (Megillus knows Homer's poetry, and its teaching, while Kleinias does not) and 804b5-6 and 842a4-6 (Megillus immediately sees the radical import of the Stranger's arguments; Kleinias needs more time to think).

[19] Pangle offers a long list of applicable citations (502).

Chapter Two:
Edifying Sod

Freedom or Food?

One of the old chestnuts that textbooks on education often toss to their readers, usually on the first page or so, is a pious reminder that "education" derives from the Latin *educere*, "to lead out." Modern educationists seem to find this etymology overwhelmingly attractive, no doubt because it justifies their viewing education both as progressive—leading "out" becomes the same as lifting "up"—and as liberating—any place that people want to get "out of" must be oppressive, after all.

Lately, some especially sensitive educators have worried that "leading out" implies that the teacher leads, in an authoritarian fashion, while the student is led. This is hardly an unreasonable concern. However, these same thinkers tend to soothe their consciences by explaining that since the "leading out" is not a "leading into"—that is, since it merely removes old prejudices without (they claim) instilling new ones—"education" poses no threat to the freedom that they so conspicuously revere.

But even a cursory examination of the etymology of "education" should unsettle these claims. The old Romans rarely used *educere* in the sense of "to bring up or rear" (see Lewis and Short, s.v., II.A.4.b.(a)). Rather, they used the closely related but distinct verb *educare*. *Educare* may have itself derived from *educere* in the unrecorded past. But in the best classical authors the two terms stand distinct.

More importantly, *educare* retains none of the sense of "to lead out" that its relative possesses. Instead, in addition to "educate," *educare* takes on the earthy meaning of "to nourish or to support" (see Lewis and Short, s.v., II.B). Thus Lewis and Short quote Varro: *Educit obstetrix, educat nutrix, instituit paedagogus, docet magister*: "The midwife draws one out, the nurse nourishes, the tutor rears, the professor teaches." Contemporary educators rarely mention this more direct etymological root of the name of their field. "Nourishing"—perhaps we might even say, with a view to the nurse, "spoon-feeding"—no doubt seems to them an activity much less directly connected with progress and freedom than "leading out."[1]

Contemporary confusion about the meaning of education thus has deep roots—though not necessarily tangled ones—roots that even reach back to the Greeks and which Plato, in his usual fashion, fully exposes to light. For example, Socrates famously describes himself as a midwife, not a drawer-forth of babies, to be sure, but someone who can "lead out" another's thoughts (see *Theaetetus* 149a ff.). True, as a midwife, he appears to have a deadly touch: in the labors that we, the readers of the dialogues, witness, the thoughts that Socrates helps birth always turn out to be still-born. But Socrates is known for his irony, and his admission of failure slyly points to his true goal. While he cannot draw forth, from others or from himself, substantial truths, he can lead people out of the darkness of their false beliefs. The thoughts that die on the birthing table are, it turns out, the prejudices and false opinions that had blinded their possessors. In the best cases, the midwife Socrates helps "lead out" a knowledge of one's own ignorance.

But the most famous example of Socratic education is offered, by Socrates himself, in the *Republic*, in the allegory of the cave. As seen in the first chapter, this image represents "human nature" in its "education and lack of education" (514a). According to the allegory, the would-be philosopher, the would-be educated man, must be freed from his bonds in the cave of conventional political and social life, dragged from amid his companions, and pulled upwards into the light of the sun. If this is not education as "leading out," what could be?

However, in contrast to these two Socratic examples of education as *educere*, the *Laws* describes education much more in manner of *educare*, "nourishing." Indeed, even when the stranger proposes something he calls "liberal education"—the first mention of such education in the history of Western thought—he does not invoke images of "freeing" people "from" their constraints or leading them "out" of their conventional places or beliefs. In what follows, we shall attend to the seemingly un-Socratic discussion of education found in the first and second books of the *Laws*, and then return to consider, for a moment, its relation to the more famous image of the *Republic*.

A Long Road

Kleinias, Megillus, and the Athenian stranger are imaginary travelers on an imaginary road. We, the readers of the dialogue, are metaphorical travelers as we hike along towards Plato's city in speech. It has already been noticed that Plato uses his extraordinary art to impose certain similarities to the characters' journey upon the readers' one. The characters in the dialogue set out with one goal in view: the cave and temple of Zeus. We begin with one puzzling word: God. Their conversation opens with a question, an inquiry; so does ours. There is another resemblance between the conversation in the *Laws* and our reading of the *Laws* that we should observe, one that dominates the second half of Book One and the whole of Book Two. This resemblance concerns education.

After giving his speech on the goods to which a good law must lead its citizens, the stranger engages Kleinias and Megillus in a discussion of how the Cretan and Spartan laws lead their citizens to these goods. They begin with courage and moderation. It does not take very long for the stranger to convince his interlocutors that he thinks that their laws lead only to a bastardized form of courage—being afraid of public humiliation—and to moderation not at all.

This realization sparks controversy (636e-637a). Megillus, the most patriotic of the three, it seems, charges that the Athenian laws do not do well in promoting moderation either; in fact, he argues, they encourage immoderacy by allowing for public drunkenness. This attack on his homeland gives the stranger a perfect opportunity to defend his own laws or a version of his own laws (Pangle 395). He thus sets out to defend public drinking parties.

But he admits that his defense must be set in a rather broad context. He must talk about "the whole of education" (641b6), since he intends to show that public drinking parties serve inestimable educational purposes. (An ancient defense of frat parties?) Educating people in what education is, is a large project, a very large project. Thus the stranger says, "First, for the purposes of the argument, let's define education—saying what it is and what power it has. That's the way we assert the argument we have now taken in hand should go, until it arrives at the god." (643a4-7) This last reference to "the god" shares the ambiguity of the first one, in the first line. But if "the god" that the stranger refers to is Zeus, then what he means is that the rest of their conversation in the *Laws* is in truth a conversation about education. In this case, the entire book is, as Strauss suggests, a book about education (*Argument and Action* 17).

Kleinias eagerly agrees to take up this conversation. So these three are not only traveling to the cave and temple of a god. They are educating themselves about education. And in this respect, we, the readers, once again find ourselves resembling the characters of the dialogue. No one picks up a copy of Plato's *Laws* for light, diversionary reading. It is always turned to, when it is turned to, as a source of education. Now, there are myriad branches of education, and different people seek to educate themselves in different things. Still, if one is to educate oneself in anything, one must have some idea of what education is and is not. Otherwise, how can one be sure that one is not engaging in something other than education—such as fooling, deceiving, corrupting, or merely diverting oneself?

The conversation in the *Laws* forces the characters—and the readers—to step back for a moment from the branches of education and ask the most basic questions: What is education itself? And how does one become educated? Unlike the initial question about god, these are questions that anyone today can easily feel in all their power. One could say that these are especially important questions for those of us living under modern democracy, as we must rule ourselves and find our own ways in life. If we do not discover, for ourselves, what education is, no one else is going to do it for us.

Three in One

If we take the stranger's question seriously, we must observe that something odd then occurs in the conversation: the stranger and his interlocutors soon come upon not one but three answers to this question. In what follows in this section, these three definitions of education will be listed and then some discussion of their similarities and differences will be offered.

The first definition is found at 643e-644a. It defines what the stranger calls "liberal education"; in fact, this passage offers the first definition of "liberal education," so called, in the history of Western thought. The definition is as follows, in the stranger's words:

> The argument now would be that education is the education from childhood towards virtue, which makes one desire and love to become a perfect citizen, knowing how to rule and be ruled with justice. It is this nurture[2] alone, it appears to me, that this argument should wish to proclaim as the only education. But as for a nurture that strives for money, or for some sort of strength, or for some other sort of wisdom without intellect and justice, the argument should wish to proclaim it to be vulgar, and illiberal, and unworthy to be called complete education. (643e3-644a5)

The stranger's second definition comes in the small speech he gives at the beginning of Book Two. The three characters had been discussing the use of public drinking in order to test the souls of the adult citizens. At the beginning of Book Two they turn to a new use of public drinking: as a safeguard for education. Thus the stranger says he would

like to "recollect again what we say, in our view, is correct education."
(652b3-653a1) He then defines it in the following, strange, way:

> I, for my part, say that the first infantile perception in children
> is the perception of pleasure and pain, and that in these do
> virtue and vice first come into being in the soul; as for
> prudence and true, firm opinions, lucky is the person to
> whom they come even in old age. He who does possess them
> [i.e. prudence and true opinions], and all the good things that
> go along with them, is a perfect human being. Education,
> then, I say, is the virtue that first comes into being in children.
> Pleasure and attraction, pain and hatred, become correctly
> arranged in the souls of those who yet have no reason, but
> when the souls do grasp reason, these passions can, in
> symphony with reason, affirm that they have been correctly
> habituated in fitting habits. This symphony is virtue as a
> whole[3]; that part of virtue which amounts to correct nurture
> concerning pleasures and pains so as to hate what one should
> hate right from the beginning till the end, and to love what
> one should love—if you cut this off in speech and proclaim
> that this is education, you will, in my view at least, be making
> a correct proclamation. (653a5-c4)

Kleinias then responds: "Indeed, stranger, what you said earlier about
education and what you have said now both seem correct to us." (653c5-6)
One must remember again that Plato is an artist and this conversation is
imaginary. Such a statement by an interlocutor is a sure hint from Plato to
readers that we should check to see whether the two definitions of correct
education do in fact say the same thing or something different.

But before we do that, let us observe the stranger's third
definition of good education. Throughout Book Two Kleinias and the
stranger discuss music, dancing, and what the stranger suggests calling the
"first education" (654a5-7), choral education. In this section the stranger
spends a fair amount of time trying to illuminate what is the "fine" or
"beautiful" way to sing and dance and, furthermore, what is the "correct
use" of a chorus of singers and dancers in public. It is at the end of this
latter discussion—the discussion of the correct use of public choruses—
that he offers his, for now, final definition of correct education:

> It seems to me [he says] that for the third or fourth time the
> argument has come around to the same point: that education
> is the dragging and pulling of children toward the argument
> that is said to be correct by the law and is also believed, on
> account of experience, to be really correct by those who are
> most decent and oldest. Therefore, that the child's soul not

> become habituated to feeling joy and pain in opposition to the
> law and to those who have been persuaded by the law, but
> rather that it follow the joys and pains of these same people—
> for these reasons, what we call songs, but which are really
> incantations for souls, have now come into being. These
> strive seriously for that symphony we are discussing. But
> since the souls of young people cannot bear seriousness, these
> incantations are called and treated as "games" and "songs."
> (659c9-e5)

Again, by giving a vague enumeration of their definitions of education and by speaking of returning to the "same thing" the stranger hints that his listeners should consider whether this definition of education really is the same as those previous.

This is one of those many places where we, as readers, must take a different path than our fellow travelers in the dialogue. They do not compare the three definitions of education; we must. In doing so, we could find numerous similarities among the three. In the interest of clarity rather than completeness, let us observe only one: all three definitions present an education that is quite unlike what today usually goes by that name. Educators today prominently dispute with one another about the priority of learning "the facts" and "learning to think." The stranger does not say a word about such things here; he makes no mention of facts, figures, or method. Instead, all three definitions present something that today is at best called "moral training." That is, all prescribe the shaping of people's, especially young people's, habits, manners, and opinions. All three, in fact, recommend that the state actively "arrange" people's souls (653b3). In modern democracies, such moral training, when publicly prescribed, meets deep suspicion. That, many would say, is the business of parents, not the state. For the stranger, in contrast, moral training is the core, and perhaps the whole, of public education.[4]

But we can learn even more about education if we consider the differences among these three definitions. They are striking. First, the most important difference: the three definitions seem to present correct education as aiming at three different goals. For example, according to the first, the goal of liberal education is to make the child love and desire to become a perfect citizen. According to this definition, the goal of a good education is perfect citizenship, which the stranger seems to define in that context as "knowledge of how to rule and be ruled with justice." In contrast, it seems, the second definition describes good education as a "nurture" that finds its culmination in a possible "consonance" of the passions with reason, a consonance called "virtue as a whole." The person who has this whole virtue is, it seems, a perfect human being. So, according to this second definition, the ultimate goal of a good education is perfect virtue or perfect humanity. It does not take a lot of imagination to see how these two goals could be different. A person may be a perfect citizen of a wicked nation; he may obey the laws with fidelity and sacrifice all he has for his fatherland. He may do all that, but his humanity or virtue in general may still be questionable.

The third definition presents the goal of correct education as habituating the child's soul to accept what the law commands, or, to be more precise, to accept what those who have been best persuaded by the law, the old men, believe that the law commands. The goal of this education appears to be perfect lawfulness, such as that of an old man. Again, it is not hard to see how this education and the second, in particular, may conflict. Perfect lawfulness is attainable by anyone who understands what the law commands and does it. But is perfect obedience to the law of Iran or of Communist China or of the United States the same as being a perfect human being? That seems doubtful, to say the least. Likewise, the perfectly lawful person may differ from the perfect citizen. The lawful person may do only what the law commands—and no more. The perfect citizen does not do merely what is commanded, but instead actively seeks further ways to benefit his nation. The perfect citizen is, at the right times, a commander.

To put the same point somewhat differently, the three kinds of education inculcate three different virtues, if all of them can even be called virtues. The first aims, at its height, at justice. Justice, it seems, is the most important virtue for becoming a perfect citizen, one who will know when and how to rule and when to accept the rule of others. According to this definition, the definition of what the stranger calls "liberal education," justice seems to be the most comprehensive virtue, the one most needful for leading a complete and good life.

The goal of the second type of education seems not to be justice but prudence. More precisely, the goal is to nurture (i.e., educate) the child's passions in such a way that if he someday attains prudence or reason his passions will be in consonant with it. That is, if he attains prudence, his soul will not be a discordant chaos. To be sure, that means that the stranger does not think that this education will teach prudence itself. It cannot put prudence "into" the child or adult's soul. Indeed, the cause of prudence seems to be a mystery: "He is a fortunate person to whom prudence or true opinion comes even in old age" (653a7-9). Nonetheless, it seems that this education is meant to be the best preparation for the possible arrival of prudence. There has been no discussion, yet, about what justice is or what prudence is. But, in his speeches, the stranger does seem to treat them as two different virtues. In the stranger's list of "divine goods," prudence is "first and leader," then moderation, then justice, and then courage as fourth (631c5-d1). Justice is still a virtue, but it is only third out of four. It seems very far from the "first and leader," prudence.

Finally, it is not clear that the third type of education teaches a virtue at all. It aims, as seen, at lawfulness, especially the lawfulness of the old man. But it is doubtful whether being lawful, acting in the conservative and cautious manner of an old man, is the same thing as being virtuous— say, as being courageous, just, moderate, or intelligent. Is every old person, by being old, virtuous? If so, people would have only to grow old in order to become good. But no one believes that this is simply the case.

What are we to make of all this? The stranger and his interlocutors say that these various definitions of education come to the same point. But now it seems that three aim at different goals and inculcate different virtues. Has the stranger forgotten his own thoughts from one moment to the next? Has Plato lost himself in contradictions?

It is reasonable to conclude that, in most circumstance, in the "usual" cases, in the cases that most people are most familiar with, these three types of education and their three goals will look quite discordant. Under the "usual" circumstances the perfect citizen, the perfect human being, and the lawful person might look very different from one another. But in what case, if any, would this dissimilarity disappear? This is the critical question: is there some case in which these three goals and hence these three kinds of education could be united into one?

It is not difficult to imagine, at least, a situation that unites the first and third definitions and their goals. That is, one could easily imagine congruence between perfect citizenship and perfect lawfulness. The stranger has hinted already, in fact, what this congruence would demand: Since the perfect citizen possesses justice, the congruence of perfect citizenship and perfect lawfulness would require that the law, to which one is perfectly obedient, be in accord with justice. That is, the law could not thwart justice or lead people away from justice in any way.

This is not as outlandish a possibility as it might seem at first. After all, it is a very common experience to assume, because one sees someone acting in a lawful manner (e.g., stopping at stop signs, paying taxes, or returning lost property), that that person is, as is commonly said, "a good person," or a just person. All people tend to assume, at some very deep level, that lawfulness is the same as justice—even if or especially if they do not clearly know what justice is. Of course people are also faced sometimes with doubts about the justice of their laws. But this initial identification of lawfulness with justice relies upon a common hope, maybe a premonition of sorts, that there can be a congruence of justice and law. So perhaps such a unification of the first and third definitions is possible, in the best case.

This focus on the "best case" may also be able to help, then, in uniting the second definition of education with the other two. The unification of the first and third requires that the law which people obey prepare them for and be in no way opposed to justice—whatever justice is. But the second sort of education is a preparation for prudence; it is a preparation for one's becoming not a "perfect citizen" but rather a "perfect human being." How can this apparent discrepancy be settled?

Perhaps it is helpful to notice again that, just as the first kind of education does not simply make people just but rather prepares in children a desire for justice, so too the second kind of education does not claim to instill prudence itself—whatever prudence is. Whether or not someone in fact becomes prudent seems to be up to some obscure power. If this power is not the chance of birth, or some other type of education, perhaps it is a beneficent god? So, instead of inculcating prudence itself, this second kind of education prepares the child's passions to be consonant with prudence, should the child ever become prudent.

But might it be that the just law—the law that is in accord with justice—is the law that would do the best job of preparing one's soul to be consonant with prudence? Perhaps it is precisely obedience to the just law that will prepare one's soul to be consonant with prudence? After all, as the stranger asserted in Book One that justice itself is a virtue that is composed of a mixture of the other three virtues—courage, moderation, and prudence. That is, justice cannot exist without the prior or contemporaneous existence of prudence. So if the three definitions of correct education are to be harmonized, this truly just law that we are imagining—the law which prepares its followers to acquire justice or at least does not thwart the exercise of justice—must also prepare those obedient to it to become prudent. This best law, then, would not only not hinder but would actively cultivate the ground for one's becoming both a perfect citizen and a perfect human being. In this "best case," in obedience to the best law, one could be a perfect citizen without fearing that one is somehow mutilating oneself, that is, that one is cutting oneself off from one's human perfection.

Here, then, is a hypothetical unification of the stranger's apparently three very different definitions of education. In the best political community, that is, in the community governed by the best law, one would live in whole-hearted obedience to that law, knowing full well that the public education you receive from that law will never lead you astray from or thwart your approach to your natural perfection as a human being; that this education will never force you to choose between your lawfulness or your allegiance to the community as a perfect citizen and your desire to reach the pinnacle of simply human excellence; that under such a law—and only under such a law—with such an education—and only with such an education, might there be a possibility for you to live as an undivided, whole human being.

The "dream" of such a law must fire the interests of anyone who does not want to live a divided life. Anyone who wishes to live with such wholeness, not abandoning or ignoring any part of his or her soul, must be interested to discover such a law, if it can be found. As implied at the end of Chapter One, the search for such a law, and such an education, seems to be what motivates this Athenian stranger. Indeed, the possibility of such a comprehensive education and law also seems to appeal greatly to his companions Kleinias and Megillus. The truly divine law, they all implicitly agree, would offer this comprehensive education. And so, the discussion of education, a type of education that goes far beyond facts and figures and "learning to think," leads us too back to the law. By showing us the attractiveness of such an education, the stranger (and Plato) adds the reader to his band of seekers after the divine law.

Still, this is all hypothetical. Does such a law exist? It is very hard for us to know without having some idea of what justice and prudence and the other virtues are. It is very hard for us to know without having some idea whether or not speaking of such virtues makes sense. It is very hard for us to know without having some idea whether justice does in fact lead to perfect citizenship and prudence does in fact make one a perfect human being—or not. We do not yet know these things. We have to keep these questions—and this dream—in mind as we proceed.

Getting Shamefaced

Though Plato has acquired a reputation as an "idealist," he in fact never allows his readers to dwell for long in such dreamy hypotheses as we have just enjoyed. In all of his dialogues, even those least restrained by reality (e.g., the *Republic*), Plato intrudes notes—sour or whimsical—that disturb the stately harmonies humming in the ears of the interlocutors or the readers or both. He does this in a particularly obvious way here in the *Laws*, by suffusing this initial discussion of education with talk of drunkenness, lying, and shame. As observers, our job is to listen to all the songs that Plato sings, not only the pretty ones. And we should note that Plato introduces these disturbing elements not to be troublesome or petulant but because as an artist and a philosopher he seeks to be true to nature in all its complexity.

The difficulty of studying Plato is in large part alleviated by the lively topics that one finds at the heart of his work. One such topic is drunkenness. Today, as in many ages of the past, alcohol is in general something that is seen as desirable but mysterious, even dangerous. The conflicting cultural norms that surround alcohol and drunkenness today mean that these matters are more the subjects of moralistic manuals than scholarly books. But in this book it is not only permitted to discuss the merits of public drinking; it is necessary. For drinking or at least the discussion of drinking plays a very large part at the beginning of the *Laws*. Those who do not know Plato may think it a surprising topic to find at the beginning of his long, serious work about political philosophy. So we must make all the more effort to see why it is needed.

As noted already, the Athenian stranger proposes in Book One that public drinking parties are a great benefit to well-run cities. The encouragement, by the state, of public drunkenness no doubt strikes many people today as shocking or ludicrous; some of us would agree with Megillus in condemning the Athenian penchant for drunkenness (637a-b). But we also have to admit that the Athenian does not appear to approach drinking in a drunken or frivolous manner; he seems quite sober in talking about the public benefits of drinking parties. So, to understand the book and to understand ourselves, we should ask why. Maybe he knows something about public drunkenness that our own politicians and laws have overlooked?

Drinking comes up at the beginning of a discussion of the virtue, the divine good, of moderation (see 635e and 637a). Prior to that, the three of them had discussed the virtue of courage (633a-635d). Kleinias and Megillus, who come from very militant cities, claim to know a great deal about courage. Many of their laws and institutions seem to aim at inculcating courage. But they cannot think of any of their laws or institutions that teach their citizens moderation. In fact, the Athenian points out that their laws promote immoderacy, when it comes to sex. Megillus gets angry at this slight against his homeland and makes a counter-charge. The Cretan and Spartan laws do prohibit the drinking of alcohol, he notes. Thus their laws are not so bad compared to the Athenian institution of public drunkenness (637a-b).

As noted, Megillus hands the Athenian a plum opportunity to defend his own laws and to prove the great benefit to moderation that public drinking brings. But the stranger does more than that. The Athenian argues that public drinking parties will contribute a great deal to education (641d). The Athenian therefore greatly broadens the discussion. They will now talk not about one virtue alone, moderation, but about education as a whole. The stranger will answer this question: how does public drinking contribute to education?

The stranger's first answer to this question is that public drinking parties help inculcate a sense of shame in the citizens who participate (see 646e-649c). But is this not absurd? After all, as they note, drinking makes the drunk bolder, freer, and ready, "without hesitation, to say or even to do anything" (649b5). Most people do things when they are drunk that they would never consider doing when sober. Most people, when very drunk, seem to lose all sense of shame. The stories of such drunkenness and its results are myriad. An example of such a tale even older than the *Laws* is the story of Noah, who after the flood plants a vineyard, becomes drunk, and falls asleep naked not far out of the sight of his family members. This unhappy lapse leads to acts of insubordination, accusation, recrimination, and finally the severing of family ties (Genesis 9:18-27). Because of its power to induce shamelessness, drinking seems to be dangerous business.

Drinking dulls or erases most people's sense of shame. But, the stranger insists, this very power could be a good thing, properly controlled. The stranger argues that public drinking can be used to test individual citizens' sense of shame. The drinking party official will get you drunk: then he will watch. He will watch to see whether and how far you become "filled with freedom and fearlessness." Are you the type to get naked or will you keep your clothes on? The master of the public drinking party will look to see, that is, how strong your sense of shame is. If it is very weak, then only a little drink will send you off to break the rules. If it is quite strong, in contrast, it will take a lot of drinking even to get you to think about doing such things; perhaps you could not be persuaded to under any circumstances. The stranger argues that this public and publicly supervised test of shame through alcohol is a safe way—safe both for the one being tested and for the rest of society—to see what your friends and neighbors are made of.

This proposal might not sound so promising today, in the political climate of the modern democratic West. It would, no doubt, be denounced as "snooping," if not something worse. Such publicly organized snooping into other people's souls is not something modern democratic political communities would allow. But clearly Plato's stranger is not so solicitous about personal privacy. More precisely, he is not so willing to let shamelessness or potential shameless hide its face. At the end of Book One he describes "the business of politics" to be the "care of souls" (650b7-9). The business of politics is certainly not just business. Nor is it merely the safety or defense of the city from external foes. The good city, in his view, must take a serious interest in the behavior and morals of its citizens. It consciously tries to inculcate in them certain rules of acting, at the least. A "sense of shame" is the individual's acknowledgment that these rules rule.

So this is the first goal of public drinking: to help inculcate a sense of shame (see 672d). It looks snoopy. But those of us who have become excited by the stranger's discussion of education now face an even more serious dilemma: the stranger defends public drinking as a contribution to education (641d). That education, according to the stranger, finds its height in leading the citizens towards the "divine goods" of justice or prudence. The problem is that these supposedly educational drinking parties do not inculcate, directly or indirectly, any of those four virtues. Rather, they inculcate a sense of shame.

Shame does bear some resemblance to the virtue of moderation. Both the moderate person and the person with a strong sense of shame will not do certain things, such as displaying himself naked after getting drunk. So, given this resemblance, it is not surprising that shame comes up within or in the place of the discussion of moderation. But shame is most definitely not the same thing as moderation. Shame is attentiveness to public opinion, to the public "rules."

More precisely, as the stranger defines it (646e), the sense of shame is a fear of public opinion or of a bad reputation. Shame, in other words, is a passion, in this case fear. And it is passion that responds not to knowledge but to opinion. In contrast, moderation, however the stranger would exactly define it, is not for him and the others simply a passion and is certainly not a sort of fear. In fact, the stranger argues at 636d-e, and his two interlocutors there agree, that moderation is a kind of knowledge. It is the knowledge that governs pleasure; it is a knowledge of when to enjoy certain pleasures and how much to enjoy them. For example, the moderate person would choose not to get drunk and naked because he knows it would be wrong, not because he fears it would get him a bad reputation.

Most succinctly: moderation, or any other virtue, is the furthest thing from "brainwashing." But using drinking in order to inculcate or reinforce a sense of shame looks much more like brainwashing than the promotion of true virtue. So this use of drinking, at least, does not seem to be a true part of that exemplary education that the stranger praises in Book One. To use an image to further explain this difference, one could say that the shameless person is a criminal on the loose; the person with a good sense of shame is a criminal living in a prison, a prison formed by his own fear of public opinion; and the moderate person is a free man with no criminal inclinations. Still, as good as it would be to live only among free man, rather than among criminals free or caged, it is certainly better to have criminals living in prison than running the streets.

Geriatric Chorale

There is a second use of public drinking that the stranger recommends, in Book Two. This use is restricted to the old, and is not said to be part of education itself. Rather it is said to be a safeguard to education (653a). It is to use public drinking to make the old men friendlier and readier to sing in choruses (666a-b). This use of drinking likely sounds even more outlandish to today's readers than the first. After all, not only are there no publicly organized drinking parties today, there are certainly no public choruses. But these choruses of old-folks sound quite outlandish to Kleinias, the Cretan, too (665b). So once more we find ourselves in a position that at least resembles that of the characters of the dialogue.

Every citizen, the stranger proposes, should sing in some chorus. But the older men, those over 30, have an especially important part to play in this civic chorus system. The whole enterprise is not just for fun. It is devoted to education, the education of the young. The choruses educate through song and dance—a very powerful method. One of the goals of this education is, as has been seen, to "draw" the young towards the lawfulness of old men. The old men are the most authoritative figures in this city. Their opinions and views carry the most weight.

This too may sound odd today, but it is not unbelievable. Today's society puts as little weight as possible, it seems, on the opinion of the old. It always hungers for what is "cutting-edge," not what is "out-of-date." It is always looking to the future, not to the past. Still, even here, when there is a crisis, people often turn their eyes to "elder statesmen" for help. Society today revels in and glorifies youth, but even it turns to the old when it counts. Because the old men have the best habituation, and are possibly the most prudent, it is most necessary for them to sing to the rest, and especially to the young people, in order to help persuade them to be lawful, just and prudent as well (see 665c-d). The choruses of old men play the critical role in "drawing" young souls to the law, i.e., in public education.

One problem with choruses of older men can be seen readily by imagining an "elder statesman" such as George Washington or Winston Churchill dancing and singing before a crowd of onlookers. The sight would be ridiculous at best. Many people enjoy going to the ballet or the opera and seeing performances by beautiful young people with excellent bodies, voices, and training. But who would want to see an exclusively geriatric ballet? Would not the wrinkly bodies and cackling voices provoke laughter or disgust?

Even if the onlookers kept from laughing out of a sense of

propriety, would not the old singers and dancers be too embarrassed to perform? This is one problem the stranger must address: as authoritative and powerful as their advice may be, old people do not want to make public spectacles of themselves. And that is where drinking comes in: if the city can get these old choristers drunk, then their stage-fright will disappear. By drinking, the old folks lose some of their sense of shame. They become friendlier towards each other and towards the rest of the city. Thus they become ready to sing and dance for the benefit of the younger generations.

So that is one reason public drinking is needed: to souse the older men so that they are not ashamed to perform in the public choruses, for the public education of the young. The first use of public drinking tests young people's sense of shame by assaulting it with alcohol. This second use intends to strengthen young people's sense of shame by, temporarily, weakening it among the old. But there is another problem with these choruses of old-timers that such drinking addresses. It concerns their message.

The choruses sing the message of the civic education as a whole: that no one who lives unjustly can take pleasure in his or her life (661b-c). In other words, the unjust life is not only more shameful and wicked, it is also truly more unpleasant than the just and pious life. Or, to put it most succinctly, injustice is most painful and justice most pleasant (661c-663e). The whole city is to sing these things, with one voice, and the most authoritative part of the city most of all. Why would old people not sing such morally edifying things about justice?

Very helpfully, Kleinias offers himself as an example of an old man who is not comfortable with this message. When the stranger proposes that justice and pleasure are inseparable, Kleinias resists the argument every step of the way (661d ff.). That does not mean that Kleinias is hungering for the unjust life or thinks injustice is better than justice. But he seems enough impressed, by long experience, with the burdens and sacrifices that justice often brings so as to doubt whether justice and pleasure always go hand and hand. For example, he might say, it is just and right to suffer wounds, even death, fighting for your family and your nation; but do not tell the hero that such suffering or death is pleasant! The hero loves those for whom he makes the sacrifice, but he does not love the sacrifice itself.

The stranger tries to entice Kleinias with promises of pleasing fame for doing just deeds in order to win his agreement that justice is most pleasant, but Kleinias rightly does not accept these bribes (663a-c). In the end he will only accept the stranger's statements about justice and pleasure when the stranger holds out the possibility that this view is a lie, a highly profitable lie, but a lie nonetheless (663d-e). In other words, the hesitation of the old to sing and dance may not be due only to stage fright. They may also balk at the message they must give to the young, a message they themselves may doubt, i.e., a message they may think is a lie. Drinking, then, not only loosens their sense of shame so that they will exhibit themselves in public. It also may muddle their mind, making them more willing to believe in the pleasant message that they may not be so accepting of in their more just and sharp-eyed sober state.

Consonance

This chapter began by elucidating the image of a wonderful education, an education by a just law, an education that would prepare human beings for perfect virtue and perfect citizenship, an education that would leave no part of their souls stunted or unattended. That is the education one might hope that the stranger would describe. Instead he speaks of a state-run system of administering drugs (i.e., wine) and requiring public sing-a-longs in order to brainwash people with a fear of public opinion and to get them to swallow stories about justice and pleasure that the old story-tellers themselves may doubt in more sober moments. This so-called education seems to give us fear, lies, and drunkenness instead of virtue. Has it turned out that the stranger has the puny soul of some dictator from *Brave New World*? Or did he somehow decide that this was the best that education could do? If so, why? And why should we pay attention to someone who makes proposals that would seem to stunt the souls of anyone guided by them?

First, we cannot simply conclude that the complete end or goal of this public education is the swallowing of certain lies. The stranger wants the city to sing, with one voice, that justice and pleasure are inseparable. Kleinias refuses to agree that this is the case; so the stranger agrees not to force the issue and leaves the truth or falsity of this claim up in the air. But this is not the stranger's last word about justice. And we should not forget what he says is his own view, right from the beginning. He says that, "To me these things [namely, that injustice is unpleasant and harmful to the unjust person] appear so necessary, dear Kleinias, even more necessary than that Crete is clearly an island" (662b2-4). This is an amazingly strong statement. It is his senses, his observations, that tell the Athenian that Crete is an island. But he says that even more than the testimony of his senses he trusts his moral sense or his moral understanding that tells him that injustice is most unpleasant. That does not sound like a man who believes that this most important "message" of the city's singing is a lie.

Still, why all the emphasis on the sense of shame? Why the need for fear of public opinion? To understand the stranger's dilemma, we need to recall here briefly the image of the "divine puppets" that the stranger uses in Book One (644d-645c). Humans, he explains, are jerked around by the passions. By themselves, people have little control over the direction of their lives. They can try to hold fast to the "golden cord" of reason, but it is hard to grasp, soft, and easily lost.

Put in other terms, the stranger's view is that there are very many different ways for human beings to go wrong in their growth and only one way to go right. Thus chances are, if left to themselves, they will go wrong. Things would be much easier if human beings could, from the beginning, understand what the right path is, and follow it. But it seems that passions take hold of them much earlier than reason does. That fact makes chances for holding fast to reason when people grow up very small. In other words, since the passions are unruly, and since they attain their strength much earlier than reason does, it is very unlikely that the passions will grow up, if left by themselves, to be "consonant" with reason. But such "consonance," one should remember, is the "whole of virtue" (653b6).

That is why, at this stage in the argument, the stranger focuses on the passions and not reason. And to educate the passions a lawmaker must use such things as song, dance, myths, drinking, and shame. One cannot simply appeal to arguments or reasoning if one is trying to shape the passions of a child—or the passions of an adult who lives as a child, without reason. Even if the lawmaker is trying to present a fundamental claim—such as that injustice is unpleasant—he may not present it as the conclusion of an argument but as a myth or as something that simply must be believed.

So we should not be hard on the stranger for speaking about song, dance, myths, drinking, and shame. These are, he himself would say, not the full flowering of a true education. But, the lesson seems to be that one cannot reach the blossom of true education if one's roots are not firm. The consideration of how one must prepare oneself for true education is a constant theme throughout the *Laws*, and by making it a constant theme Plato shows that it must be a primary consideration for any "divine law." The stranger prudently spends this time fertilizing the soil of the soul not because he enjoys speaking about low matters but precisely because he wants to grow something very lofty. It is the kind of "spade-work" that contemporary democratic communities may ignore, but only at their peril and the peril of the souls of those who grow up within them. Still, we should wonder: how will dubious treatment of the roots of education affect the final growth?

Notes

[1] Rousseau explores the nutritive aspect of education in Book One of his *Emile*, at the beginning of which he pointedly compares the child to a plant.

[2] I translate as "nurture" what Pangle renders as "upbringing" (24). The Greek word, *trophe*, comes from a verb meaning "to eat." "Nurture" captures the nutritive aspect of this very down-to-earth word for education. It also reminds readers of the Latin *educare*. "Nurture" is not the same word as "education," *paedeia*, which comes from the word for child.

[3] This is the alternative rendering offered by Pangle (518n.2), and fits better with the interpretation offered in this book.

[4] The contemporary suspicions that public moral education meets with in modern democracy have not always been a marked feature of this regime. The founders of the United States certainly thought that republican government must rely upon public moral and even some religious instruction. For example, consider Article III of the "Declaration of Rights" in the Massachusetts State Constitution (written largely by John Adams in 1780), George Washington's "Farewell Address" (1796), or Jefferson's Northwest Ordinance (1807). A typical expression occurs in James Madison's speech before the Virginia convention to ratify the Constitution of 1787: "To suppose that any form of government can secure liberty or happiness without virtue in the people is a chimerical idea."

Chapter Three:
That Old Time Baloney

The Ancient One?

"Kennewick Man," a largely intact human skeleton over 9000 years old, emerged from his long rest in July 1996, after students watching the "Water Follies" hydroboat show on the Columbia River in Kennewick, Washington, stumbled over his skull. Since then, he has shuffled from one locked casket to another throughout the American northwest, pursued by a pack of scientists, government official, Indian activists, and lawyers.

His unquiet rambles result from a striking conflict between the claims of science and those of something that at least poses as filial piety. Archeologists and anthropologists want to study Kennewick Man's remains in order to understand better his way of life and the world in which he lived so many millennia ago. Their interest is all the more keen, given the relative paucity of pre-Columbian remains, especially complete ones, of such great age.

But to many others, the Kennewick Man is not a fossil—he is an ancestor. The leaders of the Yakama, Nez Perce, Colville, and Wanapum Indian tribes refer to him as the "Ancient One," and they have marshalled a large effort to stop the scientific study of the remains, return the skeleton to the tribes, and bury it anew in a secret location. To date the Indians have succeeded in persuading the federal administration that, by law, they have the right to the Ancient One's bones, resting their case on—and even convincing President Clinton's Interior Department of—their oral traditions, which teach that they and their ancestors have inhabited the land "since the beginning of time."[1]

However, the Indians are not alone in claiming Kennewick Man as a forefather. A cult of pagans from California, known as the Asatru Folk Assembly, also asserted a familial connection to him, though they eventually had to abandon their court case for lack of funds. The Asatrus—who worship Odin, Thor, and Freya—locate their heritage in ancient Scandinavia, and believe that the Kennewick Man's descendants migrated to far-off Europe. Then, after the Norsemen got out of the case, a Polynesian-turned California paralegal got in, arguing that Kennewick Man's descendants in fact travelled south, to South America, and then across the Pacific to Samoa, where his line still lives. This pious fellow demanded the 9000-year old remains as "simply a relative who wants the best for his kinsman."[2]

The Indian tribes (not to speak of the pagans or Polynesians) have pressed their claim for Kennewick Man in the face of significant factual obstacles. Their own tribes can at best be shown to belong to a culture that has existed in the northwest for about 2000-3000 years, thus falling short of "the Ancient One's" demise by at least six millennia. What is known of his culture indicates its great difference from theirs, in its mobility, trade of raw materials, and types of tools used. Just as strikingly, Kennewick Man's physique differs considerably from that of his supposed descendants, possessing some features akin to those of modern caucasoids, others found in south Asians, and still others foreign to all presently known racial types.[3]

But still they, and their government allies, come back to the "oral tradition." The story of Kennewick Man thus presents a noteworthy case of the conflict between story and history, myth and science. And it illustrates that science pursues its work within a political context, one subject to, if not ruled by, passions of reverence and respect that put a great weight on ancient things. In Book Three of the *Laws*, the Athenian stranger confronts similar passions, and uses arguments meant both to expose them and to turn them to the support of his own political plans. As far removed as his plans are from our own political sphere—and though none of us can convincingly claim his creator, Plato, as our ancestor—the story of Kennewick Man reveals that we have something to learn from the stranger's confrontation with this deep stratum of human politics.

Stranger Rhetoric

In Book Three the stranger completes his movement from apparent student of the Doric laws to actual instructor of the Doric lawgivers. He repeatedly emphasizes what he thinks any good lawgiver should seek: that his city should be free, intelligent, and a friend to itself (see 693b and 701d). He also stipulates (693c) that these goals are equivalent to any that he has mentioned previously, such as prudence (631b and 688b) and harmony (628a).

The stranger argues for these goals in the three major sections of this book. First, he provides his own account of "the beginning of political regimes," namely, an account of human pre-history, from the earliest times down to the beginning of recorded events. Then, after briefly speaking about Greek politics before the Persian Wars, he speaks at length about "the seven worthy titles to rule." Finally, he takes his two interlocutors through a sketchy presentation of the two "mothers" of all regimes, here epitomized by Persian monarchy and Athenian democracy.

By speaking of "the beginning of all political regimes," "the seven worthy titles to rule," and the "mothers" of all regimes, the stranger gives his conversation in this book the appearance of being his presentation of the foundations of his own political theory. Still free from any consideration of practical politics, the stranger seems almost to be leading a class on the "first things" of political science. Certainly this appearance of objectivity impresses his interlocutors and many of his readers.[4]

However, if we consider what he says closely, it should become apparent that the stranger is himself engaged in story-telling in all three sections of this book. What appears the most theoretical part of the *Laws* is in fact the most mythical. As will also become clear, the stranger engages in this less-than-scientific discourse in order to meet and move the less-than-scientific passions of his interlocutors. In contemporary terms, one could not simply identify the stranger with the Indian leaders of the Umatilla tribes, but his way of speaking is certainly closer to that of the would-be descendants of the "Ancient One" than that of their scientific opponents.

A New Beginning?

Book Three of the *Laws* begins abruptly. The end of Book Two completes the discussion of drinking and the discussion, for now, of music education. Then, at the beginning of Book Three the stranger asks what seems to be a new question: "The beginning[5] of political regimes—how do we say that it ever came about?" (676a1-2) What is the origin or the beginning of all politics and political life, simply? This new question echoes the question that began the *Laws* itself, the question, "A god or some human being, strangers, which is the cause of the laying down of your laws?" But instead of talking about gods or human beings, here the stranger asks, more abstractly, about "beginnings" of "regimes."

If we briefly look ahead, we can observe that the end of Book Three marks another break. At the end of Book Three the stranger explains the purpose of their entire conversation up till then. He says: "All these things [in Books One, Two, and Three] have been discussed for the sake of spying out how a city might best be founded sometime, and how, in private, someone might best lead his life" (702a7-b1). He then asks his interlocutors: "But if we have made something useful, what sort of test could we have, a test in conversation with ourselves, Megillus and Kleinias?" (702b1-3) No doubt a leading question, and Kleinias takes the bait.

At this point Kleinias reveals to his two fellow interlocutors something he has kept hidden up till then. He, Kleinias, as a distinguished member of his city, has been commissioned by his city and indeed the whole of Crete to set down laws for a new colony that Crete is founding. His commission gives him the latitude to use the old laws of Crete, if he likes, or, if he thinks he can find better ones, to use those. This is quite an amazing bit of freedom. Can one imagine the United States (or any other nation) founding a new state, say, on the Moon, and telling the settlers that they can use American laws, if they like, or other, foreign laws, if they think those new laws are better? At any rate, one thing that Kleinias reveals here is that the preceding conversation has impressed him so much with the abilities of the Athenian, and has made him so doubt the obvious excellence of his own Cretan laws, that he is now willing to suspend his patriotic prejudices and inquire with this foreigner into what laws he should give to the new colony.

If we put these two observations together—the observations about the beginning and the end of Book Three—we can see that Plato matches the very lineaments of this book to the stranger's rhetoric in it. A book that poses as a searching study of the beginnings of politics or the foundations of rule intrudes into the conversation as an apparently new beginning, and it leads to a new undertaking by the interlocutors: the setting-down of laws, in speech, for a new colony. But, as will be seen, the study of the political beginnings in this book are perhaps not as objective as they appear. Nor, as has been seen, is the stranger a stranger to Kleinias' political duties even at the beginning of the *Laws*. For all this talk of beginnings, it is good to remember that the dialogue of Book Three finds itself firmly enmeshed in a larger whole.

The Hellenic Deluge

After his question about the "beginning of political regimes," the stranger and Kleinias pose an abstract of human history. They begin with the supposition of recurring catastrophes, floods, plagues, and other such disasters. They consider the case of flood, in particular—a disaster that is no doubt familiar to readers of the Bible (see 676a9 ff. and Genesis 7-8). After the flood there are just a few "sparks" of humanity left, on the tops of mountains.

These people, they claim, either never possessed or soon lose all knowledge of arts and sciences. They have to recreate civilization, from the ground up, so to speak. The first community they form is something like a familial clan. The stranger later calls this familial clan "the first city," a surprising title for a family (683a4). After some time, these families band together into hillside villages. These villages have walls and common rulers, and the stranger calls them the "second city" (681e1).

Again, as time passes and the human race proliferates, the stranger suggests that the hillside people forget their understandable fear of the water and form large cities on the coast; they engage in trade and end up fighting large wars, such as the Trojan War, against one another. The stranger classifies these seaside cities proper as "the third city" (681e2). Finally, as a result of these inter-city wars and due to domestic strife, the stranger explains that entire "nations" or "tribes" take shape; one of these nations is the Dorian people, the people to whom both Kleinias and Megillus or Crete and Sparta belong. The tribe or nation the stranger calls, again rather surprisingly, "the fourth city" (683a7). With the description of this "fourth city" the stranger brings the conversation into the realm of what the Kleinias and Megillus know by experience or by fairly reliable report.

It is not hard to see that the stranger's tale cannot stand as reliable history. He offers no proof or evidence for his statements. He also begins his account in an arbitrary manner. Why a flood rather than a fire or a plague? The answer reveals that the stranger's words more likely reflect his estimation of Kleinias' opinions rather than his speculations about the truth.

A fire or a plague might wipe out most of a city. But it would leave the survivors a chance to rebuild. Also, these scourges would not leave that convenient remnant locked at the top of mountains, far from the scene of once-civilized habitations. His choice of this particular new beginning looks less arbitrary when it becomes clear that he has selected for one that strips the survivors of precisely any civilizing influences.

The "Good" Old Times

One cannot forget that, whatever his own views, the stranger addresses this account of the past to Kleinias. In fact, the stranger's account is not an address, but emerges in a conversation in which Kleinias has a part to play. That part decisively influences the picture the stranger paints.

If we look past the initial horror of the flood, the picture seems pretty rosy. Indeed, the stranger's account seems to show that the oldest times were best, and that human beings, in their original or 'natural' state are much better and much better off than human beings in their civilized, sophisticated state, such as they are now. His seems to be the view that human beings start off in a state of innocence and bliss and that the increase of human knowledge and human power only brings an increase in misery.

This is point of view that the stranger's tale would seem to share with the Bible, and with several other religious traditions. In Genesis one learns that the first civilizer, the first founder of a city, is also the first murderer—Cain. This view would also, strangely enough, seem to be at the heart of certain sorts of modern romanticism. For example, the hearts of many modern sophisticates appear plagued by the suspicion that the only way one can be truly happy is to throw off the burdens of modern civilization, escape from the cities, and 'return to nature' and to a very simple existence. All these very different attitudes still share the belief that the oldest times, before the rise of cities and the arts and science, were best.

These ancient, religious, or romantic views all differ from one of the most influential depictions of the human origins in modern political thought, that of Hobbes. He famously describes man's life in the state of nature, the state from which all human civilization struggles to escape, as "brutish, nasty, and short" (*Leviathan* Chapter 13). Though for Hobbes, as for several other Enlightenment thinkers, man's beginning is marked by the greatest freedom, it is very far from best. Rousseau, who famously opposed Hobbes' portrait of early human life, and who deeply influenced the modern science of anthropology, takes a more ambiguous stance. The first half of his *Discourse on the Origin of Inequality* presents original man as living in a sort of godless Eden; but it also suggests that this original man was not yet human but something like a promising ape. Both of these thinkers, in characteristically modern fashion, also present original man as solitary.

How does the stranger paint this picture of the past? First, he claims that all the wickedness of civilized life, all the lying and cheating and tricking would be absent in the oldest times (678a). For example, in a world lacking the most rudimentary arts and social structure, there is no need to worry about someone stealing your identity and charging up huge bills on your credit card through Internet shopping. Likewise, due to these people's simplicity and their being dispersed, he asserts that they will be very "glad" whenever they see each other, as rare as that might be (678c5 and e9). In contrast, many people today who live in big cities can barely smile at each other on the street; people who do smile at or greet strangers are viewed with suspicion.

And with so few people around, the stranger claims, there will be no lack of food and other necessities: no poor, no homeless, no starving children. Because of this natural friendliness and natural abundance, there will be no reason to fight (679a). Compare that peacefulness to the conflicts and wars that rage endlessly today, so much so that one might turn on his television and barely notice the deaths of hundreds in armed conflict. Finally, the "first city," the family "dynasty," where the parents rule by virtue of their advanced age, is, the stranger says, a sort of kingship that is the "most just" (680e3). He does not call any of the other three "cities" "most just." The advance of political forms away from the family leads to a decrease in justice.

The stranger sums up all this evidence and then asks Kleinias this question: "Shall we not say that the [people who lived then, at the beginning]...were simpler and more courageous and at the same time more moderate and altogether more just?" (679d2, e2-3) Kleinias responds enthusiastically: "You speak correctly" (679e5). To put this all another way, as far as moral virtue is concerned, that is, courage, moderation, and justice, the oldest times seem much better than anything that comes later. If, then, someone is serious about moral goodness above all, maybe he should long for some sort of return to the original state, something like the innocence of the Garden of Eden. Maybe he should not assume too readily that history progresses; maybe history is a chronicle of moral corruption?

However, the stranger does not abandon civilization and head for the forests to eat grass and acorns. After all, he uses this dialogue itself to propose the founding a new city, not a familial clan. Why?

One should reconsider the stranger's characterization of the earliest people: simpler, more courageous, more moderate, and more just. Four virtues, it seems. This list should readily remind us of the four divine goods or human virtues that the stranger said, in Book One, any good law should aim at: courage, justice, moderation, and prudence or intelligence. For the people in the oldest time, simplicity takes the place of prudence or intelligence. That is to say, they seem morally sound, but stupid—or, if one prefers, naive. One way that the stranger hints at this view is by saying, "No one had the wisdom, as they do nowadays, to know how to be on the lookout for lies. They believed that what they heard about gods as well as about human beings was true, and they lived according to these things" (679c). The earliest people live in the greatest ignorance about the greatest things. They may appear to live peaceably and justly, but they are certainly missing something.

This view of what the earliest people are missing must, then, affect the stranger's view of civilization. Indeed, one could say that the oldsters' lack of prudence or intelligence becomes and is the justification for the founding of political communities, the founding of true cities. The justification is the fostering of intelligence. But is the fostering of intelligence—which no one doubts the ancient people lacked—worth the apparent loss of moral purity? Universities, think tanks, and wise men are all very well and good, but does their gain offset mankind's loss of its supposed pristine goodness? How could the stranger win Kleinias over to such a conclusion?

The "Bad" Old Times

The key to answering these questions is to observe that the stranger's fanciful account also suggests that the beginning times might not have been so idyllic. As Pangle notes (427-28), following Aristotle's *Politics* Book One and the hints of Farabi (III.2), the stranger adds plenty of details to his picture to suggest that the uncivilized human beings were savage and cruel to one another. In places where food was scarce, they may have even been "glad" to see each other because they were hungry and needed something to eat. After all, the image that the stranger uses of the "first city," the familial clan, is that of Homer's vicious Cyclopes.

To the consternation of many indigenous people around the world, such a picture is the one also painted by anthropologists and archeologists today in many different locales. Whether true or not—and, again, the stranger at least offers no evidence to support his claims—it wins the politician Kleinias' approval. And it certainly entails a different view or appreciation of the political community than did the earlier, more idyllic picture of the oldest people. If the oldest times were savage and vicious, then politics attains a whole new justification. This justification is symbolized by the city's wall. Politics finds its justification in protecting our skins, first and foremost—protecting the skins of "us" insiders against "them" outsiders. Perhaps political life could also allow for a fostering of human gentleness or what many call "humanity." But if the oldest and most original state is a truly nasty one, the fundamental concern of the political community must be to keep that original nastiness from breaking out once more. Under this view of politics, a view not unfamiliar to many people today, the guardian of the wall or, as Bloom put it, the policeman, becomes the preeminent political personage (*Closing* 110-112).

What are we to conclude from this complex story, suited by the stranger to his interlocutor's attitudes? It preserves a nostalgia for the simplicity of the old times, a nostalgia that might be felt especially by an old man, who has suffered something of the world's troubles. But it also flatters its listener's realism by suggesting that the simple old times were marked by stupidity and cruelty. It thus clarifies for this legislator why civilization, cities, and lawgiving are so important: to provide a home for intellectual growth and personal security. Neither does it imply, in the end, that the growth of culture comes simply at the price of morality. The stranger clearly rescinds what he says about the first people's virtue with his hints about their viciousness. Intellect and morality can only grow together.

Still, the stranger's Kleinian vision of the past also brings to the fore some of the limitations of legislation. If the oldest times were truly nasty, as they seem to agree, then that nastiness has consequences. The later mischief and even cruelty that so-called "civilized" people inflict upon one another does not look like degeneration or corruption, but a constant eruption of our constantly nasty nature. However much we might progress, we may not be able to extinguish that part of our nature completely. The constancy of human nature, and its constant political problems, is hinted at in the odd way that the stranger speaks of even the family and the nation as "cities." In any event, it seems that they agree that the police will always be with us.

The political community can still try to foster good morals and intelligence. But if this underlying nastiness must always be dealt with, and if keeping the "Cyclopean" part of human nature down must always be on legislators' minds, then the city cannot devote itself wholly to fostering these things. Indeed, depending upon the state of civilization, political communities may be able to devote themselves only indirectly to what is truly highest in human beings. Policemen and armies protect higher culture, but they are not the higher culture themselves. This agreement would mark quite a demotion from Book One, where the characters agreed that a truly good law would aim above all at the divine goods, the moral virtues and prudence. That may be the ideal, but it may be an ideal at which even the stranger recognizes no human city can simply aim. Such conclusions perhaps indicate why, even while he accepts the stranger's disturbing hints about the oldest times, Kleinias—like most people—looks back upon them with some nostalgia.

Spartan Games

The stranger's account of the past is an artful creation, fit to the opinions of his audience and designed to lead them (or him) to particular political conclusions. It also reflects the stranger's own political ambitions in this conversations. Though it emerges in a conversation, this account does not challenge the interlocutors' fundamental beliefs. Rather, it uses the conversation to bring about agreement upon fundamental matters. To us observers, it provides an example of how one might move an auditor who feels some piety, but also has misgivings about the oldest times and so is committed to the worthiness of political life. Here, as elsewhere in the *Laws*, the stranger seeks to elevate—rather than to overturn—politics with his words.

Still, the stranger wraps this practical discussion in the mantle of theory, an appearance which persists into the latter half of Book Three. Here he appears to raise the question, "Who should rule?", a question that strikes at the heart of any community's most settled opinions.

The stranger's treatment of this exceedingly important question arises in the midst of his discussion of Sparta. His "history" of humankind brings him up to the present, or nearly to the present. It actually brings him up to the founding of Sparta. Sparta is of special concern to the stranger, for it is renowned as the best-run city of all the Greek cities. Certainly he says that it had a very good founding. But its promised goodness never materialized. Sparta soon began attacking other Greek cities and generally sowing mayhem. What went wrong?

It is not that the Spartans are lacking in something like courage; as Megillus has said already, they train incessantly for war. Instead, the stranger argues, what they lack is prudence. What he means by prudence, he says, is a "consonance" between desires and opinions. The prudent person has an opinion of what is good and his desires harmonize with that opinion (689a). The Spartans, for all their training, lack this consonance or, as the stranger puts it, are "ignorant of the greatest of human things" (688c).

Strikingly, though Kleinias admits that he and Megillus cannot openly praise the stranger's words, they do not challenge his conclusions about Sparta, conclusions which are hardly evident, even upon the basis of Sparta's treatment of Argos and Messene. They seem to recognize that the stranger's approach partakes more of games than seriousness (see 685a). They play along. And so, based on his claims, the stranger and Kleinias conclude that rule of cities should only be given to those human beings who possess the consonance of prudence.

Very well: Let the prudent rule. But why is it not that easy? Why do things not happen this way? Does something get in the way of the rule of the prudent? Or are the prudent unwilling to rule? The stranger does not raise these questions explicitly. But it is in response to such implicit questions that he abruptly turns to consider what he calls the seven "worthy titles to rule and be ruled" (690a1).

Title Search

His worthy titles to rule and be ruled are parenthood, high birth, age, mastery, strength, prudence, and luck. Some of these titles to rule and be ruled no doubt sound familiar; others may not. All of them are claims to rule that people do put forward. But are they a complete list of such titles? Are any particular worthy titles or claims to rule are missing here?

One might be surprised that wealth does not make it into the list of worthy titles to rule. After all, it is undeniable that wealth has played a significant factor in historical states in the determination of who shall rule. For example, later in this very book the stranger talks about Athens in the old days, before the advent of radical democracy, when the citizen-body was divided into four classes—on the basis of wealth—and the ruling offices were divvied up among these four classes (698b ff.). In other words, in old-time Athens wealth was not the sole title to rule, but it did affect who would rule and who would be ruled. Is wealth ever, by itself, considered a worthy title to rule? The stranger does not argue against the possibility. But if it ever does happen, it would seem, in his view, to be an "unworthy" title.

There is another apparent omission, one that should be evident to citizens brought up with the Declaration of Independence. Where is the claim of "the People" to rule? The Athenian does not mention this claim, the claim of "the people," explicitly. But that is certainly not because he could not imagine it; after all, his home was a democracy. But what do "the people" offer as justification for ruling? That "the people" are all older? or well-born? or luckier? Not likely.

Someone might say that "the people" as a whole are prudent. But is that true? The stranger seems to equate prudence with intelligence (recall 631c). No doubt the majority of the people must be, by definition, of average intelligence. There will be, among the people, some who are very intelligent; but there will also be some who are very stupid. Within the context of the stranger's definitions, it would seem that the people, if they have any title to rule, possess that title only by their strength—for they are, no doubt, very strong.

But this exchange only forces us to see a deeper omission in the stranger's list. For certainly many, especially within American democracy, would defend the people's rule on the grounds that it is most decent, most morally sound. Where is moral virtue or justice on the stranger's list of worthy titles to rule? Is justice simply an expression attached to one of these other titles? Is it not the title most believers give to God, the greatest ruler of all: "I am not a God of iniquity"?

The stranger may mean moral virtue to be encompassed by prudence or intelligence. (See again 631c: prudence is the leader of the other three, explicitly moral, divine goods. Also, in the preceding discussion of Sparta, prudence is equated with a sort of moral consonance.) Still, even if moral virtue were its own title to rule, it would not support the rule of all the people, unless all the people possessed this moral virtue to an equal degree. The stranger does not make the case, but his omission indicates that he does not think such a moral multitude possible. To answer the question why he thinks this way, we will have to wait, to delve more deeply in his views as they emerge in the laws themselves.

Given that this conversation unfolds between two Dorians and an Ionic (Athenian) Greek, and that they go on to discuss Persians and other barbarians, what about race as a title to rule? Again, history suggests that physical, racial differences are easily seized upon by rulers to justify their rule, or by the ruled to explain their subjection. The qualifications so advanced—skin color, hair color, height, and so forth—do seem extraneous to the task of ruling. Perhaps that is why the stranger omits them from the "worthy" list. But that does not make them practically negligible.

Finally, one may also be surprised that the stranger's list makes no reference to sex as a worthy title of rule. He, at least, does not seem to think that either sex has a superior claim to rule the other, or, put otherwise, that when it comes to ruling, sex is irrelevant as the presence or absence of hair (see *Republic* 454c ff.). Accordingly, as we will see in Book Six, he apportions several important political offices in the new city for women.

A Tale of Two Titles

While the stranger's list is broad, then, it does omit a number of possible titles. No doubt the stranger could respond, as indicated above, by saying that such titles propose criteria that having nothing to do with ruling, thus making them "unworthy." But the habit of eliminating such titles as "extraneous" to the business of ruling seems especially fraught with danger for circular reasoning. Also problematic is the stranger's insistence that these titles "are by nature opposed to one another" (690d3-4). That means that, in his view, no more than one claim to rule can be operative in each political community at a time.

In a certain sense, and in some cases, the point seems valid. If we demand that every title operate in the same person, then it seems unlikely that both the eldest and the strongest could rule at the same time. But are parenthood, age, high birth, and prudence exclusive of one another? And why insist that rule be unified in single individuals? What about mixed regimes, of the sort that the stranger had praised only a few moments before in Sparta? Actual regimes seem to operate with much more complexity, even in their fundamental opinions about rule, than the stranger allows here.

These problems should not be taken as evidence of the stranger's stupidity or mendacity, however. Again, he is not simply engaged in a lecture on theory here. His arguments, such as they are, are directed at a particular rhetorical end.

What is that end? To see it, we need, for the moment, to take his discussion as a sort of lecture. If we do so, we face the question of which of these titles, if any, are superior, better, than the others. Is there some rank to them? Are some dependent on others? What, if any, are the relations among the seven?

Strauss (*Argument and Action* 46-47) offers a few hints that sketch out a possible answer to this question. His own hints follow closely the argument of the last chapters of Aristotle's *Politics* Book Three, which also considers this fundamental question, "Who shall rule?" The following paragraphs lay out, following Strauss' hints, his "straight" reading of the stranger's discussion of these titles.

In this discussion, two of the titles stand out. One is the fifth, the claim that the stronger rule and the weaker be ruled. This is the only rule that Kleinias calls "very necessary" (690b6). This is also the title that the poet Pindar, whom the stranger calls "wise" (690c1), says is "in accord with nature" (690b8). The other is the sixth, that bids the ignorant to follow and the prudent to lead and to rule. The stranger himself says that it, and no other, is in accord with nature, and Kleinias agrees, answering that "you speak most correctly" (690c4). These two are the only titles to rule and be ruled that anyone says are "in accord with nature."

Strauss then sketches ways that the other five titles can be linked to these two, as secondary to primary. For example, the first three titles or claims to rule—the claims of parents to rule over descendants, high-born to rule over low-born, and elderly to rule over the younger—all make some reference to age, age of persons or families. But why should the elder rule over the younger? One of the primary reasons would be that they have more experience than the young. But that means that the rule of the older over the younger is itself a sort of reflection of the rule of the prudent over the ignorant, the sixth title.

Likewise, the fourth, that slaves be ruled and masters rule, also reveals itself to be secondary. The stranger never speaks of "natural" slavery or "natural slaves." He does not admit that some people, as Jefferson put it, are born with "saddles on their backs" and others are born "booted and spurred" to ride them. So how do some people come to be masters and others come to be slaves? History shows that slaves are forced into their slavery and are kept in slavery by force. At the bottom of the relation of master and slave is the presence of strength and weakness.

Finally, then, there is the odd seventh claim, that the one who draws a winning lot should rule and those who draw losing lots should give way and be ruled. This title to rule may sound outlandish to people today, but it was not odd to the Athenians of the heyday of the 5th century BC. As a democracy, they treated all citizens as equals, and they took that equality very seriously. So, when their offices came time to be filled, they wanted to make sure that every citizen had an equal opportunity to hold each office. But what is the least discriminatory way to choose a leader, the way that treats all people as completely equal to one another? The roll of the dice. If the lot decides who rules, there can be no charges of favoritism or prejudice of various sorts. Even "free and fair" elections, as exist in contemporary western democracies, allow all sorts of prejudices to reign in the voting booth.

But this title to rule, a title that seems especially at home in pure democracy, is also secondary, according to Strauss' exposition. The lottery, it is true, will never guarantee that only the more prudent or more experienced rule. Nonetheless, it has its attractions. The lottery is attractive because it gives every citizen, no matter how young, or how low-born, or how weak or how stupid, the chance to rule. Even if it picks only this one or other person as a ruler, favors the rule of the people as a whole. But what title do the people as a whole have to decide how rulers shall be chosen? As discussed above, contrary to the moderns, the stranger seems to grant them only the title of strength. But strength is one of those two "natural" titles to rule.

An Insoluble Problem?

What about these two "natural" titles, then? Can they be harmonized? This question is of great importance, for if there exists two fundamental and irreconcilable titles to rule, then the promise of a harmonious, wholly just political community is rendered impossible. If there are two fundamental worthy titles, and a community chooses one, then some people could always complain, justly, "Why not the other?"

So why should not the claim of the prudent and the claim of the strong be harmonized or combined in some manner? Strauss finds the answer to this question in the analysis of the seventh title: The fundamental dilemma is, in his view, that the prudent or wise tend to be very few. Therefore they tend to be very weak. Or, to put the matter positively, the people or the "many" are everywhere and always the strongest, but there is no such thing as a prudent or wise "many." There can only be a prudent or wise "few."

The dilemma becomes most apparent if one looks at it the following way, the way offered in *Politics* Book Three. The many or the people recognize this much, that the rule of the prudent or wise is exclusive. The prudent are not prudent today and imprudent tomorrow. The prudent are necessarily much more prudent than others and they stay that way. Thus, if the prudent were to rule, then by far and away most people would be excluded from the honor of ruling throughout their entire lives. But ruling oneself rather than being ruled is seen by almost everyone to be good thing, one of the best things in fact. Thus, if the prudent or wise were to rule, then by far and away most people would be excluded from this very good thing throughout their whole lives.

But for a community to be a community it must share certain good things; it must have a "common good." This fact is almost so obvious that it must be pointed out from time to time. But what kind of community would it be that excludes the vast majority of people from one of the greatest common benefits and instead relegates this benefit, rule, to a very few all the time? (Consider the anger, on both the left and the right, at the United States Supreme Court's recent decision of a presidential election in *Bush v. Gore.*) It would cease to be a community, since there would not be a truly common good.

After all, the claim of the people to share in the rule, on the basis of their strength, is not just a stupid or brutish claim; it cannot be easily waved aside. The people are strong, and as the strongest they carry the greatest burdens of any community. (For example, in wars, especially in democratic times, it is "the people" who do the dying.) By virtue of their strength, the people share in each community's sacrifices. Why should they not also share in its goods? If this is truly a community, why should the people not share in the common good of rule?

This is, in Strauss' account, the fundamental political dilemma, one that emerges in the stranger's account. The source of this dilemma is that, while it is quite obvious that the people are very strong, it seems quite impossible for the people to become very wise. Both the strong and the wise seem left with defensible claims to rule. The wise could say that their wisdom would lead the community to what is truly good. But the rule of the wise cannot be truly good if it excludes the vast majority of the community from ruling. Instead of good it would be insufferably bad. After all, the people would say, for there even to be a community there must be a sharing of good things, including rule above all. There can be no community without a people, and so the people, by their very "manyness," by their strength in numbers, possess a firm title to rule.

And yet who would not admit, in his most sober moments, that he would prefer to be ruled over by wise and prudent rulers rather than mediocre, fickle, or foolish ordinary folks? We take our cars to experts for fixing. Why should we not entrust our most important public matters to the most intelligent? That is, both claims—the claims of the prudent and the claims of the people—seem irreconcilable and indispensable. But this means that at the heart of political life there is a fundamental dilemma, and it is unavoidable.

Such is one way to take the stranger's discussion of the seven "worthy titles to rule," as a sort of lecture, in which he delivers (in veiled terms) his deepest understanding of the fundamental problem of political life. His treatment of the "mothers" of regimes that follows—his discussion of Persia and Athens, which, as Pangle notes, is riddled with historical inaccuracies and omissions (523-524)—could be taken in a similar way. There the stranger could be said to argue that each "mother"—empire and freedom—has a certain logic to it, and each seeks to rule unopposed. But each also destroys itself when left to rule unopposed. Thus they must be mixed, but the mixture of these fundamental ruling positions means that no nation can spare itself from tension at the deepest level.

But this line of argument, while impressive in the sweep of its theory and its claim—that there can be no just regime among human beings—fails to deal adequately with the stranger's rhetorical stance in this book. He is not just lecturing here, directly or indirectly. The conclusion of Book Three quite clearly shows him maneuvering Kleinias into a practical conversation, a conversation about the city he is charged to found. By the end of the book the stranger has convinced Kleinias that he is the type of man with whom he (Kleinias) may safely share that most difficult and sensitive project.

He does not convince Kleinias of this view by showing him that politics is doomed to temporize among less-than-just options. Nor should we accept that understanding of the stranger's speeches here. Such a view, as mentioned, ignores the omissions—in fact and in theory—in the stranger's statements. It also ignores the conclusion that the stranger offers on the basis of his discussion of the seven worthy titles to rule, and which introduces his discussion of the "mothers" of regimes: that a mixed regime, one that mixes these various titles, is best. He does not seem to have any qualms about a regime's embracing several different titles or claims about who should rule. He does not seem to be a "purist" in this matter. Finally, even if he were, we have not omitted the possibility, forced upon us by the opening of the *Laws*, that the stranger thinks that human beings, left to themselves, do make a mess of their political communities; but that with God's aid, they can live together well. Indeed, far from forgetting or rejecting this possibility, he explores it more fully in Book Four.

How then to explain the stranger's rhetoric here? He does paint a sober picture of the old times and he does suggest that politics is beset by fundamental problems over who should rule and the relation of freedom and empire. But he does these things offering in some cases no evidence and in other little evidence marked by inaccuracies and omissions. His sleight of hand convinces the would-be realist Kleinias that he is a man who does not shy away from the tough choices in political life. But the lack of rigor of his account also leave secure—as they must—Kleinias' vague respect for the old times and his ambition to do good in politics. After all, the stranger gives no indication here that he takes the would-be gloomy messages of his words all too seriously. How could he, and still pursue this political project?

There is a parallel to the stranger's rhetoric in that of the Native Americans so interested in the skeleton of "Kennewick Man." With nothing to go on but "what's said"—and in the face of considerable though not conclusive material evidence to the contrary—they insist that these exceedingly ancient bones belong to one of "their own." Their passion for Kennewick Man rests upon their beliefs, especially their belief that they have "always" lived where they live now, and this passion both grows out of this belief and, importantly, reinforces it. They clearly feel a respect for "the Ancient One," a respect that issues in anger at the treatment his bones are receiving. Nonetheless, as respectful or as angry as they are, none of them suggest returning to the life enjoyed by the Ancient One or even by their much nearer ancestors. Their piety is tempered by a realistic, sometimes even shrewd, understanding of the political situation at the present, and they show no hope or desire to exit that situation. After all, none of the devoted descendants of Kennewick Man have denied that he died from the thrust of a stone-tipped spear into his right side, a spear wielded no doubt by one of their other forebears.

Notes

[1] See the position paper by Chairman Armand Minthorn of the Umatilla Reservation, dated September 1996, at http://www.umatilla.nsn.us/kennman.html. The Interior Department's summarizes its amazing defense of its position in several documents at http://www.cr.nps.gov/aad/kennewick/.

[2] On the Samoan connection, see *Tri-City Herald*, "Polynesian 'relative' lays claim to Kennewick Man," Mike Lee, 26 July 2001. On the Pagan claims, consult "Pagan sect blasts corps' handling of Kennewick Man," Associated Press, 31 August 1997.

[3] For a brief technical description of Kennewick Man, see archeologist James C. Chatters' account at http://www.mnh.si.edu/arctic/html/kennewick_man.html.

[4] See, for example, Pangle's introduction to Book Three, which argues that the

book presents the stranger's account of "man's prepolitical condition" or "the natural necessity of man's historical evolution from precivil to civil life" (423). He thus explains the mythical character of the stranger's statements as softening the blow that the stranger's objective view of "natural necessity" offers to conventional belief (424). Strauss (*Argument and Action* 38-44) also appears to take the stranger's account of the human beginnings as the stranger's own truthful view of the matter, touched up with the appropriate mythical daubings.

[5] In Greek, the same word can be translated as "beginning" or "rule." Thus this question could be asking how the rule involved in political life ever came to establish itself.

Chapter Four:
Upholding the Law

First, a Tyrant

In Book Four the three speakers finally turn to legislating—or almost to legislating. Kleinias, as revealed in Book Three, has to frame laws for a proposed new colony in Crete. He could simply take the old Doric laws and apply them to the new colony. But he has the remarkable freedom to adopt other laws if he thinks he has found better. By the end of Book Three he has become convinced of at least two things: that the Doric laws are not necessarily the best laws, and that the stranger—from Athens of all places—has the knowledge to propose better laws. So Kleinias is undoubtedly eager for the stranger to start proposing.

But the stranger takes his time. They begin, in Book Four, to consider the question of who should rule in the new city. This—the question of who should rule—is the primary political question; there can be no political community without some answer to this question. But the question of who should rule arises here in the context of another question: What is "the best way" to found a new city? (See 707d9.)

To this question the stranger gives an odd answer. He argues that the best way would not be to start a new city from scratch. If a founder does that he runs into the problem of where to find new citizens. They have to come from somewhere, and that somewhere may not be very good. Also, for a city to survive its people need to share customs and beliefs; a truly new city would lack this foundation and possibly collapse from internal weakness. The best way to proceed, instead, would be to transform an already existing city, one that is already "grown together" (708d5). But that means changing, fundamentally, the already existing laws and customs of the place, and this is no easy task. For example, one could observe how long it took in the United States, even with its Declaration of Independence, to bring liberty to its that part of its population descended from African slaves. It required a Civil War, decades of legal wrangling, and some would say that the work is still not finished.

So, the stranger proposes, the best way to found a city would be to start with an already existing community—one ruled by a tyrant (709e ff.). Why a tyranny? A tyrannized city is the easiest to transform, because it is used to bowing to the dictates or even the whims of one man (see 711b). For example, when Stalin announced that National Socialism posed no threat to Communism, communists in the USSR and around the world defended Hitler. When he then denounced the Nazis in the face of Hitler's betrayal, communists around the world just as quickly followed suit. A tyrannical founding, the stranger explains, will be "best and fastest"—if there is a wise legislator present, and if the legislator has the tyrant on his side, and if the tyrant has certain good qualities, such as being young, a good learner, possessing a good memory, courageous, generous, and self-restrained (see 709e-710b). But obviously these are a lot of "ifs."

Kleinias finds it particularly hard to imagine that the wise legislator will find a tyrant who is "self-restrained." (Kleinias may also be surprised that the tyrant should be young. The stranger has ceased to pretend to worship gerontocracy of the Doric type.) After all, tyrants do not usually start out self-restrained, and even if one did, he usually soon loses all self-restraint. One need only recall a few of the tyrants of the past century—Hitler, Stalin, Pol Pot, or Mobutu. These men were not known for their moderation.

Perhaps this is why, in the end, the stranger modifies his argument and concludes that "whenever in the same human being the greatest power coincides with prudence and moderation, then occurs the natural genesis of the best regime and similar laws; but otherwise it will never happen" (711e8-712a3). That is, the best way to the best regime must proceed through something like the tyranny of a very good and wise human being; the wise legislator must himself be the tyrant. But how often does this happen? Has it ever happened? One cannot assume, then, that the stranger means this talk of tyranny as a practical proposal. He is not asking Kleinias to look for a tyranny to take over, nor is he telling him to wait around until a very good and wise man somewhere becomes a tyrant. The stranger's entire argument here serves to show Kleinias and us observers that right at the beginning of their proposed founding there lie overwhelming obstacles to getting it done well.

Divine Rule

Still, even though he does not mean for Kleinias to wait around until some wise man somewhere becomes a tyrant, how can the stranger even be sure that the tyrannical rule of a wise human being really would be best? The stranger answers that question by discussing, in the very middle of Book Four, this most important matter, what "regime" or type of rule and rulers their city should have (712b-715d).

In this context he reveals that the truly best regime or rule would be a theocracy—literally, the rule of a god over human beings (see 713e). He talks about this presumed "divine rule" and what it would look like. He then goes on to give a speech to the hypothetical colonists of their new city (715e-718a). It is the first speech directly aimed at the new citizens. It is wholly concerned with their stance towards the gods or towards the divine. Even though the stranger's laws will not be "divine law" in the traditional sense, that is, laws handed down by a god to human beings, they certainly rest on an understanding of God and God's place in human life. The stranger begins to explain this part of his thought here in Book Four. One could say that, addressed as it is the people of the new city, this speech offers the stranger's "popular" understanding of divine law.

The Advantage of the Stronger

The stranger first asks his interlocutors what kind of "regime" or type of rule this new city will have—again, that most basic of political questions, "Who is to rule?" Kleinias wonders whether it will be one of the usual regimes: democracy (rule of the people), oligarchy (rule of the few), aristocracy (rule of the well-born), or monarchy (rule of one). Megillus adds that his own regime, Sparta, seems to be a mixture of all these regimes. But the stranger rebukes them both. All these usual so-called "regimes" are just forms of "administration," he says, in which one person or one group of persons tyrannizes over or enslaves the others (713a). That is, oligarchy, aristocracy, monarchy, even democracy are all just different forms or permutations of the same thing: tyranny, despotism, or slavery.

How could he say such a surprising, not to say shocking, thing? He seems to have in mind political reflections of the following sort. Each political community is known by a sort of regime, e.g., democracy, oligarchy, aristocracy, or monarchy. As these very words show, a regime is known by nothing other than that part of the community that does the ruling. Again, democracy is the rule "of the people, by the people, for the people." Monarchy is the rule of the one; as Louis XIV is supposed to have said, "L'etat, c'est moi." "The State? That's me."

Every human community is ruled by a certain part of the community, and that part is, by the arrangement of the political regime, the stronger part. So each regime is an instance of the rule of the stronger. But what does that part look to in ruling? The stranger replies: to its own advantage, as a part (see 713a). Thus, in a democracy, the people (who are generally not rich) legislate what is good for the poor (e.g., Social

Security, Medicare, public transportation, etc.). Or in an oligarchy, the few (who are most often the rich) legislate what is good for the rich (e.g., taxes on necessities, no taxes on luxuries or assets).

In every regime, the ruling part legislates for the good of the ruling part, the stronger part. And each regime calls its laws "just." E.g., when democracy by legal taxes redistributes the property of the rich, it calls that "just." Likewise, when oligarchs gobble up the property of the poor in legal debts, they call that "just." Justice is the name given to what is advantageous for this stronger, ruling part. And this is why politics is often such a rough-and-tumble pursuit. Each part or faction wants to get control, and once it does rule it wants to stay ruling. It wants these things because with rule comes the good things. As long as politics is in the hands of human beings, and as long as blood flows through their veins, that is, as long as they are selfish beings, politics will never be peaceful (see 713e4-6). This is the understanding of politics that the stranger begins with here.

The Myth

But, one might well protest, is that all there is to justice? Is justice, true justice, nothing more than what is good for the stronger, the party that is in power? As the stranger himself warns us, this discussion about regimes is not an argument about something minor. "It concerns the greatest thing: again the argument has come back to us about the just and unjust, to what each must look" (714b6-8). It would be very unconvincing if the stranger's criticisms of human regimes were based on nothing more than cynicism about justice. The stranger is not a cynic; he is not the sort of person who simply says, "Everybody's crooked." He does not describe these human regimes as the only regimes. He does not call their crooked justice the whole of justice; indeed their justice is only justice in name. The stranger has his eyes set on a justice of a higher sort, on a more-than-human regime. It is in answer to these pleas about true justice that the stranger brings in the rule of the god.

He mentions (713c ff.) that he has once heard an oracle (or rumor). Now, at this point, hard-boiled readers might be tempted to turn aside in disgust, saying, "Oh, well: he ran out of intelligent things to say, so now here come the tall-tales!" But we should be more patient. The stranger does not turn to this myth as a way to bolster a failing argument. He introduces the myth to show the consequences of something that his very interlocutors—and perhaps even hard-boiled readers too—care deeply about: justice. The myth is the stranger's "popular" way of revealing what true justice demands.

So, he says, he once heard an oracle or rumor that once, long ago, human beings lived a completely blessed life. This life was blessed because they lived justly, that is, in accord with a completely just regime. This regime was completely just because it was ruled not by a human being or by some group of human beings, but by a god, the god Kronos, the father of Zeus. This god Kronos knew that humans could not rule themselves justly. When we rule ourselves we become "stuffed with insolence and injustice" (713c). So he set over us certain super-human rulers, "demons" (good demons), the way we ourselves set human rulers over cattle or over sheep. These super-human rulers provided justice without any grudging. So, unless a god rules, there cannot be a rest from evils for political communities. The only truly just regime is theocracy.

At present, then, even though Kronos and his demons rule over us no longer, we human beings still have a reminder of truly just rule in the stranger's "oracle." And even though we are very far from divine, we should try to imitate this god as much as possible. We should try, through this imitation, to come as close to that most just "rule of god" as possible. But the most godlike part of our mortal selves, according to the stranger, is our intelligence, our "immortal" intellect (713e8). Therefore, "whatsoever in us partakes of immortality, this we should obey...giving the name 'law' to the distribution of the intellect" (713e8-714a2). The only way we human beings can approximate true justice is by letting intelligence rule.

This is the stranger's myth and the political conclusion that follows from it. But no doubt all of this seems to be quite a leap. Is the stranger serious that the rule of god, a theocracy, is best? And how does he move from the mythical rule of Kronos to the present rule of intelligence? Let us consider each of these two questions in order.

Just Kronos?

It is tempting to abstract from the particularities of the stranger's tale and to conclude that, underneath its mythic trappings, it teaches that impersonal "divine justice" is the only hope for the righteous. What sort of argument, then, would support this particular interpretation of the myth?[1]

Assume that when he speaks of justice, the stranger has in mind some general expression of that principle, for example, that of those to whom much has been given, much shall be demanded, and likewise, that those who, by their good deeds, deserve much should get their just deserts. How do we identify those with true merit, who deserve much? In practice, every community reserves its greatest honors (such as political office) to those who are members of the community, excluding even meritorious outsiders. In order to be truly just, then, a political community would have to drop this qualification of membership, the difference between "us" and "them." Limited political communities would have to be transformed into a world-community.

But then one must ask oneself that fundamental question, "Who will rule this world-community?" Given the weakness of human nature, and its propensity for corruption, no human being or group of human beings could do the job well. And even if we could find some "incorruptible" to rule the world, this just ruler must, by the principle of justice, give every person what he deserves. That means the just ruler must know everyone, his abilities and his weaknesses, his accomplishments and his failures, his merit or desert—an obvious impossibility. So, what is divined when one speaks of the need for a "world-community" as an all-encompassing human society subject to one government is in truth a community ruled by a more-than-human power. What is divined by speaking of a world-community, in other words, is the universe ruled by God. The universe ruled by God is then the only truly just regime, the only true community. Anything else falls short of true justice.

Such, then, is one attempt to present the "truth" that might underlie the stranger's "popular" story. But surely the stranger does not invent this story (if he does construct it) with complete disregard to its details. For example, it seems important that he identifies Kronos, and not some impersonal "God," as the beneficent and most just ruler of the old times. Kronos is, as mentioned, the father of Zeus. But the very cave to which the stranger, Kleinias, and Megillus are trekking is the cave in which Zeus hid from his father who, in a bid to preserve his own power, had eagerly devoured all his previous children.

Kleinias does not interrupt the stranger's myth in order to question making the murderous Kronos the exemplar of just rule. But presumably the stranger's choice of deity makes him wonder and renders him all the more likely to accept what the stranger says in the following paragraphs about justice being the advantage of the stronger. It is an ambiguous comment, in the light of the story of Zeus, to say that Kronos ruled human beings as shepherds rule their flock (713d). Likewise, the ancient rule of Kronos might remind us, and the interlocutors, of the stranger's account of the ancient savagery of human beings. It seems hardly plausible, then, to argue that the stranger believes, according to this passage at least, that in divine rule and only in divine rule can we find true justice.

Nomos as *Nous*

If the stranger's myth teaches anything, it shows the difficulty that human beings have distinguishing absolute justice from absolute despotism—the rule of the good shepherd from the rule of the man who shears or even devours his flock. But it also teaches that, whatever the true character of Kronos' regime, he and his demons rule no longer. We human beings are now on our own.

Thus the stranger tells his imaginary colonists that they must make up for the absence of directly divine rule by substituting the rule of their own intellect (*nous*). What does this mean? And why should the present "imitation" of the most just, theocratic rule take the form of obeying intellect as law? Why should true justice today amount to being intelligent or, as one could also put it, using the stranger's language, being prudent (recall 631c)?

The stranger's recommendation supports our surmise that, for him, true justice requires knowledge. If true justice gives to each what he deserves, how does one determine what each person deserves? The usual and most obvious answer would be that the law sets forth what each person deserves. To modify the famous example from the beginning of Plato's *Republic*, if someone owns a gun and he lends it to an acquaintance, the property laws would say that the owner should get the gun back. But the law, as everyone knows, cannot deal with every particular circumstance. And that means that the law, by itself, sometimes seems to command stupid things. To return to the gun example, if the owner of the gun demands his weapon in a state of frenzy, the property laws would still say that he should get his gun back. But no just person would think that giving a gun to a madman is right. Justice should give to each what he deserves—and that giving should produce good, not evil. Justice, as is obvious, should advance the right, not the wicked. So justice cannot blindly follow the law.

Instead, justice must take into account all those particular circumstances. And that means above all accounting for the abilities, intentions, and deserts of each person. But these may differ for a young person as for an old person, just as they differ between the sane and the insane. So, in part, the one who would be just must consider the nature of each person in order to determine what is right. But, to say the least, not everyone knows what the nature of each particular person. E.g., only doctors—who are rather rare—have some vague idea of the nature of bodies. So justice depends on a certain, very exalted type of knowledge— the knowledge of the nature of human beings, the nature not only of their bodies but of their souls. Justice is impossible without wisdom. This wisdom is what, perhaps in the case of Kronos, was combined with world-encompassing power. A beneficent God could provide justice not only because he possessed super-human strength, but also because he possessed perfect wisdom.

So what about human beings? Whether humanity can attain world-encompassing power, through technology, is open to question. But even if humanity had or has such power, human beings would still need this perfect wisdom in order to bring about justice. That is, people would need a union between world-encompassing power and the knowledge of the nature of each and every human being. Such knowledge, the knowledge of every particular person's nature, seems beyond the human ken. That means that universal justice is certainly not politically possible. But, the stranger appears to say, the knowledge of the nature of a few particular human beings—above all, of one's own nature—may not be impossible. Thus one would do what is right, do what is just, by becoming as wise as possible about human nature and acting in accord with it for oneself and for whomever else one could, within the narrow limits of human intellect. This seems to be the meaning of the stranger's call for human beings to obey their intellect, and even, in happy pun, to call the distribution of the intellect (*nous*) the "law" (*nomos*).

What is Law?

If we consider what we have seen thus far in Book Four, the main point is the following: Each and every political community claims that it teaches justice, namely, the giving to each person what he deserves or merits. But different regimes define that merit or desert in different ways. In general, human political regimes define merit or desert in the interest of the ruling part. In democracy the poor are seen as deserving; in oligarchies the rich; in monarchies the monarchs. But that means that these communities are divided: divided within themselves and divided against one another from without. So, where do people turn if they want true and uncompromising justice, to give each and every person what he deserves?

The stranger's "popular" answer is that human beings must turn to the divine. Only the rule of a god provides the world-community that true justice demands. Only the rule of a god combines power with the wisdom or knowledge of human nature that true justice demands. That is, human longing for justice directs humanity's eyes to god.

But, the stranger intimates, no such good god rules at present. So human beings must rule themselves in imitation of such a god. His just rule depended on his wisdom. So, in imitation, human beings must obey their intelligence, their divine part; they must be prudent. True justice—in the limited form human beings can attain—amounts to prudence. This proposal is quite far from the "divine law" discussed at the beginning of the book. But, as the drama of the dialogue reveals, it is the natural point to which concern for that divine law leads.

In the rest of Book Four the stranger talks with Kleinias and Megillus about the form of their new laws. That is, he does not offer any actual legislation yet. This next discussion is preparatory to the actual legislating, which will begin very soon. But this preparatory discussion makes sense, for in it these would-be legislators discuss what law is.

Now, the astute observer might have thought that the characters of this dialogue, the *Laws*, would have discussed this critical question— "What is law?"—long before Book Four. After all, if one does not know what a law is, then how can one be a legislator, a maker of laws? Indeed, one could say that it will be impossible for a person ignorant of law even to be a citizen, since every citizen must distinguish between the law, which he or she must follow, and whatever is not law, as well as between those people who are lawful and those who are not. But how can he do that if he does not even know what a law is? And how can one know what a law is if one do not know what law itself is? So why did the characters not take this question up openly, right at the beginning?

One very obvious reason is that Kleinias and Megillus, like most people then or now, assume that they know what law is. But this observation forces the question more strongly: why do they—or we— never wonder what law is? A second reason for not approaching this question openly, from the start, may be its intrinsic difficulty. Brief consideration of the question, "What is law?" reveals that it is not an easy one.

But there is a third, perhaps obvious, reason why they—and we—did not turn immediately or easily to discussing this question. To answer the question "What is law?" means to offer a definition of law. A "definition" involves drawing a line or a border. That border defines a certain class; it includes some things and excludes others. All the things within the definition share a certain character or likeness. And they are unlike the things outside the definition.

In most matters, such inclusion and exclusion are no big deal. Distinguishing cats from dogs does not offend anyone. Likewise distinguishing oak trees from birch trees causes no disputes. But the matter is altogether different when dealing with laws. For the definition of law implies that some things that people may currently hold to be laws may not, in fact, be laws. That is, the existence of a definition would allow people to test all presumed laws to determine whether they truly deserve that designation. One can easily see the importance of such a designation by considering the slightly different, but still consequential, tests that the United States Supreme Court applies, through judicial review, to determine laws' "constitutionality."

Now such determinations matter, obviously, because law normally commands obedience. And obedience is very difficult, even impossible, to offer if one thinks that the supposed law is not a law at all. In short, the question of "What is law" is a difficult question not only because people hardly ever think of it, nor only because of the intrinsic complexity of the subject, but above all because it threatens to undermine loyalty or allegiance to the existing laws themselves, in particular the laws of one's own community. This cannot help but be a very troubling prospect to any responsible, serious person.

Nous Revisited

In Book Four the stranger offers three different views of what law is. Each one has its attractions but also its detractions. There is no simple answer to this difficult question. So we should consider each in turn, and feel the force of each definition's attractions and detractions.

The stranger's first definition of law has already been mentioned. After describing the idyllic rule of Kronos, the stranger says that today "whatsoever in us partakes of immortality, this we should obey...giving the name 'law' to the distribution of the intellect" (713e8-714a2). No doubt this is a very opaque description of law. What is the "distribution ordained by the intellect"? It would seem to indicate some sort of intellectual insight. Maybe it is knowledge, knowledge of the world and of human beings.

The context seems to suggest that this knowledge would, in particular, concern human nature. Our intellect would seem to "distribute" to us this knowledge. This is why it was said before that law, in this view, would come to look something like prudence. This seems to be a very lofty, not to say pretensious, definition of law. It appears to turn law into something like science or philosophy. Law, in other words, in order to be law, would have to be purely rational, the pure product of intellect.

But, because of its loftiness, this is in a way the least satisfactory of the stranger's definitions of law. First, in order to obey the law, one has to know it. That only makes sense. But prudence, the stranger says in Book Two, is very rare (653a). So, if law is equivalent to prudence, what happens to all those who do not possess prudence? Are they left without law? Or do they possess law in only a metaphorical sense, as the products of other people's intellects (see 645b)?

Second, one must face the practical problem of where this

definition would leave all the supposed current laws. It is a very big thing to claim that true law, as law, must be the distribution of the intellect. How many so-called laws could one say are truly and purely rational? The United States Constitution? Traffic laws? Will even the stranger's laws be purely rational? But if no so-called laws are purely rational, then this definition would undermine allegiance to all such "laws" and would make communal life unstable.

Finally, is it even right to suggest that law could be intellect alone? Consider the case of laws that are "on the books," but which no one respects or enforces. If such laws are purely rational, but everyone ignores them, are they still law? Does not law require the support of some powers, some force, something beyond reason? To put it graphically, does not law have to have "teeth"?

None of these objections are meant to say that the stranger's first view of law as the distribution ordained by the intellect is foolish. After all, it points human beings to what might be said to be the most lawful life, the life of obeying the law as formulated by intelligence, the life of imitating a just god. And it answers to the natural human respect for law, which requires people to admit that they would be unhappy with a law that they thought was mindless or foolish. Law, it seems, cannot be wholly divorced from reason if it is to garner respect, as law. But this respect should not blind readers to the fact that law seems to be more than pure reason as well.

Persuasive Preludes

Let us turn then to the stranger's second view of law. After giving his speech to the prospective citizens, a speech that encourages their humility before the gods and their ancestors and encourages their hopes for justice, the stranger returns to the subject of what law is. Here he emphasizes a very important political problem (718b ff.). Law, he points out, must address everyone, the entire community. There is not one law for me and another for you and so on by individuals. Thus the law must speak in a general manner. But the fact is that human beings are not all alike. They have different natures, and so they have different desires. How are legislators to reconcile the need for generality with the need to speak to individuals?

The stranger suggests that they include a preface or prelude to each law to persuade the citizens why they should act in this way and only in this way, why this way is best. Thus the stranger and the interlocutors adopt what Kleinias calls the "double" legislation (720e6). Each law will contain two parts: a prelude and a command. The stranger offers, as an example, a hypothetical marriage law. The law will command people to marry between certain ages or else suffer certain penalties. But the law will also contain a prelude that gives certain reasons for marrying, i.e., that explains why obeying the law is actually quite fitting for each individual. In other words, this argument presents law as a combination of both persuasion and force.

This presentation of law as a combination of persuasion and force is in some ways the most attractive. This view of law would accord with the characteristically modern argument that law relies upon consent. Law is not merely tyrannical, not merely a matter of force. It is a self-evident truth, according to the Declaration of Independence, that government derives its "just powers" from the consent of the governed.

Also, this view of law as a combination of persuasion and force seems to make it possible for people to respect law while not taking any overly lofty, unrealistic view of law. One of the problems of the first definition, which treated the distribution of intellect as law, is that it seems to leave no room for force, for the "teeth" that law must have. This, second view of law would allow listeners to respect law as involving some sort of appeal to thinking, in the form of persuasion. But it would also acknowledge that this appeal is still in the service of getting people to obey a certain command, a command backed up by the threat of force and punishment.

But this view of law, as a combination of persuasion and force, as attractive as it is, has its own difficulties too. First, the very appeal to persuasion creates a certain difficulty. The stranger says that the prelude will persuade the citizens in the same way that a "free doctor" persuades his patients to take certain drugs. It is not like a slavish doctor who merely orders his patients to do such and such without explanation (720a-e).

But, one should observe, the free doctor persuades the patient to allow him to better the patient's physical condition. Persuasion, in this case, aims at the patient's own health. Persuasion in general tries to move people to a certain action by appealing to their own interest. So, the difficulty caused by making persuasion an integral part of law would be that it involves appealing to individual selfishness. Or, if the stranger does not quite make that appeal, making persuasion an integral part of law would at least hold out the possibility that the preludes themselves, the law itself, would corrupt certain citizens, if not all citizens, by leading them to focus on their own selfish interests. Instead of asking what they can do for their country, these citizens would always being looking to the law for a persuasive explanation of what it will do for them.

A second, and related, difficulty of viewing law as a combination of persuasion and force can also be discerned from the example the stranger gives of the "free doctor." He likens the lawgiver to the "free doctor" (720a). But they are quite different. The free doctor uses only persuasion to help his patient; the lawgiver must also use force. The lawgiver seems to combine both the free and the slavish doctors' techniques.

This obvious difference between the lawgiver and the free doctor points out an even more significant difference. The doctor's whole concern, if he is a good doctor, is with the patient, with curing or bettering that individual patient. The case is not the same with the lawgiver. The lawgiver must care for an entire city, not for individuals. His concern is the common good, not simply the good of individuals. To take the most obvious and painful example, cities sometimes must defend themselves in war. In doing so, statesmen must order some people into harm's way, even to their deaths, in order to preserve the community "as a whole." To be sure, those who die often do so gladly, as it is a noble thing. But they themselves recognize, and everyone else recognizes, that they are making a sacrifice, even "the ultimate sacrifice," that they are giving up something good for the sake of what is right.

A doctor may persuade you to cut off your arm, if it is diseased, for your own good. But a statesman cannot tell you that giving your life in battle is for your own good. In other words, the law, by its very nature, cannot rely on persuasion alone; it must hold out the option of force and punishments, because it sometimes must ask people to do very painful things. However appealing persuasion may be, to overemphasize the place of persuasion in law may not only be corrupting, it may actually lead to misunderstandings of what law actually is.

Forceful Commands

We are thus prepared for the third and last response to the question "What is law?" that the stranger offers here, in this critical discussion in Book Four. This response comes at the end of the Book, after the stranger has offered the example of the marriage law as a sort of "double" law. He tells his interlocutors here that what they have done is to discover the need for "preludes" (722d). This is a very great step forward in the art of legislation. But here the stranger clearly distinguishes between the prelude and the law itself. One should consider the relevant passage in full (722e):

> But the discussion we've been having, so it seems to me,
> shows us that the very laws that were called 'double' seemed
> to me just not to be simply double, but rather two things: a

> law and a prelude to the law. What was called a tyrannical
> order, and likened to the orders of doctors whom we called
> unfree—this seemed to be unmixed law. But what was
> mentioned before this, and was said to be persuasive on
> behalf of this law, really did seem to be persuasive, but
> seemed to have the power of a prelude in speeches. For it
> became apparent to me that this whole speech, which the one
> speaking gives in order to persuade, is spoken for the sake of
> this: so that he to whom the legislator speaks the law may
> now receive the command—which is, in fact, the law—gently
> and account of his gentleness more apt to learn something.

This is a very rich passage, but its obvious point is hammered home: the
persuasive preludes are not, strictly speaking, a part of the law. The law
is not the persuasion. The persuasive speeches are added to the law, to
make listeners well disposed to the law. But these persuasive speeches are
not the law nor even, properly speaking, part of the law. The law as law is
the command, a command that is backed up by the threat of force and
punishment.

The law is command backed up by force. Obviously this answer
to the question poses deep problems. Not the least problem is that law
itself is often defined, in practice, by contrasting it with force. For
example, compare these two situations. In the first, you are stopped on the
street by a man with a gun who commands you to give him your wallet or
else he will shoot you. In the second you get a notice from the IRS
commanding you to pay certain taxes and threatening that if you do not
pay you will face penalties and jail time. Most people would say that
although these two situations have some resemblance, they are in fact very
different. Both do involve a command and the threat of force. But the
second is called lawful and the first is decried as lawless. Still, the
stranger's argument and the movement of his thought would seem to
indicate that, in his view, the two are essentially the same.

But this conclusion does not seem to be exactly correct, even by
the stranger's difficult argument. Everyone, as noted before, recognizes
that the law often demands painful things, like handing over money on tax
day or much more painful things than that too. But people, or at least
decent people, do not complain about these demands they way they would
about the demands made by a mugger. Decent people do not complain
because they say that these demands are just. The law is a just command,
backed up by just force. A mugger issues an unjust command, and follows
it up with an unjust use of force. Or, to look to the consequences, the just
commands of the law lead to noble sacrifices. The unjust commands of a
criminal lead to losses or harm. Sacrificing for what is right is a lot
different from handing over your wallet to a robber.

Now, someone might complain, is the law-abiding person only "sacrificing" because the law commands and threatens? The decent person would respond that of course some people merely obey the law out of fear. Maybe some lowly, selfish people would not sacrifice if the law did not threaten punishment. But not all people are lowly and selfish.

Decent people look to the law not as a harsh taskmaster or tyrant, holding a big stick over their heads. Rather they look to the law for instruction, to show them what their duties are, what sacrifices they should make, and how to make them. That is why, in part at least, the stranger suggests that people can learn from the law. The law itself, and politics as a whole, is a sort of education, an education first of all in virtue. The fact that the law is essentially a command backed up by force—and not an appeal to our intellect or to our selfishness—is no reason for despair but rather an opportunity. It means that the law itself responds to, reflects, and educates the decent desire to do what is right.

As his speech to the prospective colonists and his dialogue with Kleinias reveals, the stranger does not think that any human law, by itself, can wholly direct citizens to do what is right. But some laws do so better than others. Laws prefaced by preludes, themselves largely a product or distribution of the intellect, may do very well indeed. Thus, by this point in the dialogue, Plato has fully justified the reader's interest in law. Law is not a matter for would-be philosophers or Kronoses to despise. Nor is it an object of thoughtless obedience. Careful consideration of law provides our first and most comprehensive instruction in justice.

Note

[1]The details of this argument appear in Strauss, *Natural Right and History* 146-152.

Chapter Five:
Union, Now and Forever

Payback

In the middle of Book Five of the *Nicomachean Ethics* Aristotle debunks the view, held in intellectual circles by the Pythagoreans, that reciprocity constitutes justice. Reciprocity literally means "suffering in response," and popular mythology puts its definition into the mouth of Rhadamanthus, the judge of the afterlife: "If one suffers what one did, that would be the straight upright way" (88). Aristotle argues that such suffering cannot constitute justice, since a policeman who strikes a criminal should not receive a blow in return; nor should a criminal who strikes a policeman simply receive a blow himself; nor should tradesmen expect to sell their goods for exactly what they put into them (1132b).

But though Aristotle refuses to call reciprocity justice, he does admit its great importance to human communities. As he explains,

> For a city stays together by paying things back, since people seek either to pay back evil, and if they cannot, that seems to be slavery, or to pay back good, and if they cannot do that, exchange does not happen, and they stay together by means of exchange. This is also why people put a temple of the Graces by the roadway... (*Ethics* 88).

Reciprocity may not be true justice, but, whether it takes the form of paying back evils or exchanging kindness, it holds cities together

Shared Suffering

Machiavelli describes the same phenomenon, though in different terms, in his *Prince*. In general, he advises princes to found their power upon their own possessions, that is, the matters under their own control, and to trust not in others' good will or in fortune. One of the greatest possessions a prince can and should make his own, Machiavelli recommends, is the people of his city. Contrary to aristocratic authors who condemn the people as fickle and cowardly, Machiavelli identifies them as the major source of power in any community and as eminently worthy of the wise prince's careful attention (41). Machiavelli thus becomes the modern father both of propaganda and populism.

But how does a prince make the people his own? Machiavelli outlines several maneuvers in his book, but two of the most colorful concern shared suffering. The first involves the prince who finds himself besieged by enemies. Machiavelli recommends that he bring his subjects into the city's walls, abandoning their farms and possessions to the enemy's ravages. One might think that seeing their homes destroyed would turn the people against the prince. But no, Machiavelli concludes: "At that time they [the people] come to unite with their prince so much the more, since it appears he has an obligation towards them, their houses having been burned and their possessions ruined in his defense" (44).

In the second case, Machiavelli describes Cesare Borgia's success at pacifying the Romagna, which he conquered and found in a state of disunion, "full of robberies, quarrels, and every other kind of insolence" (29). Borgia famously set up a "cruel and ready" overlord named Remirro de Orco, whose cruelty quickly put lesser brigands out of business. But then comes Cesare's masterstroke:

> Because he knew that past rigors had generated some hatred for Remirro, to purge the spirits of that people and to gain them entirely to himself, he wished to show that if any cruelty had been committed, this had not come from him but from the harsh nature of his minister. And having seized this opportunity, he had him placed one morning in the piazza at Cesena in two pieces, with a piece of wood and a bloody knife beside him. The ferocity of this spectacle left the people at once satisfied and stupefied (30).

Remirro's cruelty enforced a certain sort of peace, what two recent authors call "the peace of the prison" (Seabury and Codevilla 265-267). But such peace is inherently unstable, the more so the more time passes. Cesare's cruelty reminds the people of their past suffering under Remirro and reminds them of what might happen to them if they step out of line. But more importantly, by destroying their apparent oppressor, Cesare wins their gratitude and creates a more settled tranquillity.

Union

Both Cesare and the prince under siege make the people their own. Both rely upon the same wellspring of trust in the people's hearts. As Machiavelli explains when discussing the case of siege, "The nature of men is to be obligated as much by benefits they give as by benefits they receive" (44).

That is, people want to believe that when they receive good it is not just a bit of luck they should blithely pocket, but part of a larger scheme of things which demands a return of benefits to some good purpose. Likewise, people want to believe that when they receive harm it is not simply a loss to be regretted or forgotten, but part of a larger scheme of things, a sacrifice, which interests them in the fate of others. Some of those others become the possible objects of their anger, while some stand out in the people's minds as the recipients of their sacrifice. From these recipients they then expect, in turn, a benefit at some point. The principle of reciprocity thus underlies Machiavelli's teaching as well as Aristotle's. Aristotle, however, tries to elevate reciprocity, a principle he criticizes, by emphasizing its quasi-divine status—the temple of the Graces. Machiavelli, in contrast, gives us Cesare and Remirra de Orco.

Thoughts about reciprocity, shared suffering, retribution, exchange, friendship, and unity very much animate the discussion in Book Five of the *Laws*, though their importance may not be obvious on the surface. Their importance in political life is, however, unmistakable.

For example, anger, frustration, and the desire for retribution dominated American political life following the attacks on Pearl Harbor or the World Trade Center. Likewise, after each of these attacks, though serious questions were raised about government officials' negligence as contributing to the disasters, in general the people expressed great willingness to grant the government much greater powers than it possessed before the attacks. In each case observers also discerned a stronger sense of social unity than preceded, especially notable in a society often described as individualistic or atomistic.

Book Five of the *Laws* explores the roots of civic unity. It also makes conjectures about the different possible types of civic unity. Finally, this chapter will argue that while liberal democracy cannot attain the ideal unity postulated by Book Five—a unity that the city of the *Laws* cannot attain either—it might make possible a type of union and civic friendship that even the stranger could have approved.

The First Prelude

Thus far in the *Laws* we have seen that the Athenian stranger claims to have made a very great innovation in legislation. He claims to have invented legal "preludes," persuasive speeches that precede the actual laws, and which make the listeners more disposed to and hence ready to learn from the law (723a). The prelude is not pure reason; it is meant to be persuasive, not demonstrative. It is meant to persuade the citizens to do what the law commands and forces them to do. The prelude and the law, then, are not the same.

This invention of preludes allows the stranger to explain the conversation to this point. Everything they have been speaking of so far, he says, has been a prelude to actual legislation (722d). In particular, the stranger's imagined speech to the citizens of the city they are going to found, which began in the middle of Book Four (716a), is the first prelude to that proposed law-code (see 724a). That speech, which concerns how the citizens are to honor the gods and their ancestors, runs from 716a-718a. At the end of Book Four Kleinias asks the stranger to complete this first prelude (723e). So, the beginning of Book Five, from 726a-734d, offers the rest of this first prelude. Only after this prelude is completed do the three characters turn, in the middle of Book Five, to the laws themselves. So, before we come at last to those laws, we too must try to understand, at least in outline or in small part, this first and most fundamental prelude to the *Laws*, a prelude that is meant to prepare our minds for all that follows.

This prelude, as seen, takes the form of a speech from the stranger to the would-be citizens of the new city. It has four parts (see Strauss, *Argument and Action* 67-71). The first part is the section in the middle of Book Four (716a-718a). This part is meant to persuade the citizens to become servants of the law (see 715d). To do so, it speaks to them about the divine things. It encourages the citizens to try to imitate the god by being moderate (716c). It encourages the citizens to sacrifice and pray to the gods (716d-e). Likewise it orders the citizens to honor their ancestors and to respect their parents (717a-e). If they do these things, the stranger claims, then they will get what we deserve from the gods and they will live in good hope (718a).

The stranger says that the remaining three parts of this prelude, which come at the beginning of Book Five, concern how the citizens "should be serious and how they should relax as regards the matters of their own souls, their bodies, and their property...so as to attain education—as much as they can." (724a7-b3) That is, the next three parts of this first prelude are particularly important to the listeners' education.

The second part of this first prelude runs from 726a-730a. This part concerns how one should or should not honor one's soul, body, and possessions. First the stranger describes how one should not "honor one's own soul."

- One should not avoid taking responsibility for one's own

wickedness.
- One should not give in to pleasures or pains.
- One should not fear death.
- One should not value physical beauty over virtue.
- One should not try to honor one's own soul with the acquisition of wealth and riches.

In other words, "to honor" means to lead the soul to virtue. One does not "honor" one's soul by pursuing self-esteem, pleasure, security, beauty, or wealth above virtue.

From one's own soul the stranger then turns to one's body and material possessions. Surprisingly, he says that one should not try to be the most beautiful, strongest, even healthiest. That is, one should seek moderate bodily beauty, strength, health and wealth; the stranger thus continues, in a way, the praise of moderation that he began back in Book One.

Finally, the stranger turns from one's soul, one's body, and one's material possessions, to one's social possessions, so to speak: one's family, friends, city, and the other human beings who inhabit one's world. In general, one should avoid being haughty, proud, arrogant, or harsh when dealing with these other people. That is, one should be reverential or modest in dealing with one's family, friends, fellow-citizens, and even strangers. Again, this second part of the first prelude concerns how one should or should not honor one's soul, body and possessions.

The third part runs from 730b-732d. In it the stranger says that they will explain "what kind of person one should be if one is to lead the most noble sort of life" (730b4). Everything up till now in the prelude has been a model for legislation. The citizens should honor the gods, their ancestors, their parents, their souls, their bodies, and their possessions, in such or such a manner. Everything up till now has been as much a guide for lawgivers as for citizens. But this third part does not speak of lawgivers or laws. It offers praise or blame. Its purpose is not to ease the way for any particular laws (such as regarding the honoring of the gods), but to make the citizens "gentler and well disposed to the laws" that in general will be laid down (730b5-7).

So, in this part, the stranger praises the truthful or trustworthy man. He also praises what he calls the "great man in the city," "the perfect citizen" (730d6-7). The perfect citizen is the one who eagerly assists the magistrates in punishing wrongdoers—the executioner, one could say, with only a little exaggeration. The stranger also praises generosity and lack of envy. He then argues that the "real man" in this city is spirited, that is, prone to anger, yet also gentle. And, the stranger adds, everyone should love justice even more than he loves himself. Finally, he says, each person's foremost emotion or passion should be a calm hope that god will give him and his city what is best. None of these passions or ways of acting are, obviously, things that the law can command. The law cannot command people to be spirited or gentle or lovers of justice. But this part of the prelude tries to praise such states of soul as clearly as possible.

The fourth and last part of this long, first prelude runs from 732e-734d. At the beginning of this part the stranger says that everything they have said thus far concerns "divine things." He seems to have in mind the talk about honoring the gods or honoring the soul or trying to attain certain praiseworthy states of soul. But, he says, we are not talking to gods. We are in dialogue with human beings. So we must discuss human things. And in this fourth part he discusses very human things: pleasure and pain. He takes up this question: is the noblest life also the most pleasant, or are they two different lives? He concludes that the virtuous life in general is more pleasant than the vicious one. This surprising lesson, then, is the end to this first, great prelude, a prelude whose purpose is, again, to persuade the citizens to be faithful servants of the laws.

The Noblest Life?

All four parts of this prelude are rich, interesting, and deserve careful study. To do so properly would require a whole other book. Instead, let us focus on the third part of this first prelude. There are at least two reasons for doing so (see 730b). First, it is in this third part that the stranger claims to explain "what kind of person one should be if one is to lead the noblest sort of life." This is a pretty big claim. It is worth seeing what this life is. Second, the stranger also says, in moving from the second part to this third part, that "After this, these are the things we must speak about—not so much law but rather how praise and blame can make each of the citizens gentler and well-disposed to the laws that are going to be laid down" (730b5-c1). This third part of the prelude most obviously and self-consciously sets the ground for the citizens' acceptance of the laws as a whole. It most of all tries to educate the citizens to receive the laws willingly. It thus describes the basics of civic unity.

If we look at this part of the long first prelude, we meet a remarkable character. The stranger says there that "the one who brings aid to the ruling powers in inflicting punishment, the great and perfect man in the city—let this one be proclaimed a bearer of victory in virtue" (730d5-7). This fellow is the perfect human being—in the eyes of the city. This man sits at the pinnacle of virtue—according to the city. This is the great man—according to the city. If we get to know this "great man" better, perhaps then we can better understand the "noblest life." At the very least we will understand better the civic point of view.

This great man in the city distinguishes himself, according to the prelude, by one characteristic activity: the great man in the city is "the one who brings aid to the ruling powers in inflicting punishment" (730d5-6). He is, again, a sort of executioner, so to speak. This "great man" may sound to some readers rather harsh. And he is. But that does not mean that people today do not appreciate such individuals—though they are, as Remirro de Orco illustrates, most appreciated in their absence. Popular movies, nonetheless, are full of such men. John Wayne played them all the time. Sometimes it took a lot to move him to get involved, but even if he was not wearing a badge, he eventually got the bad guys and got them good. Clint Eastwood also played such a "great man in the city" in both his Western and his "Dirty Harry" films.

A more recent example can be found in the movie *The Untouchables*. The Kevin Costner character, Eliot Ness, fits the bill of the "great man in the city" exactly. His whole life as a Justice Department agent is consumed with a hatred of Al Capone and his criminal exploits. And so Agent Ness devotes himself to crushing Capone by any means possible. Viewers like John Wayne, Clint Eastwood, Kevin Costner—and one can add to that list Charles Bronson, Sylvester Stalone, Arnold Shwarzenegger, Chuck Norris, and a hundred other tough guys. People at least like it when they beat up bad guys.

But what makes people, what makes the city, think that this "great man" is so great? The stranger explains it this way. Everyone thinks it is fine not to do injustice. But, most people would say, it is at least twice as fine to stop others from doing injustice. That is, at the core of the "great man in the city," at the core of this "perfect" human being, at the core of this "bearer of victory in virtue," is a passion for justice or, more precisely, for stopping injustice.

Again, these popular movies or television shows bear out the stranger's point. The main characters in them are always trying to stop injustice or to punish the injustice that has already been done; they all seek to get the wrongdoers. And most people would say that this point of view—the view that says the great man loves to stop injustice—makes some sense. One may recall here the stranger's first definition of education, in Book One, in which he describes the peak of liberal education as learning how to fall in love with becoming "a perfect citizen, who knows how to rule and be ruled with justice." (643e5-6) Perfect citizenship and justice are undoubtedly linked.

However, one should note the limitations of this popular point of view, the point of view that says the one who punishes injustice is the great or perfect man. First, according to it, the punishment of injustice is the highest virtue, above all the others. In contrast, the stranger has said that a city should aim at prudence, friendship, and freedom (693b and 701d). The stranger has also said that the law should prepare citizens for prudence above all (631c and 688e). But when it comes to persuading actual citizens, when it comes to addressing the city as it is, he must acknowledge that the highest most people will aim is at justice—not prudence.

And is it even justice that they aim at? When the stranger talks about a liberal education back in Book One he implies that the perfect citizen is the one who know how to rule and be ruled with justice. Justice looks there to be the virtue of ruling oneself and others. The same is the case in Book Four, in which the stranger wishes that human beings could turn justice into prudence, which would mean ruling ourselves as individuals justly and wisely. Here, in Book Five, the emphasis is on punishment. Remirro de Orco, Eliot Ness, or the characters of John Wayne and Clint Eastwood—these men are not rulers.

The stranger does not deny that rule is an important part of justice, maybe the most important part. But he focuses here, in his speech to the would-be citizens, not on what is best but on what is most necessary. In politics it is necessary to take most people where they are. And most people focus their eyes not on ruling but on punishing those who transgress the laws. Justice, for most people, means "throwing the book" at law-breakers. They assume that "the book" has already been written. Justice, for most, does not mean ruling themselves or others wisely. So one cannot ignore this fact: the "perfect citizen" of this prelude seems to fall very short of the well-educated, just person whom the stranger praises in the earlier books.

Real Men

But the stranger admits, even within this part of the prelude, that this "great and perfect man in the city" cannot simply talk the palm for victory in virtue. He does not ignore the popular view, which praises the punisher. But he also indicates that this popular view should stand as only part of the true view.

As noted, this part of the prelude, which describes the "noblest life," first praises truthfulness and trust. Then, after praising the punisher, it condemns envy. The stranger then describes someone he calls the "real man." The stranger's prelude praises "the real man," who "should be spirited, but also as gentle as possible" (731b3-4). The description of the real man highlights the shortcomings of the tough guy.

The real man's combination of spirit and gentleness is hard to fathom. By calling him "spirited," the stranger indicates that this real man readily gets angry. When he sees someone doing wrong he does not turn the corner or close his window. He tries to stop the wrong. Still, the stranger adds here, the real man must recognize that no one does wrong voluntarily. His argument is complex, but in short he offers the famous Socratic argument that when someone does wrong he makes himself worse (see *Apology* 25c ff., *Meno* 77c-78a, and, for a fuller exposition, see *Laws* 860c ff.). But, the stranger adds, no one would voluntarily harm himself. Thus those who do wrong must do so out of ignorance, involuntarily. Therefore, the real man must also be gentle to those wrongdoers who can be "cured," who can have that evil removed from their souls. However, towards those who are incurable, he should let his spirit rage unchecked.

So, there is some resemblance between this real man and the "great man in the city." Both of them can get angry; both are ready to punish. But the great man in the city is characterized only by a readiness to punish. He does not need, or it is not asked of him, to have the gentleness of the real man. That is, the great man in the city need only be half of a real man.

The Greatness of the Great Man

However popular tough guy characters may be in movies, it is likely that few people in our times would criticize the stranger's "real man" for his gentleness. Indeed, to the contrary, many people might imagine that a real man never really gets angry. Still, we must remember that the stranger's "noblest life"—while free of lying, envy, selfishness—mixes together both anger and gentleness. Because of our times, we run the risk of condemning the "great man in the city" as all anger and praising the real man as all kindness and gentility.[1]

The brief against anger is one that particularly appeals to the modern American temper. Without a doubt, one critically important characteristic of the "great man" in the American "city" is tolerance. Negatively put, the good American is not a zealot or a fanatic. Indeed, even before September 11th, "zealous," "zealot," "fanatic," and "fanaticism" had become nasty words in modern American usage. Likewise, "tolerant" has become a term of praise. The attack on the World Trade Center seems not to have seriously upset this order of values, even strengthening it in some people's minds.

What does this toleration amount to? In general, one could say, the tolerant person does not "judge" other people. Most people today are especially easy-going, or squeamish, when it comes to judging other people's beliefs about the highest or most important things (e.g., god, politics, morality, etc.). Contemporary good citizens try to get along. They try to put aside such differences so that they can work together, "getting things done." They are so non-judgmental and so focused on business that our contemporary good citizens are sometimes squeamish about applying even their own laws in a rigorous fashion. Legislatures attempt again and again to get American courts to apply even their minimum sentences in a rigorous way. And contemporary citizens almost reflexively react against serving on juries.

Most people today are just too nice—and too busy—to punish others. The good American works hard and pursues his own prosperity, but without stomping on others—or at least without stomping on others he can see. The good American dreams about following "his own drummer," but he always keeps careful watch that his drumming does not overpower that of other individuals. The good American citizen is a nice person especially when it comes to judging others. He or she is always ready to see the best in other people, to look for reforms to be made, and if someone must be punished, the good American does so only after much deliberation and hand-wringing—and then makes sure to pay someone else to do the actual deed. Perhaps one reason people today like Dirty Harry so much is that no one wants to do the dirty work of punishing himself.

What is at the bottom of this toleration, this niceness, this non-judgmental streak, or this desire to work together above all else? At the bottom of these sentiments is what is at the bottom of most political sentiments in America: a particular interpretation of the principle of equality. Everyone is human, one might say. Everyone is equal. Even people we disagree with deeply. Even criminals. Even terrorists.

For example, the American reaction to the obviously religious overtones of the September 11th attacks has revealed that, even in a state of war, this particular form of toleration—one that forbids "judging" others—is alive and well. The problem with the terrorists is not their beliefs, it is said, specifically their Islamic faith. The problem is with *how* they believed, the intensity of their hatred, their intolerance for others' equal right to life. Thus in the consequent war Americans have done little to try to change their enemies' minds and beliefs—or even to identify their enemies too precisely—and have focused instead on securing or destroying certain weapons, promoting institutional change in other countries (as if "democracy" automatically makes a country good and friendly to other democracies), and strengthening their own internal security. Even the latter attempt has run afoul of the fear of treating suspected classes of individuals "intolerantly," that is to say, not exactly the same as everyone else. For very practical reasons, the war on terrorism may reveal whether this peculiar interpretation of equality, one that leaves political equality far behind and instead levels all human beings to the same moral level, can continue to hold its lofty place in the national mind.

Compared to the tolerant American citizen, the "great man in the city" of the *Laws* looks like a fanatic. After all, as the stranger explains in the second part of the prelude, the "great man in the city" cares above all about the bettering of his soul. The person who talks about soul today, especially in public life, stands out as an object of curiosity. And he, the perfect civic-man, is ready to assist the magistrates in punishing the unjust. Most people today, again, are very uneasy about punishment.

At bottom, the real difference is this: the good citizen of the *Laws* is not impressed at all by claims that one must offer all human beings equal respect. He sees a hierarchy of goods in this world. And, corresponding to this hierarchy of goods, there is a hierarchy of human beings. One's place in that hierarchy does not depend on one's political rank; indeed, the two may be unrelated. One's place in the hierarchy of human beings depends on what good or evil one's soul pursues. The best people are those who pursue wholeheartedly the best things, and so on down the line. One can choose to pursue rather lowly goods, such as fame or wealth or even personal health and security, but, the "great man" would say, one cannot choose that there be no hierarchy of better and worse. Thus, from the point of view of the good citizen of the *Laws*, the "great man" in contemporary American would not look wicked. Instead, this tolerant American would look frankly insensitive—insensitive to the difference between human greatness and littleness, right and wrong, goodness and viciousness.

One-sided Dialogue

The stranger's discussion of the "great man in the city" thus offers insight into one element of civic unity: anger. Every community arranges itself around certain goods. Every city devotes itself to one or a few goods above all. But most people think about those goods only when they are threatened. They then become angry, or they praise those who repulse the threat. Anger and a desire to punish do not provide the highest ground for civic unity, according to the stranger. The rest of the first prelude reveals the limitations of that simply reactive stance. But anger and the desire to punish do reveal, in their limited way, the deeper grounds for that unity, in the moral goods that angry citizens seek to defend.

What then does Book Five reveal about those deeper grounds? Let us turn back from the details of the argument to the appearance of the book as a whole.

Book Five is one of the strangest books in the dialogue, for several reasons. The most obvious sign of its oddity is that it is entirely lacking in dialogue. That is, Book Five is a monologue by the stranger, till the very last line when Kleinias basically says, "I agree." No other book of the *Laws* is so monologic. This characteristic obviously stands out in a work called a platonic "dialogue."

So why is Book Five so strikingly a monologue? The most obvious reason for a monologue is that the main speaker, here the stranger, does not allow any interruptions, and in particular, any questions. He keeps talking without a break, with barely a breath. But why would he do that? It may be that he is trying to sneak something by Kleinias, his main interlocutor, in this flood of words. Still, Kleinias has already proved himself ready to dispute what displeases him. And Kleinias never interrupts or demands to ask a question.

Instead, it is better to assume that in this book the stranger is presenting material which he thinks must be presented as one whole, without breaks or digressions. This material may itself be very questionable, which would be the reason that digressions are a real danger here. That is, he may be presenting material that he knows Kleinias will not entirely understand, but which he wants Kleinias to hear and then think about. This is material that we readers may also not understand and would have to think about at length after reading it. That is, this is material which, if the stranger let us, could very easily lead to all sorts of questions and long digressions—discussions which would entirely destroy the stated goal of talking about laws.

Still, the stranger clearly thinks that, for this legislative purpose, this difficult material must be heard. So, it is precisely for Kleinias' good, and the good of his legislative project, that the stranger dominates the discussion here. He presents things that he thinks Kleinias, as a prospective legislator, must think about. But he does so without room for present discussions that would get in the way of his helping Kleinias' legislation by talking about actual laws. So, the stranger's monologue, his "lecturing," one could say, is exactly suited to Kleinias' practical situation.

The Ground of the Laws

So what is this difficult material that has to be presented but cannot be discussed here in Book Five? The first half of the book has been considered already: The first half completes the fundamental prelude to the laws as a whole. It presents highly important material. It aims, above all, at making the prospective citizens good servants of the laws. So the second half of Book Five, from 734e to the end, should turn at last from the prelude to law. But what law? Which law is the primary or fundamental law of Plato's *Laws*?

It seems at first as if it is going to be the law concerning magistrates and their selection, the law that define the government of the political regime. For example, one should consider 734e3-735a6:

> Let the prelude to the laws spoken to this point find an end to its speeches; but after the prelude it is surely necessary for a law to follow—or rather, in truth, to sketch the laws of a political regime. ... Let there be two parts to a political regime: the establishment of each kind of ruler, and the laws given to the ruling offices.

But, in fact, the stranger then puts off the discussion of ruling offices till Book Six. Something else, it seems, must come first. That something else is the consideration of property and the citizen-body's attitudes towards property. That is, the first and most fundamental laws of Plato's *Laws*, those upon which all the remainder rests, are the property laws. What we must do, then, is to review these property laws and then consider the most odd of all their odd features.

Staking Claim

As founders of a new colony, Kleinias and his friends have it easier, in one sense, than most legislators—when it comes to property. Because they are founding a new colony, Kleinias and his fellow-legislators do not have to worry about working out old arguments about debt or about the distribution of land.

Most legislators are faced with old property claims and hence old arguments about property, and these arguments are very divisive. For example, for the last few years the African nation of Zimbabwe has suffered armed conflict, and now famine, as the government has seized vast farms owned by a very small white minority and has distributed the land to much larger numbers of poor blacks. A much less violent and less tragic example of conflict over property has animated the United States Congress for several years concerning bankruptcy law, which now makes it harder for debtors to escape their creditors. Or, finally, there are the immense political fights that arise whenever people propose either lowering or raising the U.S. income or corporate tax rates; it is always said that one side or the other is trying to benefit the rich and harm the poor or vice-versa. Because he is founding a new city, Kleinias does not have to worry about these arguments and divisions. He need only watch out whom he lets in to the new city.

Now, the stranger does not propose that they make wealth a

criterion for entrance, far from it. They merely should turn away from their new city any homeless, poor people who are also eager to take property away from those richer than themselves (735e). Such ravenous types would, the stranger says, be a "disease" in the city (736a1). The stranger of course is not here saying that all poor people are bad; he is only warning them to keep out poor people who want only to seize property from the rich and not earn it themselves. So, Kleinias must conduct "entrance interviews" of a sort to make sure to admit only colonists who are moderate with regard to acquiring property.

Casting Plots

But once the people start to arrive, how then should property be handled? The stranger ordains that they should take all the arable land of the city and divide it into a certain number of plots. They should then give one plot of land to each colonist family. The number of these plots will depend on the size of the land itself and upon the number of people whom they need in order to defend the city from its neighbors. For the sake of argument, and because it is so divisible, the stranger picks 5040 as the fixed number of civic plots of land. But here is the main point of this law: once the number of plots is fixed—whatever it is—it will not be changed. By law, the plots of land cannot be divided, combined, or otherwise altered. That is the fundamental law of Plato's *Laws*, the allotment of the land and this fixed number of plots (see 737e-738e). All sorts of sacred injunctions follow, which are meant to safeguard the fixity of the number of plots.

Other laws follow as a consequence of this fundamental law. Since each plot is given to one family, fixing the number of plots means fixing the number of families in the city. That is, the population in this city must stay roughly fixed. So "familial legislation," as people would call it today, is part or a consequence of property law.

For instance, because the familial plots cannot be divided, the father of each family must pick only one heir to inherit the familial land. While this heir must be a son, the heir does not have to be the oldest son. The heir can be whoever of his children the father thinks is best. The stranger's law does not assume that the oldest child is the best choice. Thus the father must marry his daughters into other families to support them. And if he has more than one son, these sons must be "adopted" by other, sonless fathers if they are to become landowners. And, most strikingly, if these "excess sons" are not adopted, they must be sent away from the city to form other colonies. There will be no homeless people or tenants living in this new city. (See 740b ff.) The familial consequences of this fundamental law are shocking.[2]

Likewise, fixing the number of plots obviously restricts work or pursuit of wealth in the new city. There is certainly no money to be made in real estate, since no family can sell its land. And the great importance given to the familial land indicates that the basis of the economy here is to be agriculture. This is why every family gets not an equal amount of land, but equally fertile land. Since agriculture is the basis of the economy, and not trade, there is not a great need for a separate form of currency. And, indeed, the stranger tells them here that the law should forbid colonists from even owning gold or silver (741e). Instead they will use, if they must, a useless form of local currency. In this respect they colonist would resemble modern Americans: dollar bills, in contrast to gold dollars, are in themselves worthless.

Finally, the value of all a family's possessions—all the goods that each family may bring into the new colony or possess there after the founding—cannot, by law, exceed four times the value of the lot itself. That is, no matter how industrious or innovative a farmer is, his wealth is capped at a certain very limited level. The ceiling of wealth is four times the plot of land; the floor is the plot of land itself. No one will fall below that floor and no one will go above that ceiling. Thus this city, while it will have four classes based on this property distinction, will not suffer from great extremes of rich and poor, such as people complain about today and in every previous age.

Surveying the Goal

This then is the overview of the property law and its consequences for family and economy. The goal of the property law is, the stranger says, to make the citizens as happy and friendly to one another as possible (743c). Presumably that friendship is critical to their happiness. And it seems that this friendship grows because of the absence of disputes about property. Because everyone will have roughly the same amount of property, there will be little room for the arrogance of the rich or the envy of the poor. And because there will be little opportunity for people to make money off one another or their mistakes, there will be little room for quarrels over property.

This is, obviously, not a prescription for a rich city. Economists today would say it is a prescription for an agrarian, "underdeveloped" economy that will stagnate and remain indefinitely at the same "standard of living." But that is exactly what the stranger and his fellow legislators want. They do not want ever increasing wealth or the demand for ever-increasing wealth.

The reasons they do not want such acquisitiveness are many. But the reason that the stranger offers here is, most simply, that he does not think that great wealth and justice—and hence friendliness and happiness—can go together (743a-c). If a person wants wealth above all, there will always be some point at which he can get wealthier by taking money from where he should not or by avoiding spending it where he should. That is, the people who amass and keep the most wealth tend to rapacious and stingy, not just and generous. But the stranger would much rather encourage just and generous citizens than possessive individuals.

Finally, we should note that the stranger is not sure that such laws will be acceptable in practice, once they get around to founding the actual colony (745e-746a). Even starting from scratch, with a new colony and a new population, he is not sure that people will accept the consequences— especially for their families and work—that these property laws would demand. But, he tells Kleinias, their job as actual legislators would be to approximate this scenario, as a model for their legislation. They should try, in practice, to get as close as possible to this scheme. And who knows? In some very lucky circumstances a very close approximation may just be possible.

True Friendship?

This, then, is an overview of the fundamental law of Plato's *Laws*, the property laws. The property law has, as one can clearly see, some very odd features and very odd consequence. These oddities, and the questions they must raise, may be one reason for the stranger's monologue. But we have not yet considered the oddest feature of the stranger's monologue here.

All the laws that the stranger offers are, he says, second best. These laws do not form the basis of the best city or the best regime, in his view. Indeed, these fundamental laws, the laws distributing property, themselves mark the cardinal deviation from the best city. This is a point worth repeating: in a dialogue entitled *Laws*, Plato reveals that the fundamental law, that upon which all the others rest and which must precede all the others, the fundamental law precisely marks the place where this city falls short of the best city. So, it is in this context, in the context of discussing property, that the stranger describes what, in his view, is the best form of political community or the best regime—and it is certainly a very strange description (739c-e).

The stranger's best regime is, as he puts it, a city of friends. As he explains, "Now, that city and regime and laws are first—and best, where the old utterance grows up in the entire city and most of all: for it is said that really 'the things of friends are common'" (739b8-c3).

But this friendship takes on an extreme form. Following the old proverb, people today might rather call it a communistic regime. And it is not just like Soviet communism, which demanded state-ownership of the means of production (land, factories, etc.). In the stranger's best regime, everything must be common: property, family, one's own body—as much as possible. There would be no "my house" and "your house." There would be no "my money" or "your money." There would not even be "my wife" or "my mother" or "my children" versus "your family." And the citizens would even forget, as much as possible, the differences between their own bodies. The stranger envisions a friendship, on a civic scale, in which the friends not only love each other, they are each other.

(The stranger thus includes the first and second "waves" of *Republic* Book Five—the communism of property and of women and children—but does not mention the third and greatest wave, the rule of philosophers. As has been noticed before, philosophy is barely present on the horizon of the *Laws*. Law obtrudes in philosophy's place.)

This complete communism, or true friendship—and nothing else—is the hallmark, according to the stranger, of the very best political community or best regime. However, this best regime is not one attainable by humans. It belongs only to gods, to beings who are immortal or deathless (739d6). Nevertheless, the stranger argues, this godly regime can and should still serve as a model for human beings to approximate. Humans can never live in this complete friendship, but they should not pretend that it is not the best way for them to live. Thus, even though he allows private property in his most fundamental law, the stranger tries to draw this regime that is tainted by private property as close to the communistic regime as possible. As we proceed in the *Laws* we will see the very many ways that the stranger tries to wean people away from their attachment to their own private goods and turn them instead to care for the common good.

Friendly Response

Still, the stranger's profession of his view of the best regime must strike today's readers as very odd. Here is where latter-day Kleiniases or later readers must raise questions and digressions and discussions and turn this monologue into a dialogue. One must ask, "Why would anyone hold up complete and total communism as the best political order?" Surely those of us who have lived through the monumental collapse of communistic schemes around the world must wonder at the stranger's words. And even if we never saw the Soviet Union fall, we must wonder because what the stranger says is best seems so opposed to the spirit of the American regime. It is not outlandish to say that this regime defends, at its very core, the rights to life, liberty, and property as fundamental rights. As Locke might say, no right to property, no freedom. And where freedom is in question, life itself is threatened. That is, the right to property—to our "own" things—is one, perhaps the greatest, safeguard of our very freedom and lives.

Another way to put this same point is this. The man without property must live in the service of others in order to eat. That is, the propertyless man is a slave or nearly a slave. And the very life of a slave is always in danger, depending on the master's will. That is why the right to property is so fundamental to the American nation and its regime. So, if even for a matter of national interest the State must take away my property, it must still fairly pay me for it.

Clearly the stranger's judgment about the best regime seems squarely opposed to the judgments of the American founders. So why does he say that complete communism is best? We can do little more than frame this question here. Let us note again the goals, the legislative goals, which are at issue. The American regime, which enshrines the right to own property and have private families, aims above all at the protection of individual liberty or freedom. Again, no right to property, no freedom. In contrast, the stranger's approximation to the very best regime, the communistic regime, aims above all at making the citizens happy and friendly with one another (743c).

Therefore, the stranger's notion of the best regime rests upon his previous reflection on friendship. The best regime is a gathering, not of mere partners, not to speak of individuals, but of friends. And in the best friendships, as the proverb says, all things are common. The best friends, we know, will even give their lives and liberty for one another, as well as lesser goods or possessions. The communistic regime is best because it is the only one where true friendship and friendship alone reigns.

Now this community of friends is not as outlandish as might first appear. Such a friendly regime is approximated in everyday life by the family, in which almost everything is common and members regularly make sacrifices for one another. Thus another way to describe the best regime would be to say that it is a civic family; it is an entire city that acts, feels, and thinks as one family. Indeed, even today, people who are concerned about justice or the betterment of political life speak regularly about the need to view our nation and our world even as one big family, and to view ourselves as brothers and sisters. So this complete communism is not as odd as may first appear. People to this day have a dim taste of it, and longings for it, in their social and political lives.

Also, we should remember what the stranger said back in Book Three, in his history of the human race, about the first type of political community—the familial tribe or dynasty. He said it was by nature the most just community (680e4). He says that about no other type of community. So, since it is the most familial-like of communities, because it is the friendliest, one could also say that this communistic community is also most just.

What we have seen here is, in general, the vast difference between the stranger's view of the best political regime—complete communism—and the contemporary view, the modern liberal democratic view. We can now see more clearly at least the fundamental difference between the two. This difference concerns the place of friendship in human life. The contemporary American regime treats the security and freedom of the individual as primary and paramount. This is why it is called a liberal regime. One makes attachments, friendships, and alliances only after that fundamental concern, for oneself, is secured.

The stranger, on the other hand, certainly does not ignore this deep concern people have for themselves. Indeed, he implies that the best regime is beyond human capacities precisely because of such self-concern. But that does not mean that he pretends that the best political order caters to that self-concern, the concern for one's own freedom and security. Political life itself, in his view, strives for something—a commonality, a friendship—that humans, as such, cannot attain in its completeness. In the best political situation human beings would live not primarily as individuals but as friends, with no concern for "mine and thine" but only for the common good. Such a friendly state of affairs is, the stranger thinks, what politics, even in its disappointing or low day-to-day forms, points to—the longings for such a friendly state are there. So, he reasons, it would be politically perverse and distorting, distorting of the citizens souls, for the law not to acknowledge this friendly community as the true and actual goal of the city's often faltering striving.

The stark difference between the goals of the stranger's best regime and the goals of modern liberal democracy thus force us to ask about the place of friendship in human life. But this difference also forces us to think about the character of friendship. Does true friendship demand or even hope for the complete erasing of private differences between the friends? Is that its ideal? Or does it rather love these differences as differences belonging to the loved ones?

"True friendship" emerges as the deepest ground of civic unity in the stranger's eyes, one much deeper, though far harder to attain, than anger or the desire to punish. "True friendship" transcends shared suffering, exchange of goods, or any other forms of reciprocity. But is this "true friendship," as described in the context of the best regime, truthful or a caricature? The latter case would not simply vindicate liberal democracy. Liberal democracy may still make more sound forms of friendship difficult to cultivate. Yet one must admit that modern liberal democracies are not held together solely by shared suffering or anger. The very equality upon which they found themselves destroys hierarchies but also encourages sympathy and a sort of fellow-feeling. This sympathy may not constitute true friendship either. But its existence at least raises the question of whether modern liberal democracy might achieve what the stranger seeks but by vastly different, and perhaps better means.

Notes

[1] Pangle goes quite far in this direction, offering a brief against *thymos*, or the anger that characterizes both the "great man in the city" and the "real man" (452-457). On the one hand, Pangle makes the extraordinarily large claims that *thymos* "constitutes a great part of what we mean by 'humanity'" (453), and that "the deep antagonism" between *thymos* and *eros* "is the dramatic theme of this whole dialogue" (455). On the other hand, he argues that *thymos* or "moral indignation" stands in sharp contradiction with "the truth": anger finds its roots in ignorance, an ignorance about responsibility and individuality (455). Pangle reveals his own view of the source of that ignorance in this rhetorical question: "Could anger (*thymos*) and fear be alternative expressions of the same fundamental psychic motion, which arises from a sense of one's threatened particularity?" (454) *Thymos* thus becomes, in the most basic terms, an ignorant reaction to the fear of one's own death, one lacking any moral dignity. Pangle's argument would thus dispel all people's concern with responsibility, dignity, right and wrong—all matters treated by the stranger as of great importance—with appeal to questionable statements Socrates makes about every person seeking his own good above all else. And yet it seems likely that Socrates made such statements in order to raise questions about the goods people do pursue, their possible conflict or irreconcilability, and the likelihood that people pursue things other than some good for themselves, rather than to establish a sweeping doctrine upon them. For further discussion of these points, see Chapter Nine.

[2] After reviewing property law in the ancient Greek world, Morrow concludes that "Plato's institution does not fit any of our familiar conceptions" (107).

Chapter Six:
Mixed Drinks

Uninterrupted Unity

In Book Five the stranger carefully distinguishes different types of civic unity. There is the unity formed out of anger at a perceived threat to the law. There is the unity of lot-holders, who get good things from the city which they call their own and who share those good things with one another. And then there is the unity of perfect friends, who share all things in common, who call nothing "my own." We saw that the proposed city of the *Laws*—and our own nation—enjoys the first two types of unity much more (though in different degrees) than the third. The conversation of the *Laws* raises the question of the character and the goodness of the friendship that the stranger claims underlies the most complete civic unity.

This exploration of the foundations of the city's union continues into Book Six, which forms a straightforward continuation of the monologue the stranger began in Book Five. In Book Six the stranger moves from what one might call the natural concerns he puts first— property, ruling offices—to divine matters—festivals and the institution they are designed to support: marriage. The stranger uses his treatment of these topics to explain and explore other ways in which the proposed city—or any nation—maintains itself as one. As in Book Five, he also uses these opportunities to reveal the obstacles, in every political community, to complete unity.

Promise Fulfilled

Book Six begins with the stranger's nearly monologic description of a confusing array of political offices and how they are to be filled. If one has just come from the discussion of property in Book Five, one might reasonably ask, "What's going on here?" For the answer the reader has to turn back to the middle of Book Five, to 734e, where the stranger had just finished the first, grand prelude to all the laws. There he says,

> Let the prelude to the laws spoken to this point have an end
> of its speeches here; but after the prelude it is surely
> necessary for a law to follow—or rather, in truth, to sketch
> the laws of a political regime. Now...with respect to those
> who are to rule the ruling offices in cities, it is necessary to
> discriminate, in accord with reason, between them and the
> others who have been trained by a small education. For let
> there be two parts of a political regime: the establishment of
> each of the rulers, and the laws given to the ruling offices
> (734e5-735a6).

But, as has been seen, the promise to describe the "ruling offices" is not kept in Book Five; this promise is only fulfilled in the first half of Book Six. So, what occupies Book Six 751a-771a is this: the description of the laws governing the ruling offices of the new city and the description of what means will be used to make sure the best human beings fill those offices.

Curiosities

This long list of ruling offices and their method of selection might strike the contemporary reader as rather dry. But it becomes much more interesting when one notes how many curious elements it contains, curious at least from the present point of view. These curiosities are not merely relics of ancient practice. The stranger is bound only by his own judgment when it comes to offering this political advice to Kleinias. Every odd part of his proposal has some reason for it. And so, when these proposals differ radically from contemporary ways of governing ourselves, we cannot merely write them off as "Greek" practices; we must think about the differences.[1]

Some of the most obviously odd elements, when compared to present political customs, are these. First, one of the more prevalent means that the stranger proposes for selecting office-holders is the use of lotteries. For example, one should consider the "Council" that he proposes. It is something like the United States House of Representatives. It is a large body that changes yearly and thus is in close contact with public opinion. This Council is to have 360 members. But in fact 720 are elected. The city then uses a lottery to select one half of the 720 to serve as councilors (756e). Similar use of lotteries occurs in several other offices, though not in the highest ones.

A second curious element, from the modern (not ancient) point of view, is that the stranger recommends that priests be officials in this new city. The inclusion of priests in the city government is a clear premonition that in this philosophically-guided city religion will be a public, not simply a private, matter.

A third surprising practice is that this city is to elect officials who will oversee music and gymnastics (764c f.). Now, an attentive reader of Book Two might have suspected that such a proposal would be coming, since in that earlier book the stranger praises public censorship of song, dance, and even games. Here he confirms his earlier teaching that music should not be a trivial or merely private pursuit for these citizens. It must be a significant part of their public education. Indeed, one could say that musical education emerges as the core of public education (see Book Seven).

And, concerning public education, a fourth and final curiosity for our consideration is that the greatest of all the high offices, according to the stranger, is not some generalship, presidency, judicial or legislative post. Rather, the greatest of all the high offices is the office of Supervisor of Education (765e). The proposed city takes education most seriously. And so the overseer of education will be the most powerful and honored magistrate in the land. If one makes an objective comparison with the present day United States, the result is striking. The American Secretary of Education has almost no power. And the thousands of local school board members and teachers in this nation—as diligent as they may be—are often treated by the other citizens with indifference or even contempt. Again, the stranger has his reasons for each one of these proposals. The fact that his proposals are so different, even antithetical to contemporary political practices should lead us to wonder about his thoughts and about our own.

Liberty and Limits

However, the biggest difference between the regime that the stranger proposes here in Book Six and present day modern democracy concerns the purpose of the government itself.

Many of the greatest nations in the contemporary world are liberal democracies. "Democracy" describes the form of government or who rules: it is government by, of, for the people. But the adjective "liberal" describes the purpose of this type of government. "Liberal" here is of course not a pejorative word, as in "tax and spend liberal." Rather, liberal means that this type of government's foremost concern is liberty. The goal of a liberal government is to preserve the citizens' liberties, or, as people also say, their rights. To see this goal one need look no farther than the American Declaration of Independence: "to preserve these rights [life, liberty and the pursuit of happiness] governments are instituted among men." The goal of such government is to preserve individual rights. The biggest problem, of course, recognized by all the American founders, is that very often governments are the greatest threat to individual rights. They had first-hand experience of this fact, in the person of the British King and Parliament. So, these founders thought, one must devise a government that is strong enough to protect individual rights without being strong enough to trample on those rights. They saw that no such government could exist. So they opted for the next-best thing. They devised a government that has great power, the power to protect the citizens from those who would enslave them, but which is divided against itself.

By organizing this government in three branches, and even encouraging each branch to protect its power jealously from the other two, these founders found a way to restrain the government. Indeed, this was their plan for every governmental office. As Madison puts it in *Federalist* 51, this government yokes the ambition of the office holder to the honor of the office. The American founders encourage ambitious, grasping politicians because that way these ambitious, grasping politicians will fight to keep each other off one another's turf. "Gridlock" is not at all a bad thing, in the eyes of these founders. Again, that is the case because in their view government's purpose is protect the citizens' individual rights, and to do that it cannot possess a unified strength. It must, rather, be strictly limited.

Educated Rule

When one turns to the regime described at the beginning of Book Six of the *Laws*, one finds a much different scenario. There are certainly no checks and balances. Classical liberals and those who worry about power concentrated in the hands of one man should observe that the stranger does not propose that this city should be ruled by a king or any office holder who even resembles a king. The American President, for example, bears some resemblance to a king. In the *Laws* there is no President.

However, the highest ruling body in the *Laws* is a council of 37 "Guardians of the Laws." These guardians rule for a long time (up to 20 years), and they have great power over who is selected to most of the other high offices. They are also in charge of scrutinizing the other officials, which means looking over their personal and public lives and deciding whether or not they are worthy to hold office. So these Guardians can throw other officials out of office or nullify elections. Their power, then, is immense and apparently unchecked.

Another problem, from the liberal standpoint, is that many of the magistracies in the *Laws* draw their members from one another. For example, the Supervisor of Education, called the highest official of all, is chosen from the Guardians of the Laws (766b). Likewise, all the judges in the new city will be chosen from the already-serving magistrates. So, while the stranger does propose many different magistrates to tackle many different duties, there is no true separation of powers. This makes possible, then, the accumulation of power in the hands of the Guardians of the Laws.

But this fact should bring to light something very basic about the regime proposed at the beginning of Book Six. It is not the goal of this government to limit or weaken itself or its office holders. So has the stranger simply overlooked the possible bad effects of an accumulation of power in the hands of one man or one body? Not at all. As mentioned before, the stranger does not propose that any one person hold overarching power; there is no king here. Second, the stranger would probably say that the accumulation of power is in itself a neutral thing, neither good nor bad in itself. What matters is whether this accumulated power is used for good or for bad. For example, when discussing the might of ancient Sparta in Book Three, the stranger does not criticize Sparta for its strength, but for using its strength stupidly (686d).

The most important question, in his mind, is not "How can we limit government?" but rather "How do we determine who rules?" One should recall once more a part of that section from the middle of Book Five, beginning at 735a2-4 "Now ... with respect to those who are to rule the ruling offices in cities, it is necessary to discriminate, in accord with reason, between them and the others who have been trained by a small education." The goal, in the stranger's eyes, is to make sure that the best educated get into the ruling offices. The goal of these governmental laws is not to limit the government but to try to make sure that the best educated rule.

Of course, that goal raises the important questions, "What is the best education?" and "How good is the education that will be offered in this city?" As the stranger notes at the very beginning of Book Six (751d f.), to begin with they face a very large problem in this regard. For they are founding a city that is currently uninhabited. So they must draw new citizens from elsewhere. And that likely means that none of these new citizens will possess the good education that this new city will itself offer.

They cannot merely hand over this fine law-code to a bunch of uneducated citizens. They would be sure to mess it all up. Even the Israelites had to spend forty years in the desert, until the whole generation educated in Egypt had died off, before they could enter the Promised

Land. So, the stranger says, the founders must somehow hold off the rule from the new citizens until a whole new generation has grown up under the new, good education. This is a real difficulty. It would require these old lawgivers, such as Kleinias, to live for another generation and a half, an unlikely prospect. This difficulty puts the rest of this great project into question.

But, one could say, assume that a generation has grown up under this new, good education, the kind of education that is described most fully in Book Seven. The great task and goal of the laws governing political offices is to make sure that the best educated of these citizens gets into power. Again, this is a very different goal from the modern liberal democratic regime, which, one could say, welcomes strong and ambitious souls into government and then pits them against one another.

Embarrassment of Riches

So, the goal of the governmental laws in Plato's *Laws* is to try to make sure that the best educated find their way into the ruling offices. But is that what the stranger's actual proposals do? Each one of the ruling offices presents a fascinating case study for this question. It would take another book to look at them all this way. Instead let us look at just one, where this problem is especially evident, the example of the Council (756b-758b).

As mentioned before, the Council is a body composed of 360 citizens. Each councilor holds office for one year. All are elected at once. But not all are elected from the same source. Ninety councilors are elected from each of the four property classes in the city: 90 from the first class, 90 from the second, etc. All classes, then, possess equal number of representatives. The Council is the most representative ruling body in this city. It is also the biggest.

And it has real power. One twelfth of the Council takes active rule of the city each month; these councilors are then known as "presidents." This ruling part conducts all foreign policy for that month. It also keeps watch, the stranger says, over "innovations" in the city and tries to forestall them. And, most importantly perhaps, it has the power to call or to dissolve all public meetings. The whole Council, by its size, also has de facto control over the choosing of all the judges, who themselves make many ruling decisions. Because of its size, its representative nature, and its assigned duties, then, the Council has considerable powers in the city.

Given its importance, the Council should be composed of "the best and the brightest." But the stranger offers no guarantees. And no mention of education is made when talking about the selection of the councilors. The only restriction made on their selection is that one quarter of the Council comes from each class, each property class.

Members of the first and second classes (the richest classes) are required to vote in the elections for candidates from all the classes. Members of the other classes (the poorer classes) are not required to vote. Also, the higher classes include presumably fewer citizens but possess an equal number of representative in the Council. So, the power of the richer classes in the Council will be greater than those of the poorer.

But what difference does this tilt towards the rich make when it comes to getting the best-educated citizens into the Council? One could say that the richer voters might have more leisure to get a good education. But this is not always the case. They rich may not all have the capacities to receive the best education. Certainly no one would say that because they are richer they are wiser. One should also remember that a lottery selects the one half of those elected who are actually to serve. The citizens could vote for someone whom they thought was, and is, the brightest candidate. But the luck of the draw could leave him out. In other words, the methods that the stranger describes for selecting the 360 members of this very powerful body do not, it seems, significantly improve the chances of the best-educated's taking office.

Hardly the Best

So why have this Council in the first place? And why select its members in the way the stranger proposes? The stranger explains his reasons in 757a-e. His explanation here applies not only to his proposals surrounding the Council but also to his proposals concerning all the ruling offices in general. These reasons reward careful consideration.

The stranger explains that for a city to hold itself together the citizens must enjoy equality. Equality is the glue that binds together political communities. However, there are two kinds of equality. One, he says, is arithmetic equality, of the sort found in weighing or measuring things. This is the kind of equality that people to this day rely upon when they say "One man, one vote." It is the equality of homogenous units, whether those units are pounds, or inches, or human beings: a pound is a pound the world around, an inch is always an inch, and a human being is equal—in some sense—to every other human being. In political terms, this kind of equality treats all human beings as equal because they are all viewed as belonging to the same kind, the same species.[2]

But, the stranger says, there is a second kind of equality as well. And, in fact, he calls this second kind of equality "the truest and best" equality (757b6). In particular, it is truer and better than that first equality. This second kind of equality gives equal honors or equal goods to those who are equally honorable or deserving of equal honors. That is, it gives the most to the best, more to the better, less to the worse, and least to the worst. This equality gives equal honors or equal goods to those who are equal by their nature. Like the first, this equality looks to nature. But it looks to the nature that distinguishes human beings. It reasons that human beings are not all alike. In some part of their nature, human beings differ; some are better, some are worse. This second sort of equality gives greater honors and offices to the better, to those with "virtue and education" (757c5). For, it seems, virtue and education reveal or cultivate the better natures.

But then what about the Council, and the many other concessions that the stranger makes to rule of less-than-the-best? From these concessions it seems clear that the stranger knows that he cannot simply look to the best equality in ruling or in establishing ruling offices. A city cannot simply give the best offices to the best natures and so on down the line. Why not? The stranger's answer is, to put it most simply, civil war. Ironically, the attempt to follow strictly the best equality would destroy the city.

As the stranger intimates, most human beings are not very good. Most are not even of the better sort. Most are, by nature, mediocre at best. So, according to the second sort of equality, most citizens should never get any ruling offices or similarly great public benefits. Most of them should be left without any honors and with no share in the government. That is where a strict adherence to the "best" equality would leave the city: with a deeply divided political system, a system in which the few rule and the many are subjects, with no say whatsoever, a system ripe for dissatisfaction and disaster, a system that would encourage unfriendliness among the citizens and which would, quite quickly, lead to civil war.

So the stranger cannot abide only by the second sort of equality in framing the regime of the *Laws*. He must also bow to the first kind of equality, the equality of homogeneity, the equality that pronounces, "One man, one vote." That is why this city must have a Council, and that is why this Council must have considerable powers. This must be the case even though this Council is not composed of the best and the brightest, or is composed in fact of people very far from the best and the brightest.

To be sure, the stranger tries to weaken this Council, so that its stupidity is thwarted. He tries, for example, as noted, to increase the power of the wealthy, the people who might have the leisure to pursue a better education than most. But this is no guarantee that the best will rule in this Council. In fact, it is quite far from a guarantee. It is so glaringly far from the rule of the best that it reveals to us the difficulty lurking at the heart of the stranger's proposals concerning the regime. The stranger cannot completely erase or ignore the power of the many citizens who have mediocre or even bad natures.

In sum, the stranger does set up multiple offices in this city (the Guardian of the Laws, the Council, the Judges, etc.). And he does give considerable voice to the people, to the popular power. But he does not create these multiple offices or give power to the people in order to weaken the government, as the American founders did. The stranger is not primarily (or even secondarily) interested in limited government. The stranger's goal is not to secure individual liberties or rights.

His goal, rather, is to get the best natures, the best educated, into the highest ruling offices. His goal is to get the most power to the best people. But he must also hold the city together. It is no good, politically speaking, for the rule of the best to lead to civil war. How could such an awful situation even be called "rule of the best"? So, the stranger cannot simply follow the second sort of equality. He must qualify the "truest and best" equality with another concern: the concern of friendship. For a city to be a community the citizens must be friendly towards one another. And such friendship is possible only if all of them have some say in the rule—even those with mediocre or bad natures. The need for friendship, and the mediocrity of most human beings, means that the city the stranger proposes will be very far from the best. But at least he sees clearly, and shows to his listeners clearly, his concessions and his reasons.

Questioning Marriage

If the first two-thirds of Book Six are occupied by governmental regulations, the last third is devoted to what seems to be private matters, marriage and home life. The marriage law that is unveiled towards the end of Book Six is the first law in Plato's *Laws* that looks like a law, according to the stranger's discussion of what a law should look like at the end of Book Four. It includes a law, clearly stated—a command with the threat of punishment—and it is preceded by a prelude. The laws preceding this one—concerning property, the ruling offices, and the "sacred things"—are much vaguer in their form. So, the marriage the law is the first law that follows the stranger's guideline of how a law should be spoken (see 771e-776b).

The most interesting thing about this marriage law is its prelude. In it the stranger addresses a question that is not much addressed in the present day, the question of how one should go about marrying. Obviously he does not talk about how a citizen should attract a man or woman or the "rules" one should follow to snare a mate. Though he does say something about how the city should organize courtship—with naked choral dancing performed by the boys and girls (772a). Rather, he talks about the goals one should aim at in choosing a spouse or the criteria that should guide this choice. "What kind of marriage should I seek?" This seemingly most personal of questions is the first that the law itself addresses and offers guidance on.

As mentioned, this is a question that is not much talked about today, at least not publicly. Many people in contemporary America like to think that marriage just "happens." They like to think that way because contemporary Americans are so intent on thinking of themselves as completely independent individuals. Independent individuals are totally free. Nothing pushes or pulls them around. There should be no demands placed upon them that they do not put upon themselves, freely. Parents. Politics. Nature. God. None of these should presume to point them, guide them, or tell them what to do. Again, they are totally free. If two of these free atoms do collide and join, it will be due to their own, individual, free choice. But what guides that choice? What explains that choice? Obscurity surrounds it. It is a mystery. It happens.

Once one does think about how that choice comes about—the choice of a girl friend, a lover, a spouse—one can easily recognize that there are powers or criteria that guide these choices. Consider personal ads. Even sad or desperate people have criteria that they look for. "Thin." "Pretty." "Loves to laugh." So does everyone else. For example: Someone who shares my career interests. Someone who likes the movies I like. Someone who likes the sports I like. Someone who comes from the same part of the country as I do. Someone whose family has about the same amount of money as my family does (or more). Someone who was brought up in my religion, or at least is not opposed to it. Someone who is about my age. Someone who has the same skin color as I do. Someone who kisses well, or has nice legs, etc.

These criteria, and many more, shape people's choices, whether they like to think of them or not. But if they do think about them, if they try to live thoughtful lives, they have to ask themselves, "Are these the best criteria, the best standards, for choosing a spouse? Or are they quite inferior and misleading? What would be the best standards, the best things to look for or to keep in mind?" The stranger's discussion and this marriage prelude spur one to think about these very important questions. They also lead us to think about why such questions are so important.

Mixed Marriages

So how should one marry, according to the prelude to this law? One should, the prelude sings, make a marriage that is in the interest of the city. One should ask not what your marriage can do for you, but rather ask what your marriage can do for your country. Contrary to most contemporary assumptions, the stranger treats marriage as so important precisely because of the benefit it offers to the public rather than to the private parties involved.

But how can marriage benefit the public? How can my marriage be for the common good? The stranger gives some pretty precise recommendations. His recommendations focus on familial wealth and personal dispositions. Contrary to most customs, he first advises that one should try to marry someone poorer than oneself. Marry down, not up. Second, he recommends that one marry someone whose disposition, or whose parents' disposition, is the opposite of one's own. If a man is hasty and impatient, he should marry a woman whose fathers are orderly. Or if a woman is slow and rather plodding, she should marry someone whose parents have energetic dispositions.

In short, marriage should aim at a mixture, a mixture of wealth and a mixture of dispositions. Marriage should mix the rich with the poor and those of opposite personal dispositions with one another. Imagine, he recommends, that the city is a large wine bowl: one must mix the drink well, water and wine, lest the whole thing become a maddening mess. Or, to use another culinary image more prevalent in our own times, marriage should be the spoon that stirs this melting pot.

But why is such mixing good for the city? Besides saying that mixed marriages will keep the wine-bowl relatively sober, the stranger also argues that mixing wealth, confounding the rich with the poor, will help keep the city "even-keeled" (773a6). Conversely, if the citizens do not mix wealth and personal dispositions, he says, the city will become uneven. The image of the "even-keeled" city implies that the city is like a sailboat. Just as a boat will founder and capsize if it leans too far in one direction, so too, the city where wealth and dispositions are not mixed together will tip to one side and eventually be overturned in civil strife.

That this is possible is not hard to see, especially if one thinks of the case of wealth. If there are great inequalities of wealth, and if the wealth always stays in the hands of one group of people, and if these people always inter-marry and exclude others from the wealth, then envy grows, and envy turns to anger, and anger can turn to violence and rebellion. This happened not too long ago in Haiti, to pick a recent example.

Indeed, every nation in which private property is allowed must deal with this problem. The United States deals with it in part through estate taxes, which break up large estates, but much more so through encouraging a market economy, which promises the possibility of wealth for everyone who works hard and innovates. But the stranger clearly decides not to use such means for dealing with this problem: he does not go the route of taxation or a free market. So, instead, he turns to marriage. Marriage, then, is a critical civic institution in the stranger's eyes. Marriage is an indispensable means for keeping the city upright. Without the proper sorts of marriages, it seems, the city faces very grave consequences. The stranger gives an honor and importance to marriage rarely seen today.

Tough Sell

But the stranger also knows that it is a very tall order to marry someone poorer than oneself and someone whose parents have dispositions opposed to one's own. For instance, he acknowledges in the prelude itself that to do so is against nature. Everyone, by nature, is attracted to what is similar to him. Like likes like. Birds of a feather flock together. People are more comfortable with what is familiar and fear or dislike what is unlike them. Also, he notes that pursuing marriage in this way may not bring either spouse the greatest pleasure. It may be more pleasing to marry someone rich or whose disposition is just like one's own, especially if one has a very pleasant disposition. But the stranger reminds his listeners that would not mix the city; it would not be in the city's interest. The stranger is honest enough to admit that pursuing the city's interest, in this crucial case of marriage, may be rather unpleasant.

In fact, if one compares this marriage prelude with the one offered in Book Four, the conclusion emerges that this marriage prelude, unlike the one in Book Four, greatly downplays the self-interest of the prospective spouses. The marriage prelude in Book Four, offered as a paradigmatic prelude, gave the citizens reasons why they should marry. They should marry because through marriage they will have children, who themselves will have children, and so their names will be remembered and they will not lie nameless and forgotten once dead (721b-c). Instead of oblivion, through marriage and children they will attain some sort of immortality in the face of death. The marriage prelude in Book Four puts all the emphasis on the self-interest of the prospective spouses: they want to be remembered so they decide to marry and have children. The good of the city is not mentioned at all in that prelude. Instead, the stranger mentions the civic good a little bit before he pronounces the prelude: he and Kleinias decide that marriage is good for the city because without children cities die (721a).

In Book Six the situation is almost entirely reversed. What is good for the city is emphasized. Immortality through children is barely mentioned. And even when the stranger does mention the "eternal coming-into-being" through "leaving behind children of children," he does not say that this activity is worthwhile because it wins some sort of immortality for parents. Rather, he says it is good to have children so that they can take one's place "in serving the god" (774a1). Even here, concerning children, self-interest is omitted. Everyone is going to die. But children are not to be thought of as one's ticket to immortality. Rather they are one's generously provided replacements in the service of the divine. Whether the goal is the civic good or service to the god, this prelude emphasizes the sacrifices that should be made in a good marriage, sacrifices for the benefit of others.

The reader may be wondering, "Are not these preludes supposed to persuade people to obey the law without being forced? Are not they supposed to attract the citizens to obeying the law? Some attraction—to tell them to marry in opposition to self-interest and pleasure!" These concerns are reasonable. But one should notice that this marriage prelude locates marriage within the context of the civic good—and even within the cosmic order, since children are said to be your successors in serving the god. That is, this prelude takes marriage from being something that pleases or benefits only a couple of people and transforms it into something that can benefit a whole community.

In comparison, the perspective of the original marriage prelude, back in Book Four, was exceedingly narrow. Take care of yourself. Seek your own personal immortality. This prelude, in Book Six, provides a much broader perspective. In this light, every marriage becomes a crucial tack or way to keep even the "keel" of the city. Every prospective spouse becomes a sort of captain, who must keep watch to make sure his choices do not contribute to the city's capsizing. And how would one rather live? Enslaved to one's own selfish, narrow, personal desires? Or a free member of an entire community, who can, by his actions and his choices, decisively affect that community's future, for better or for worse?

The first marriage prelude, the one in Book Four, is superior to most contemporary discussions about marriage, for it reminds the reader of his inevitable death and of his concern to "live on," somehow. That is, it enlarges the reader's possibly narrow soul by reminding him of immortality and the human interest in immortality. But this second marriage prelude, the one in Book Six, is superior to the earlier one, for it reminds the reader that there are much nobler goals for him to pursue than his own personal benefit. It enlarges the narrow soul by reminding the reader of the common good and the human concern for the common good.

Holy Marriages

There is, however, at least one more complexity here that must be observed. One must wonder whether or not, if one is to marry in such a way as to benefit the city, are the criteria which the stranger offers in this prelude the best criteria to follow in order to bring about that civic benefit? Is marrying someone poorer than oneself or of an opposite disposition the best one can do for the city (as far as marriage is concerned)? Maybe not.

The stranger, or Plato at least, knew that it is not. For in Book Five of Plato's *Republic* there is described a much different proposal for making "marriages" (so to speak) that would benefit the city most of all. In general, Plato's *Republic* presents what institutions would have to be in place for there to be the greatest and most consistent common good. In the end, for there to be such a common good, Socrates argues, the citizens would have to have all things in common—including their spouses and children. There could be no "my wife" or "my husband" or "my son" or "my daughter." That is, for there to be a true common good one must abolish private families.

That would mean, of course, abolishing marriage as our society or most societies (including Plato's) know it. Instead, the citizens would reproduce themselves through one-night stands, and anyone who got pregnant would hand over her child to the civic authorities once it was born, immediately. Also, if a citizen is to benefit the city as much as possible through these "marriages," he or she will want to make sure that the offspring of these unions are as good as possible. That means mating only the best citizens with the best citizens. It means instituting a eugenics program and allowing only the best specimens to breed.

Such would be, Socrates argues, the best way, the most effective way, to use marriage for the civic good. If we keep this proposal in mind, we can see just how very far from the best case the stranger's proposal is. Yet it points, one could say, in the right direction. It aims in the direction of serving the common good and not letting marriage be a private, selfish, nesting of couples. The stranger does all he can to make marriage benefit the whole city. Still, just as Socrates in the *Republic* knew that almost everyone would see his 'marriage' proposals as laughable or worse, so too the stranger in the *Laws* does not offer these criteria as laws: they are recommendations for what truly good citizens should try to do. They cannot be commands.

Just as in the case of property, in dealing with marriage the stranger reveals the limitations that human nature places upon a legislator who tries to aim at the best regime: people will marry whom they (or their families) wish, and they will insist upon remaining married for longer than a night. It does seem clear that he does his best to bring the institution of marriage in the proposed city closer to something like the marriage scheme of the *Republic*. But the difference between the two institutions must still remain vast.

At the same time, however, it seems perverse to conclude that private marriages represent nothing more than a falling-short from the ideal. As seen, Book Five's critical or limited endorsement of property forces us to wonder about the true character of friendship. Book Six's much more enthusiastic though still limited approval of marriage should impel us to wonder about the true character of that relation. At this point the stranger has already conveyed two, very different sets of justification for marriage. He never claims that these justification exhaust the reasons for marrying. The very eagerness with which people marry, and the tenacity with which they defend the institution of marriage, indicate that they seek more in marriage than civic betterment or the selfish dream of fame through procreation. Surely, as indicated, the stranger adds a charm to marriage, by showing how it can benefit the city as a whole. But he does not deny the possibility that one can find other goods, quite apart from public ones, only in the bosom of marriage. He explores this possibility more fully in Book Eight, when he discusses love and friendship. In this light, his sanctifying of marriage appears not only as a bow to necessity but also as a wise and moderate measure.

Notes

[1] Morrow observes that the governmental institutions in the *Laws* included "the usual organs," "familiar Greek institutions," but that even these familiar institutions take some novel forms in Plato's dialogue (157). When taken as a whole, the stranger's proposed government resembles closely no known government of the ancient world.

[2] Cf. Strauss, who calls the first kind of equality "conventional" (*Argument and Action* 86). Strauss interprets the stranger's calling the second kind of equality "truest and best" as meaning that the second is natural and the first unnatural.

Chapter Seven:
Peculiar Institutions

Switching Cornerstones

On the eve of the American Civil War, on March 21, 1861, the Georgian statesman Alexander Stephens spoke to an assembled crowd about the reasons for the recent secessions. He explained the differences between the new Confederate States of America and the former United States. They differed in interest, the latter, he charged, greedily imposing burdensome taxes on the trade of the former. They differed in principle, the Northern politicians believing in the principle that "all men are created equal," while the Confederates asserted that that principle was "fundamentally wrong." And they differed in their ways of life. Most strikingly, the Southern way of life found its basis on African slavery. Stephens skillfully used the words of the New Testament to justify this institution:

> The architect, in the construction of buildings, lays the foundation with the proper material—the granite; then comes the brick or the marble. The substratum of our society is made of material fitted by nature for it, and by experience we know that it is best, not only for the superior, but for the inferior race, that it should be so. It is, indeed, in conformity with the ordinance of the Creator...The great objects of humanity are best attained when there is conformity to his laws and decrees, in the formation of governments as well as in all things else. Our confederacy is founded upon principles in strict conformity with these laws. This stone which was rejected by the first builders 'is become the chief of the corner'—the real 'corner-stone'—in our new edifice.

Slavery was the cornerstone upon which the Southern edifice rested, he claimed, a foundation missing in the North and rejected, at least in principle, by the founders of the United States. Although he supported secession only after the fact, Stephens made clear that this "revolution" sought to preserve the distinctively Southern way of life through a change of the most radical, foundational, sort.

Resisting Change

Change and the preservation of ways of life are two of the foremost concerns of *Laws* Book Seven. In this book the stranger eloquently shows the connection between changes in the smallest and the greatest matters. He shows how resisting change requires radical thinking, of a sort that even outstrips Stephens' repudiation of the founders. And he makes the case for stability grounded upon slavery—but a slavery much different from the American variety, in fact so different that it can lead us to reevaluate the liberty we enjoy today.

But to take up these topics, we must backtrack for a moment to look at a curious sight that we breezed past in Book Six. A significant part of that book concerns the authority of ruling offices, especially the body known as the "Council." One of the Council's duties is, to use the stranger's words,

> to make sure that each and every innovation of all those that typically come to be in a city not come to be, if possible; but if one does come to be, to make that the city perceives and cures the sickness as quickly as possible (758c5-d2).

This is quite a strong, maybe even shocking, statement. The stranger calls innovation a "sickness." He says that the city needs a high office, a whole body of magistrates, to squelch innovation. To travelers from the modern world this must sound very odd.

But the Council's duty to stifle innovation does fit with many other things the stranger has said or proposed throughout the *Laws*. For example, in Book Two he praises the "Egyptian" method of regulating song and dance, by which (according to the stranger) the Egyptians made a list of approved songs and dances 10,000 years ago and have never let anyone's singing or dancing deviate, in spirit, from that list since (656d-e).[1] His economic proposals in Book Five are similar, in which he argues that the new city must have a firmly grounded and strictly limited agricultural economy (see especially 741d-742b). A farmer of course has to deal with the change of seasons. But even in this respect each year is much like the last. The seeds are sown, the crops grow, the crops are harvested, winter comes, and the whole cycle begins again. It is not a fast-paced, ever-changing economy or a fast-paced, ever-changing life.

In the same place, the stranger rails against the private possession of gold or silver or any form of currency. In other words, he tries to outlaw exactly the kind of monetary system which would make commerce and other, non-agricultural forms of business possible. As any observer of the modern economy knows well, merchants and other businessmen are always innovating, always trying to change their practices in order to maximize their income, minimize their costs, and beat their competition. Merchants and manufacturers are also always trying to convince other people—consumers—to think that they need new things, that they cannot live without the latest invention, so that they, the merchants, can sell it to them. The world of the market economy is an ever-changing world characterized by innovation. And it is precisely this kind of world that the stranger wants to avoid.

So perhaps it should be no surprise when, in turning at last to Book Seven, we learn that stranger thinks that the city should even try to watch over children's games, to keep them from changing at all (797a-799e). This proposal sounds petty and ridiculous. And even the stranger admits that he cannot make laws about children's games. But he thinks it would be a very good thing if decent citizens did their best to make sure their children's games always stay the same. He wants to nip the taste for change right in the bud.

Embracing Change

It is important to recognize just how different the city that stranger would build is from the commercial republics of the modern West. Today innovation of various sorts pervades western society. Perhaps the most obvious example is economic—the invention of new products, new services, new ways of handling and making money. This innovation is encouraged for at least one very simple reason: the invention of new products and new services creates the opportunity for new jobs, more wealth, and greater comforts. To paraphrase what Locke observed over three centuries ago, a poor man in America lives far more comfortably than a chief would have among the pre-Columbian American Indians. Without this economic innovation the West would not have suburbs or yuppies; the poor would be as numerous as they in fact are in the Third World; and, incidentally, there would be far fewer universities.

Modern society also encourages all sorts of technological or scientific innovations. These discoveries increase modern man's power in many ways: over disease, over unruly nature, and over unruly or inimical human beings. They too have greatly increased the comfort of people's lives. The importance of scientific innovation to the United States is made very clear by the Constitution. It does not mention science or learning except once, to say that the Congress shall have the power to make laws regarding patents so that inventors will be able to protect and profit from their discoveries (Article I, section 8).

Finally, contemporary American society encourages all sorts of political innovation. For example, the practice of popular referenda or "ballot questions" has become much more widespread in the last fifty years, and these referenda allow for changes of the most radical sort. And the First Amendment to the Constitution, which protects the right to political speech above all, aims to make sure that no new political ideas will be stifled. Most fundamentally, Americans praise a Revolution, a radical political change, as their most important political event, and celebrate this great political innovation every year as their most sacred national holiday. From its start this country has loved innovation, and it has continued in this path ever since.

The stranger would obviously criticize the American or Western way of life as bad in this respect, because of the praise for feverish innovation or change. But why would he do so? Does he have any good reasons for doing so? Is there anything wrong with the contemporary love of change? This is one of those places where we observers may learn from the stranger, or at least come to a more clear-sighted understanding of ourselves.

Weathering Change

As seen, the stranger proposes that the new city try to regulate children's games. Even his interlocutors, Kleinias and Megillus, think this odd. Now, they certainly do not come from liberal, innovative societies. They are conservative. But even they think the stranger may be going too far. So the stranger tries to explain his proposal. He says, "Change is by far the most dangerous thing in everything, except in bad things—in all the seasons, in the winds, in the regimens of bodies, and in the habits of souls" (797d9-e1). Change is bad in everything except in what is bad.

In one sense, this would seem to be obvious. If something is the best it can be and it changes, the change can only be for the worse. Conversely, if something is the worst it can be and it changes, the change can only be for the better. But the stranger is not just censuring change in the very best case. He is censuring change in every case, except the change from the very bad state. The examples he gives help make his point clearer. He points to changes in nature: seasons, winds, and bodies. The changes in the seasons or winds are dangerous because these changes wear down bodies or other structures. The seasons or the winds, by their variability, wear away and eventually destroy the materials subject to them. Likewise, as bodies change they develop weaknesses, they get worn out, they break in various ways, and they eventually fall apart under the accumulated stress of all those changes. One could say, according to the stranger, that the world is always changing, and this is why things always fall apart.

But how do these examples of natural changes pertain to change in the political sphere? For it is change in a city, in political life, that the stranger is worried about. He is proposing regulating children's games, not the weather. The relation seems to be something like this: The natural changes of the natural world are bad for bodies. These changes wear down and destroy bodies, whether animate or inanimate. Changes in social or political life have a much different, but also destructive, effect. Political changes do not affect bodies; rather, they affect souls. Political changes wear down people's habits or temperaments.

In particular, the stranger says, one habit that changes in social or political life wear down or destroy is human beings' sense of reverence. This reverence takes time and stability to develop and grow, just as a plant will only grow over time and in a secure environment. Conversely, constant changes in our habits and customs and activities destroy this reverence. For reverence, as the stranger observes, is closely related to fear. In fact, reverence is a kind of fear, a respectful fear (see 647a). Change diminishes this respectful fear; people lose all respect for or even disdain anything that is always changing. Under the stress of repeated changes and innovations, reverence turns into contempt.

A lack of reverence is not so important in children's games. Nor is reverence or respect critically dangerous in songs and dances. Games, songs, and dances are not, by themselves, the most important cases. The most important case is the law. To respect and revere the law differs greatly from disdaining the law. And this is why the stranger is worried about innovation and change even in comparably little things like children's games. The healthy political state is one in which people revere or even fear the law. In that state, they do all they can to avoid breaking the law. But what happens if the law changes all the time? People come to look upon those ever-changing laws with disrespect or disdain. And so they become bolder in ignoring the law. A contemporary example of this sad state is the American income tax laws. These laws change every year, sometimes radically. People have gotten so used to their variability that the complexity and variability of these laws has become something of a joke. And people do not take jokes seriously. Thus the income tax laws are by far the most violated federal laws.

So, one reason that the stranger is opposed to innovation or fears change is that he thinks it is intimately tied to lawlessness. People who think only of the present day, whose lives are always fluctuating and changing, who always shuttle from one activity to another—these people lose their sense of reverence, their sense of reverence for anything, including the law. One other small contemporary example makes this point: Most people have probably heard that Boston drivers are among the worst in the nation. One should also add that Boston pedestrians are very lawless, even walking directly in front of oncoming cars that have a green light. There are probably many reasons for this lawlessness. But could it have anything to do with Boston's being a hotbed of innovation, economic, technological and political? Drivers and pedestrians are much more law-abiding in the more conservative and less variable Midwest. This is a small matter, but sometimes the smallest habits betray the deepest causes.[2]

However, lawlessness is only one, serious consequence of pervasive innovation. The stranger is concerned about at least one other grave liability of innovation too. He says about little children who get used to ever-changing games that they "by necessity come to be men who differ from those who were children before; having become different, they seek a different way of life; and having sought it they desire different practices and laws" (798c4-6). Again, disregard for the established laws is a problem. But he also argues against a taste for different ways of life. Those who are surrounded by innovation do not abide by the previously established ways of life. They turn away from their fathers' ways and seek the ever new, whether it is found in Buddhism, or practicing the law of mergers and acquisitions, or becoming a day-trader. People say today that everyone is going to have multiple careers by the time he or she retires. Restlessness in innovation becomes restlessness in living. Ways of life become like clothes: to be worn for a while and then discarded. Ultimately it becomes difficult to take any way of life very seriously. Everything changes, after all. The 'quest for meaning' that many modern people throw themselves into becomes not a solution but an integral part of the problem it is meant to solve.

In criticizing innovation, therefore, the stranger has both public and personal dangers in mind. He is most obviously concerned about preserving a public respect or reverence for the law. But he also wants people to respect themselves, and respect the seriousness involved in a choice of a way of life. He thinks that both lawlessness and a lack of seriousness about living are the ultimate, if unintended, products of even seemingly small innovations and changes.

Sacred Games

But what can he do? What can we do? Are not innovation and change inevitable? How can one stop them? These are reasonable questions. The stranger himself admits that change is inevitable. As he says at the beginning of Book Three (among other places), in the course of human political history there have been innumerable changes: cities and nations come to be and flourish and pass away time after time. Change is inevitable. But human beings do have some control over when change happens. Lawgivers especially can do certain things to hasten change or to retard it. Clearly, the stranger is on the retarding side.

He has many means at his disposal to do this. But the greatest means, and the one the stranger emphasizes at the beginning of Book Seven, is the use of religion. In order to avoid changes in children's games, the stranger proposes that they sanctify certain games; he proposes that they make these games holy. For example: Let baseball be a holy game. Then whoever proposes the introduction of a new rule, such as the designated hitter allowance, not only tries to make a change; he commits a sin.

This proposal sounds rather silly, when applied to something as seemingly small as games. But sanctity has great power. And it is no laughing matter when applied to the law itself, when the law is pronounced holy and inviolable by the hands of mere mortals. For this sanctity calls in the power of the gods, the oldest beings of them all, the most established beings of them all. The imprimatur of god lends instant respectability, instant weight, instant authority to any practice, and immediately forestalls the development of changes. One does not try to change what is holy, unless one is a heretic, a dangerous occupation.

However, after advising that they use the power of religion to sanctify the games and songs and dances, the stranger departs on an odd and revealing tangent (799c). He says that what they have just agreed upon is puzzling. And he adds that when someone faces something puzzling, if he is smart, he will pause and think about it. The three characters do not pause here and think about it. They move on and agree to think more later. But we, the readers, should pause and think. What does the stranger think is so puzzling about his proposal to sanctify games, songs, and dances?

Radical Conservatism

One problem is that the stranger is in essence saying that the city they are founding will use religion for political ends. That is, politics appears superior to religion. The gods, or at least the public stories about the gods, will serve human ends. This is obviously not a pious position. The stranger and his interlocutors reveal themselves to be of questionable piety. But the problem runs even deeper.

A deeper problem is that they need to make up these stories. The human things are disordered; cities come to be and pass away; change is always ravaging things natural and political. In other words, human beings find themselves in a messy position. It seems that if things are going to be in a good state, human beings must put them in that state themselves. They cannot rely on the gods to take care of them. The gods have left human beings in a state that requires them to act for themselves. So, his very use of these divine stories, his very reliance on these stories, shows that the stranger does not trust the gods as much as these stories would encourage others to do.

Finally, the deepest problem is that the stranger is proposing that they invent, make anew, these sanctifying myths or stories. He is proposing, in other words, a great religious and political innovation. Consider his pointed question at 798e: "And so, do we say, every sort of contrivance must be contrived so that our children may not desire to seize upon other imitations, in dances or in songs, and so that no one may persuade them by drawing them towards all sorts of pleasures?" (798e4-7) Kleinias immediately agrees.

The stranger could not emphasize more that they, the legislators, are to come up with contrivances or inventions in order to fight against future contrivances or inventions. This is not a contradictory stance. But it is a tricky one. The stranger talks like a conservative, the most conservative of conservatives. He praises Egypt, the most conservative and pious place in the world.[3] But his conservatism and piety rest on surprising foundations. He recognizes that at the beginning of every conservative tradition is some innovation, some change, some revolution. So, he speaks and acts like a conservative, but thinks like a radical.

But the stranger is not a stupid radical. He recognizes that if human beings are to live well, they need traditions and set ways. They need laws and praiseworthy ways of life to follow. He is the exact opposite of many contemporary politicians, who never stop calling for "change" but whose ideas are usually very commonplace and far from radical. For the stranger would say that this continual call for change and innovation, while perhaps pleasing at first and not immediately destructive, ultimately makes living well impossible.

Slave City

But how well would the citizens of this new city live? What would they do with themselves all day? What kind of changeless, unvarying activities would they engage in? To begin to answer these important questions, we should make one more recourse to Book Six, to a topic that may well trouble all modern readers of the *Laws*: slavery.

Abraham Lincoln, when he was twenty-two years old, took a voyage down the Mississippi on a flat-bottom boat to do some trading.

When he reached New Orleans he was horrified to behold a slave auction, where men and women were forced to prance like livestock before eager buyers (Charnwood 18). The traveler in Plato's universe must also behold the ugly face of slavery. The slavery described in the *Laws* does not wear quite as barbaric a demeanor as that encountered by Honest Abe in the 19th century South, but we may still recoil and wonder, What in the world is this doing here?

One cannot dismiss the existence of slavery in the *Laws* by saying, in effect, "Everybody was doing it." Morrow does observe that "A Greek city without slaves was almost unknown in Plato's day" (148). But that "almost" cannot be ignored. Even more importantly, the stranger is his own man. He shows time and again that he is willing to innovate, to dismiss old customs, to start new ones. He is proposing a new city here. He has some reason for every proposal he makes. The inclusion of slavery on his part must be a conscious choice. To put it most baldly: when given a practical shot at founding a city, the founder-philosopher embraces slavery.

One cannot ignore this fact. But neither should one use it in order to dismiss the *Laws*. Should the stranger be condemned for including slavery in the proposed city? Maybe. Maybe not. He himself notes some significant problems with slavery. Unlike James C. Calhoun and many other statesmen of the ante-bellum South, the stranger does not think it a morally unquestionable institution, a "positive good." And he notes that the people he is talking with and legislating for—the Cretans and the Spartans—have slaves and have built their communities around and on the basis of slavery. He must acknowledge and deal with their prejudices. But what problems does he see surrounding slavery? And why does he accept it to some degree in the new city? These, of course, are the essential questions.

Kinder, Gentler Slavery

The slavery the stranger proposes is more complex than the slavery that Americans are used to condemning. First, for the stranger slavery does not equal racism. Modern Americans are used to the two being linked, since slavery in the United States had an overtly racial element to it. The stranger knows that there exists a temptation to enslave other races. But he advises against following this path; instead, the new city should take its slaves from many different nations and peoples (see 777c-d). Slavery is a political institution for him, not a racial institution.

Second, the slaves that he proposes are neither without rights nor, even, without remuneration. He says in Book Five, when discussing property, that currency is needed in order to pay wages: to craftsmen and to hired help, and he mentions here hired help who are "slaves and foreigners" (742a4-5). Some slaves, at least, will get paid.

Finally, the slavery that he describes is not necessarily for life. There are provisions in the law, unveiled later, for the freeing of slaves. In particular, slaves can be freed by the city itself if they perform especially noble actions. In other words, the stranger knows that slaves can do such actions and he honors that possibility. These freed slaves then can become full members of the community, equal to the other citizens. This is especially easy since slavery, in his proposal, is not tainted by race. So, for the stranger, slavery is not racial; it may earn slaves wages; and freedom, for them, is a real possibility. These striking facts remind one how complex and unusual the stranger's discussion of slavery is.

Slave Nation?

But there is one more observation that the stranger's introduction of slavery can help us make. It is an observation neither about the slaves of the *Laws* nor about 19th century America.

If we think about the work that the stranger proposes these slaves do, we must come to the conclusion that today by far most people live in a way that the Athenian stranger would call slavish. Why say this? The stranger makes clear that slaves in the new city will work largely in private, some being paid for their labor. They may do all sorts of private tasks, not just unpleasant ones. Probably the majority of them will do farm-work, since the economy of this city is agricultural (805e, 806d). Some of them will work on public projects, in a menial capacity (760e, 763a). But other slaves may do more sophisticated work such as accounting or doctoring (808a-e).

As varied as their work may be, however, as much as they may be paid, none of the slaves may take a hand in running the city; none do truly public work. And in this respect many people today resemble these slaves. By far and away most people now spend by far and away most of their time thinking about private concerns. Usually that means thinking about careers or businesses. Americans, in particular, spend more time than any people in the past thinking about their private work. But other private matters that people busy themselves with greatly include love-interests, families, hobbies, and education (an "education" which is often aimed at the advancement of personal careers).

In other words, the great majority today spends very little time engaged in political life. People may read newspapers or watch the news on TV. But that is a spectator sport. Very few get involved in or deliberate about public affairs. Some vote. (It is not always very many.) But casting a ballot once every year or every four years is about the least direct involvement in public life possible. Modern society is very efficient. It has pared down public life to a minimum.

So, most people today lead lives that resemble the lives of the stranger's proposed slaves. But this resemblance forces a series of questions upon us. How do the masters, the citizens, of his proposed city live? How do their lives differ from their slaves' lives, and hence from the lives of most modern Americans? What explains these differences? And which way of life is better? The stranger's proposals in this area are, as usual, quite unusual. But thinking about these questions and looking at the text will bring into focus a way of life almost undreamed of by the modern world. This way we travelers can truly broaden our perspective—a favorite promise of modern education, but a rare accomplishment.

Minimizing Private Life

To start this investigation into the lives of the citizens of the proposed city, we should observe what these citizens do not spend their time doing (see 806d-809a). First, these citizens do not spend their time in any arts or crafts. None of these citizens are plumbers or carpenters or masons. They have well-trained slaves for such handiwork. Nor, it seems, are there to be citizens who are musicians, or painters, or sculptors. Again, artistically educated slaves fit the bill here. And since no citizens are to be artists or craftsmen, no citizen needs to spend time training in the arts or crafts. These are all things that the great majority of citizens need not concern themselves with at all.

Second, the stranger says that the citizens' farms will be "given over to slaves" (806d9-e1). Obviously the slaves will not own the farms. But they will do the work and manage the farms. What the stranger implies here is that even the poorest class of citizens will have enough property to employ slaves to keep his farm running well. Since farm-work is very demanding, this means that none of the citizens need spend all those hours plowing and sowing and harvesting. Since the citizens are farm owners they will presumably know something about farming; as part of their civic education they certainly learn about the land they occupy. But the actual business of farming will trouble them very little.

A third point, very surprising: these citizens will not only not have to worry about cooking, they will not even eat together in private. There will be no family dinners in this city: no sitting down with the wife and kids over a cozy, private meal. Instead, the stranger proposes, the whole city will eat together at large "common meals" (806e ff.). This does not mean that the whole city will literally sit together at some huge table. The common meals will be organized in neighborhoods or some such manageable grouping. But the main point is, of course, that these meals, no matter what their exact size, will be public, not private. There will be no gabbing with the family, gossiping about the neighbors, or bad-mouthing the civic officials over the private table. Instead each family will eat with its neighbors and under the eyes of the public officials in charge of such feasts. Obviously the citizens will always have to be under pretty good behavior.

Another characteristic that makes these common meals even more unusual: the meals will be segregated by sex. Men and boys will eat in one locale, women and girls in another. This segregation serves at least one important purpose that is consistent with what the stranger has proposed thus far. If the common meals are segregated by sex, then not only will each citizen eat with his or her family in private; he or she will not eat with the whole family. One's spouse and perhaps half of one's children will spend every meal apart. This proposal cannot help but have a weakening effect on family relations and familial bonds. For example, it is very likely, based on this proposal, that over meals a citizen will get to know his or her neighbors' day-to-day concerns and thoughts better than he or she knows his or her own spouse's day-to-day concerns or thoughts. At the very least, this segregation will keep the common meals from becoming mere agglomerations of families, each sitting by itself. One cannot sit apart with one's own family if half the family is not there.

Finally, there is a fourth very surprising thing that these citizens do not spend much time on: their children. As the stranger puts it, once the day breaks and the sun comes up, children should be handed over to their teachers (808d). And by this he means any child three years and older. Once a child is three the stranger has him or her out of the house and participating in public games and basic public education. As he says, let these little tykes all gather in some "common place," such as a district temple, and be watched not by their parents but by a public official, a teacher or nurse of some sort (794a).

Even before the age of three, the stranger explains, children will not be the sole concern of the mother or under her sole supervision. At the beginning of Book Seven he gives lots of advice to mothers about how they should exercise their infants and keep them from becoming spoiled. This advice is not a law, but it is a strong recommendation. Also he makes clear that the mothers will have the help of certain nurses who may themselves be public officials. And he certainly says that the women appointed to watch over the citizens' sex-lives must take an interest in how new mothers nurture their babies. So, from day one the public takes part in the raising of children. From age three onward children will spend their days apart from their parents, at school.

And, there is one more very surprising aspect of all this: the stranger proposes that if any citizen finds any young person doing something wrong, that citizen has the authority to punish the youth, even if the young person is not his own child (809a). In fact, the law commands the citizen to punish the youth, and it says that if he does not do the punishing he himself will be punished. In other words, everyone has authority, punishing authority, over everyone else's children. As a citizen, one has no right to keep other citizens from disciplining one's children. But that means that each citizen can rest content knowing that a whole city and its laws are watching over his or her children. The burden is not just on the parents alone; in fact, it rests very lightly on the parents. The stranger certainly believes that it takes a city to raise a child well, and he puts that belief into practice.

So, there are many private activities, which people today take for granted as private responsibilities, which the citizens of this city will not busy themselves with. They will not need to be or to train to become craftsmen or artisans of any sort. They will not need to work on or even manage their own farms. They will not need to cook or even eat in private. And they will not need to take much direct care over the raising of their own children. It is not too much of an exaggeration to say that they do not have to be businessmen, housewives, or even parents. But these things—business, home, and children—are what most people today spend all their time thinking about. What time these citizens must have on their hands!

Night Life

But it is obviously not enough to notice how many things these citizens do not do, as surprising as such observations are. What do they do with all this time they have? To begin to answer this question we should look at an extended passage from Book Seven:

> For people who live this way [i.e., with little or no private concerns] the work left over is not the smallest or most contemptible, but the greatest of all the tasks ordered by a just law. For just as the life of a man who hungers for victory at the Pythian or Olympic games offers no leisure at all for all other activities, because of his preparations, so doubly or much more than doubly lacking in leisure is the life that's most correctly called a life—the life of one who concerns himself with caring for his body in all respects and for his soul as regards virtue. Not even a little bit of the other

> activities should be allowed to become an obstacle to his giving his body the fitting labors and food, and his soul teachings and habits; the entire night and day together are scarcely sufficient for the one who's doing this to attain a sufficient end to these activities (807c1-d5).

The life, the life that is most correctly called a life, is not the life of business or household chores or even of parenting; the life—the best life the stranger implies?—is one of devotion to cultivating your body in all respects and your soul as regards virtue.

In the paragraphs after this one the stranger goes on to describe how the citizens should spend their nights and days, in order, presumably, to live this life. He says, "There should be instituted a schedule for how the free men spend all their time"—a 24 hour schedule (807d6-7). "Free men" possess no "free time" in this city.

What the stranger says about the citizens' nights is particularly surprising. First, he says that the free people should spend as little time sleeping as possible. He knows that some sleep is necessary for health. But he suggests that once a person develops a good habit, he or she can live healthily with much less sleep than thought. The stranger does not make this a law: "Thou shalt not sleep more than six hours!" But he says that the free people should sleep less than their slaves do and should be ashamed if they are caught snoozing.

But what should they do at night when they are not sleeping? He says, "All citizens should be awake at night doing much of the political and household work—the rulers acting in the city and the masters and mistresses in the private homes" (808a7-b3). So, what little private business these citizens need to attend to, they will attend to late at night, when, presumably, they are not in their tip-top shape. Likewise, and more surprising, most of the political business of the city will be handled at the night hours. The stranger argues that the magistrates' nocturnal work will have salutary effects. Criminals will be more afraid in a city where the magistrates are busy working even at night. And the good citizens will feel more courageous and will honor the magistrates even more for burning the midnight oil. One can also spot a further benefit, which the stranger does not mention: if the political officials do a good part of their business at night, that leaves only a little bit of work to be done during the day.

Day School

So what then will these citizens do with the day, both the actual magistrates and the other citizens? They do not have to worry about private business. They do not have to worry about taking care of their homes. They do not have to worry about their children. And they do not even have to worry much about politics, if a good bit of the political business gets done at night. What do they do? The stranger had made it seem that the citizens' main business would be to deliberate about politics and to execute the political business. But while political action will certainly be a part of their daily concerns, what the stranger says here implies that it will not be their main daily concern. Again, their main concern is to cultivate their bodies and to cultivate their souls with regards to virtue. And while an orderly political life may be needed for such cultivation to occur, and while politics may be a good place to exercise or "work out" a virtuous soul, political business does not seem to be the primary place to cultivate that virtuous soul.

But what then do the citizens do during the day? The answer is staring us in the face in Book Seven, for the answer is the education as whole that is described therein. This education is complex and defies easy description. It certainly is a political education. The citizens participate in communal song and dance and learn such politically important matters as how to fight well in war. They cultivate their bodies in gymnastics and wrestling. They also learn what one could call "higher subjects," such as arithmetic, geometry and astronomy. But even these higher subjects they should pursue, the stranger says, "for war, for household management, and for arranging the city" (809c5) So the eventual product of their education will be excellent execution of the political business. But it is this education itself, it seems, that is the most important thing and most important part of their day.

There is clearly a problem in this proposal. The stranger has said that the life that these citizens should try to live is a life of cultivating their bodies and souls with regard to virtue. He then describes their day-to-day activities, and he makes clear that political business forms only a secondary part of their lives. And, in the whole of Book Seven, he reveals that a certain education will be their primary occupation. But then he makes it sound as though the goal of this education is the good execution of political business.

How could the education be primary and the execution of political business secondary, if the goal of the education is the good execution of the political business? It is the same as if someone were to say that the work of carpentry is properly only a secondary concern in a good life, but that an education in carpentry is the most important thing. Such a statement would be odd. For why would the knowledge of carpentry be so important, if the practice of carpentry is only of secondary importance? Would anyone pride himself on knowing how to build cabinets yet treat building them as a secondary pursuit? This would be ridiculous. So too, it seems silly to say that an education aimed at political activity should be superior to any such activity itself. What is the education good for if the activity is only a secondary concern?

To answer this question sufficiently would require looking at the whole of the education described in the *Laws*, not only here in Book Seven but in the book as a whole, and trying to see if, in fact, this education is only devoted to political action. Maybe it is not so restricted. But of course this investigation would require seeing what, if anything, in the political education or beyond the political education allows the citizens to cultivate their souls and bodies with regard to virtue. Such cultivation is, after all, the goal, the life.

Leaving Lincoln

In his many speeches against the apologists of the South Abraham Lincoln often took issue with their economic theory. Of course he attacked what he saw as the fundamental precept of slave economics, the very definition of injustice he called it, the principle that "You work and I'll eat." But he also took issue with the vision of social stratification implied by these apologists' words, the claim that some men must work solely as laborers while others act as owners and capitalists. Lincoln embraced and extolled the social fluidity made possible by the Revolution and revolutionary legislation. Economic freedom allows the same man to start out as a laborer, earn enough to buy his own tools or land, come to supervise others, and eventually hire supervisors for his own property. Today such fluidity has reached the point that the same man may be a laborer in one instance but, in another relation, an owner or capitalist, a situation one observer has called in pointed jest the "class straggle" as opposed to the Marxist class struggle (Scruton 17-18).

The stranger would no doubt mistrust Lincoln's enthusiasm. Though he proposes a slavery that would allow some fluidity, and though his property laws would not prohibit the disappearance of some families and their replacement by others, he aims at a system fixed in its hierarchy and orders. But the purpose of this fixity is not to cultivate luxury, nor commerce, nor even conquest in war. It aims at a public-spirited education that will occupy almost all of the citizens' waking days. The fluidity that Lincoln praises lifts the chains from slaves or any oppressed classes. But it also encourages people to spend almost all their waking hours on private advancement, usually of a commercial sort. There are great pleasures found in such advancement. But it leaves precious little time for education, personal or public.

Education is the "business," so to speak, of the stranger's odd city. It is for the sake of this education that his proposed citizens pare down or minimize every other element of their lives. It is for the sake of this education that they avoid private business, avoid farming, avoid family life, and even minimize political business. In other words, it is for the sake of this education, for the cultivation of their souls and bodies with respect to virtue, that they minimize all the parts of life that most people today so exalt, cherish and busy themselves with. Which is the better way—the contemporary way or the stranger's way? This is the most important practical question of the book. At least now we begin to see where the differences lie. And we see the importance for detailing more clearly the substance of the proposed civic education.

Notes

[1] Morrow observes that Plato may have known, from his own travels, of a contemporary revival in Egypt of earlier forms of artistry, a revival that prized emulation rather than slavish reproduction (355).

[2] For a similar ancient warning about the danger of innovation, see Aristotle's clear and succinct criticism of the proposal to reward people who come up with useful inventions (*Politics*, II.10, 13-14).

[3] On the goodness of Egypt, see Strauss, *Argument and Action* 25.

Chapter Eight:
Mars and Venus

Myths New and Old

In 1992, John Gray, Ph.D. published *Men are from Mars, Women are from Venus: A Practical Guide for Improving Communication and Getting What You Want in Your Relationships*. Despite its unwieldy title, the work has gone on to sell more than 15 million copies worldwide and has given birth to a litter of progeny including *Mars and Venus on a Date* (for those just forming a "relationship"), *Mars and Venus Starting Over* (for those breaking one), and even *The Mars and Venus Diet and Exercise Solution*.

At the beginning of *Men are from Mars...*, Gray imagines a race of people on the planet Mars discovering another race on Venus and, of course, falling in love. Despite their different backgrounds, nay, different worlds, the Martians and Venusians enjoy many good times together, celebrating their dissimilarities. They decide to work together to colonize a new planet of their own, Earth. But once established in their new home, a surprising ailment befalls them: "selective amnesia." They wake up forgetting their differences. The Martians expect the Venusians to act like Martians and vice-versa. Disappointment and discord take the place of amity and enjoyment.

Perhaps one reason for the success of Gray's work resides in his decision to invent his own sci-fi allegory to describe the differences and misunderstandings he ascribes to men and women, rather than to return to the ancient myths about Mars and Venus. His invented story allows him to appeal to an audience shaped more by Star Trek or the New Frontier than by Homer or the tragic poets. It also protects his recommendations from troublesome conclusions to which the old stories might have led some readers.

For Homer's tale—if it even allows us to take his deities as types of man and woman—presents the sexes in quite a different light than does Gray's. There are real differences between the two gods: Mars (or Ares) is the bloodthirsty god of War, while Venus (Aphrodite) is "crowned with flowers." These differences obviously go far beyond the tepid versions Gray assigns to modern men and women: reserved vs. outgoing, direct vs. circumlocutory, obtuse vs. sensitive, hunters vs. gatherers, and the like. Gray's men more resemble sulky cave-dwellers and his women needy dependents than they do the God and Goddess of the most stirring passions.

More fundamentally, what Gray never really explains—but which Homer dramatizes to the full—is the attraction between these two different types. At most Gray seems to suggest that women need support and men, well at least some men, like supporting them. Homer allows nothing so milquetoast. His Ares exclaims, when he sees Aphrodite's cuckolded husband Hephaestus stump away:

> Quick, my darling, come, let's go to bed
> and lose ourselves in love! Your husband's away—
> by now he must be off in the wilds of Lemnos,
> consorting with his raucous Sintian friends.

Nor does Homer ignore the goddess' desire:

> So he pressed
> and her heart raced with joy to sleep with War…(Fagles)

Off they went to bed, embraced each other, and then embraced by the crafty Hephaestus' net of chains. The reaction of the two to being caught is also revealing. After Hephaestus exhibits the naked lovers to the Gods and finally releases them, Ares proudly flies away to his belligerent friends, the Thracians, and Aphrodite flits away to Paphos, to take a bath with her nymphs, laughing the whole way. This is no tale of mutual support or dependence but of two bold lovers who know exactly what they want.

Nonetheless, while in this way Homer possibly dramatizes the difference between the sexes and their mutual attraction, he leaves as a puzzle the reason for their attraction. Why should bloody War love Love? And why should Love love War? Homer does not offer the reader the crutch of Gray's easy psychologizing, and thus prompts one to wonder not only about the sexes but also about the relation of these passions within the human heart, the passions of love and anger. It is a relation that Plato studies throughout his dialogues, but it comes to the fore in *Laws* Book Eight.

Acorns

In our journey through the first three book of Plato's *Laws*, we saw that there is ample reason to think that the central topic of concern of the *Laws* is education. If there is one lesson that the stranger stresses throughout the conversation it is that the origins of things, the beginnings of things are very imperfect. The beginnings are lowly and disorderly. That goes especially for the human things. The original human societies are rude and savage. And individual human beings, in their original or first state, are undeveloped and imperfect. Perhaps the stranger thought that babies are cute—perhaps not, given his demand that nurses shape infants' limbs (789e)—but he certainly thinks that they are very far from being completed humans. They are imperfect human beings, in need of shaping body and soul.

But this obvious imperfection of human beings in their youngest state is only half the problem. For matters would be much easier if, like oak trees from acorns, human perfection appeared, on its own, in time. Every normal acorn, if given soil and adequate sustenance, will grow into an oak tree; it will grow, without prodding, into its perfected state. Human growth is not so simple. If nourished, normal human babies will grow into physically mature human beings. But the physically mature human being is very far from the complete human being. A full-grown man may be ignorant or wicked. To perfect human beings, something more is needed beyond good weather and adequate physical nourishment.

That something more is, of course, education. Oak trees do not need education; human beings do. But what education is necessary to grow a complete human being is not obvious. That is a sign of human beings' deeper imperfection. Starting out as a needy, crying, weak baby is one sign of human imperfection. A more significant sign of imperfection is that no human being begins with knowledge of what he or she needs to learn in order to become perfect. But if human beings need education, and yet do not know what that education is, how can they perfect themselves? This ignorance of education is humanity's true, most pressing, most practical problem. We have to ask ourselves, and not let up, What is most important to learn?

All of his remarks indicate that the stranger has asked himself this question again and again, and that he continues to ask himself this question. And this question is the precursor to another question, another practical and pressing question. Since human beings grow up and live in political communities, and they receive and give education within those communities, what is it that they should teach their children, their students, themselves? What is the most important, most necessary, subject of education?

This is, of course, a question that vexes political communities, including the United States, to this day. In many contemporary American political campaigns this question arises: What should the schools be teaching the children? The typical answers may help illuminate the differences between present-day America and the city the stranger is proposing. Americans tend to answer that the most important things for children to learn are certain bodies of facts and certain skills. Children should know how to read and write English. They should also know how to manipulate numbers in a variety of basic operations. And they should possess some basic knowledge of history and of the most prominent sciences. Finally, many people argue that schools should teach children how to think, how to work together on projects, and how to tolerate others' opinions and views.

But what is all this learning for? Usually people defend this fact-based or skill-oriented education by saying that it prepares children to become productive members of society, good workers, in other words. A sign that this system of education cannot usually do this job satisfactorily is that most college-aged readers of this book must go to college in order to learn the skills they need in order to become productive workers. But at least elementary and secondary education tries to provide a good grounding for that pursuit.

Old School

The stranger, of course, proposes a much different content for education, because he aims at a much different goal. To recall briefly the three views of education he gives in Books One and Two, he first explained, in Book One, that a good education leads children to want to become perfect citizens, ones who know justice. This education seems to aim at political life above all. And certainly much of what is proposed in the *Laws* makes it seem as though this is the life citizens will be leading: a life of ruling and being ruled, which requires knowledge of justice above all.

Then, at the beginning of Book Two, the stranger suggested that the best education can do is to prepare human beings' passions so that they will sing in consonance with intelligence, and that this consonance makes for perfect humanity. That is, education cannot make people perfect. It can only prepare them to make the most out of intelligence, if they are lucky enough to have it.

Finally, later in Book Two, the stranger asserted that education drags children towards lawfulness. This lawfulness would seem to be quite a step down from perfect citizenship or perfect humanity. But it does seem to be what the stranger aims at in the rest of the book. He proposes a multitude of laws, after all. Most human beings cannot live together without laws, it seems. Nor, it seems, can there be a flourishing of humanity in the absence of political communities. So lawfulness becomes extremely important. But unless there is a law that teaches us justice and prepares us for perfect humanity, then the teaching of lawfulness will happen at the expense of these other teachings.

Military Academy

So what follows from all these proposals and suggestions early in the *Laws*? The hope was that the stranger's laws would teach justice and prepare the citizens' passions for perfect humanity. But do they? What now does the stranger say about the goal of the laws? He makes clear in Book Seven that the regime will exist to support a certain education. Education, not business, is the business of this city. But what does that education aim at? As much as one might like to say that this education aims at some lofty goal, the stranger comes to admit that, on the whole, this city's educational system will aim at military excellence. He repeats this again and again in Book Seven: he wants to make both men and women into good soldiers for the city (see 794c-795d, 803d-804b, 804d-806d, 809b, 813e-814c, and 815a-b).

Another sign of the importance of the military arts comes at the end of Book Seven. At the end of the book the stranger turns suddenly starts talking about hunting (822d-824a). He does not explain why. He goes through the different types of hunting, as he sees them. And he ends by legislating that one particular type of hunting—hunting four-footed animals with horses, dogs, and weapons—is most praiseworthy (824a). Why is that? For one, he says that it cultivates a "courage that is divine." It is not sneaky, as many other types of hunting are. And it requires the hunter to use his body extensively, to get used to riding and using weapons, and to face his foe—the hunted animal—quite directly. In other words, it is a great practical preparation for warfare.

The stranger hinted that this would be the case back in Book Six. In that book he talked about how all the young male citizens would have to spend two years in a sort of "secret service" that would roam about the country fixing things and doing various public works. In that section (763b3-6), he says,

> Probably no learning is greater than that which allows them
> all to know with accuracy their own country. It's for this

reason that a young man should study hunting with hounds
and the rest of hunting, in addition to the rest of the pleasure
and benefit that come about from such things.

Hunting prepares one for war by giving the opportunity to really get to
know the country that one has to defend.[1] So, the toughness and the
knowledge instilled by hunting are, it seems, the summit of education in
this city. No learning is more important, the stranger says. But hunting
does not necessarily teach justice, perfect humanity, or even perfect
lawfulness. It prepares one to be a better soldier.

One more sign that victory in war is the goal of this city's
education comes towards the beginning of Book Eight. In this section
(828a-835b), the stranger turns back to the subject of gymnastics. He does
so in the context of the civic festivals, and makes some rather surprising
recommendations here. For example, he begins by saying that this city
should celebrate at least 365 festivals or holy days, so that every day there
is some sort of celebration and sacrifice to a god. But what is the point of
all these festivals? Has the stranger become excessively pious?

Hardly. He says this about all these festivals: "The citizens
should always be devising certain games, noble ones, to go along with the
sacrifices, so that certain festival battles come about, resembling as much
and as clearly as possible the battles of war" (829b7-c1). For, he goes on
to say, this city is engaged against all other cities in "the greatest contests":
the contests of survival in a world of war (830a1). And so, he advises, in
addition to the major festivals with their mock battles, the lawgiver in this
city should "legislate small military exercises, without heavy arms, for
pretty much each day" (830d4-5). These exercises, major or minor, he
says, should be the goal of the choruses and the whole gymnastic art
(830d).

Such proposals seem quite surprising in the context of what was
discussed in Book Seven. The stranger insists in that book that the citizens
must have a plan for every day. They would get done whatever housework
needed to get done at night. They would also handle most of their political
business at night. That would leave all day for them to engage in
education. One might imagine them studying mathematics or poetry all
day long and become ever wiser and more "cultured," as people today
would put it. But that is not to be. Instead, every day they will be engaged
in various sorts of military exercises. They will be working out for war, so
to speak, nearly all the time. The ability to defend themselves well in
warfare emerges as the clear winner in the contest over the aim of the
city's education.

Serious Puppets

But of course we can and should ask, Why? No doubt everyone would agree that it is important to be able to defend yourself and your community in the case of war. But why should military education emerge, on the whole, as the foremost goal of the civic education? Is not this quite a disappointment, after all that has been said about education in justice or prudence? What happened to perfect citizenship or perfect humanity? Why should being a perfect soldier be all that these citizens can be? Is this truly what the stranger thinks is the most serious goal for public education to pursue?

To answer these questions we need to trek back to a puzzling passage in the middle of Book Seven (803c-804e). In this passage the stranger—in a burst of candor, it seems—tells the reader and his listeners what he thinks is serious and not serious in human life.

The stranger begins by saying that his own view of what is serious and what is play and the relation between the two is almost exactly the opposite of most people's. Most people, he explains, think that what is serious in life is conflict, such as war. Fighting, defending your family and your country, is serious business, they believe. Likewise, most people think that peace-time should be play-time. Peace should be filled with playful activities, whether that means spending time with your friends or families or pursuing various pleasures. Finally, most people suppose that the serious things—fighting and war—are endured for the sake of the playful things, such as enjoying yourself with others during peace. Human beings live to play, in other words.

This is not a crazy view. Most people today likely consider war quite serious, but would also class among the serious things work and careers. What is most serious, they might say, is scraping together enough money to provide what is needed for yourself and your family. But that means what is serious—whether war or work—is pursued for the sake of something else. And that something else is leisure. Spending time with family or friends. Playing sports. Playing other games. Pleasing oneself in various ways. Whatever the choice of pleasures, most people would say that they work—they are serious—in order to play.

The stranger is not entirely opposed to this position. He does not say, in contradiction to the regular view, that human beings live in peace in order then to fight. But he does make this much clear: play, in his view, is for the sake of what is serious, not vice-versa. The reader can observe this view play itself out in his recommendations concerning festivals. The festivals and sacrifices, the singing and dancing, that the citizens of this city engage in are all play. He calls them games, the noblest sort of games.

But what are these games or festivals for? They are for the sake of being prepared to fight well in war. The games are for the sake of war.

But here is where the complexity arises. For war, in his view, is not the most serious thing. It is certainly not play, but it is not the height of seriousness either. Again, his attitude is not outlandish. Soldiers throughout history, including those in the present day United States military, often refer to their engagement in exercises or even warfare as "play." No doubt their usage reflects, in part, gallow's humor, a happy means of dealing with grim realities. But it also reveals that they recognize something higher than the fighting—that which they are fighting for, the truly serious things.

But what is serious, in the stranger's view, if not war or military exercises? The stranger puts it this way: "What we say is for us, at least, the most serious thing" is "education" (803d6-7). But what does this education amount to? So far, it seems to amount to nothing more than preparing oneself well for war. But by the stranger's own argument that—war—does not seem to be the most serious end. But that means that the "education" that aims at it—war—would be even less serious.

To make sense of this tangle one must go beyond these remarks. The stranger also says in this passage "by nature god is worthy of a complete and blessed seriousness" (803c3-4). What is most serious for humans is education. But what is most serious simply is god. That is, the human things are, as a whole, not very serious. Human lives, human play, human wars, even human education—these are not the most serious things in the world. What is most serious, simply, is the divine, the god. Another way the stranger makes this same point is by saying that mankind is a "plaything" or "puppet" of the god (803c5). Even God does not take humanity seriously. So why should human beings do so?

These comments are most surprising. What the stranger is saying, in effect, is that this entire project that the three of them are engaged in, the project of founding and legislating for a new city, is itself not the most serious affair. All human pursuits, even political pursuits are not worthy of the greatest seriousness. The stranger, for a moment, gives voice to a view of human things that makes those things, and politics, look small, even inconsequential.

But the stranger's interlocutors rebel. Megillus butts in and complains to the stranger, saying that he is "running down the human race in every way" (804b5-6). This angry comment seems to pull the stranger back to earth. He replies, "I was looking away to the god when I said what I did just now" (804b6-7). And he acquiesces: "Let the human race not be worthless, if it's dear to you, but worthy of some seriousness" (804b7-c1). But still it is clear that in his view the stranger does not think human things are truly serious. What he does here is to acquiesce to the reality of having to live with and talk with other human beings who demand that human things, their own lives, be taken with utmost seriousness. Maybe he even acquiesces to being a human being who must, by necessity, take seriously something that is not, by itself, serious—himself.

The necessary backpedaling notwithstanding, this dramatic exchange teaches us something important about the stranger's view of what is serious and what is play. He says that for us education should be taken most seriously. But clearly he cannot mean simply the education in heavy weapons and the like. He seems to be pointing to an education that would lead human beings towards knowledge of the most serious thing simply, that is, to god.

As an aside, we can observe that this exchange with Megillus shows what gets in the way of that very rare and refined education. What gets in the way are love and anger. As Megillus shows, people hold themselves, the human race, as dear. People even like to think that the highest powers in the universe—the gods themselves—take them very seriously. They like to think, as Megillus implies, that the highest things, the gods themselves, are cognizant of human beings and care about their happenings. But the stranger's words present a much different picture. If we are the puppets of the gods, the playthings of the gods, then we cannot hold such high hopes and such a lofty view of ourselves and our place in the universe. That rejection of what others hold dear sparks a swift and angry reaction. As Megillus reveals, the education in this teaching, as serious as it may be, can never become the popular foundation of a city.

Educating Eros

To recall, the popular education aims at making good soldiers. It does so, in part, by weakening the familial bonds among the citizens, splitting up spouses, parents, and children, directing them all to different public exercises and segregating them by sex in the city's common meals. While the stranger's most serious education, the one concerning god, appears to stand open to any human being of requisite abilities, the popular education, such as it is, very much addresses citizens as men and women. Understanding this popular education thus requires thinking more about the stranger's treatment of the sexes.

In each of the books since Book Four the stranger has revealed something of his proposed treatment of private families and private life. One of the most disturbing elements of this treatment is the way the stranger's laws would weaken familial bonds, especially the bonds between husbands and wives. As seen, he calls for common meals that are segregated by sex, so that spouses will spend every meal apart from one another; he demands that both the male and female citizens spend their nights in political or household business and their days in exercises and festivals and the rest of "education," enjoying little home life in the meantime; and he frees women of most household duties and gives them an education of their own, so that they are less dependent on their husbands and less tied to their homes. All of these proposals and many more will weaken families in this city.

Now, these proposals may seem unrealistic as well as disturbing. Do men not love their wives and wives love their husbands and parents love their children and vice-versa? What people would accept the separation that the stranger wishes to impose? His response has been to emphasize what the family members are going to do instead of spend time at home: the public business and military exercises that they are going to spend their days and nights engaged in. In this city, instead of worrying about their own narrow or selfish familial concerns, citizens can devote themselves to the common good in a much fuller way. No doubt decent people will always choose to devote themselves to the common good and to sacrifice their own private interests, even if those private things are very sweet. Still, one might worry that such a "Spartan" life would require citizens who are emotionless, unerotic automatons.

But to ascribe that view to the stranger would be very unjust. He is not assuming citizens who are passionless or unloving. Far from it. If one remembers Book Four, the very first laws he discusses are laws concerning marriage (720e-721e). He knows that very great and very deep desires lead people to couple and to seek to live with one spouse and have and raise children together. Indeed, as he says in Book VIII, the very commonality of the city—that fact that in this city unlike any other the citizens will have the time to gather together in common and exercise and play together—this very commonality makes him worried (835d ff.). He is worried that young people, young men and women, will see each other at play and be drawn together into all sorts of liaisons. He knows the power of erotic desire. He knows that it is lurking beneath the surface, especially in the young. He knows that it cannot be gotten rid of, nor does he ever propose trying to get rid of it.

But—and this is decisive—he does think that it can be directed. He thinks it can be directed for good or for ill, or that erotic desire can be directed in better or worse ways. This is the point he makes at the end of Book Six: "all human things depend on a threefold need and desire, through which, for people who are led rightly, virtue results, and for those who have been led badly, the opposite" (782d10-e1).

The "third and greatest" of these needs or desires is, he says, the "erotic longing which rushes on most sharply and last of all, and makes human beings thoroughly and completely inflamed with madness: a most violent burning for the sowing of offspring" (782e6-783a4). So much for his diagnosis of human ills. The stranger's prognosis follows, in the same section: "What must happen, turning the three illnesses towards what is best and against what is said to be most pleasant, is the attempt to hold them down with the three greatest restraints—fear and law and true reason" (783a4-7). Left to itself, erotic desire amounts to a great illness. But under the direction of fear, law and true reason, it can be the support and engine of virtue itself.

Constraint and Contempt

In this last respect—in the way he thinks erotic desire can and should be regulated—the stranger is clearly at odds with much of today's society. Most people nowadays make very large claims about sexual desire. They like to think that they now understand sex better than every previous generation. They like to think that they have delved into the depths of the human soul, into the unconscious or the like, and have seen sexual possibilities that their forefathers never dreamed of. They also like to think that they are freer with regard to sex than every previous generation. But what is the result of all this exploration and freedom? Many people have concluded that sex is no big deal, a happy addendum to life, but nothing to get worked up about. Under all these influences, modern Western society prides itself on enduring no or nearly no sexual regulation.

The stranger's laws are, of course, quite different. The stranger, unlike most of today's politicians, offers extensive sexual regulation or sexual legislation. This does not mean he is going to be a repressive sexual tyrant. But he does propose rules that people today would find quite burdensome.

For example, in the various proposals he makes in Book Eight regarding sex, one restriction stays the same throughout. No homosexual sex (as it would be called today) is to be tolerated. But before one condemns the stranger for being a "puritan" or a "prude," one should acknowledge this point: the stranger proposes laws regulating erotic things because he takes those things very seriously. He thinks erotic desire is one of the most fundamental, important, and potentially dangerous desires in the life of man. And as he wants to try direct human beings to the best life possible, he must speak about and try to direct erotic desire. How could he not legislate about them? In contrast, the stranger would have this to say about the permissiveness as regards sex that society today so prides itself in: that only a people who did not take erotic things seriously would be so permissive. He might say that contemporary laxity regarding sex comes not from open-mindedness but from a sort of childish or even willful ignorance of the vital importance of eros to human life.

Sex and Men

So maybe one can learn something about erotic things from listening to this stranger. One thing that should be noticed from the start is that his discussion of sex in Book Eight is directed towards men. He assumes male listeners. Now, in a sense, the reason for this is obvious: he is talking to two old men. But clearly, as he often does, the stranger here is speaking over the heads of his two interlocutors to the citizens of the proposed city. And in this case he is speaking especially to men: not just any men but in particular to young men.

In fact, at one point in this discussion, he imagines one of these young men responding to him, as though in dialogue (see 839b). He has just laid down his view of what sexual regulations there should be, in the best case. But he says, "suppose standing here was some man, young and eager, full of a lot of sperm, who had been listening to the laying down of the law: he would probably complain violently that we have set up stupid and impossible customs, and he would fill the whole place with his cries" (839b3-6). This complaint might sound familiar. The stranger has anticipated the very complaint that arises most naturally from contemporary readers, the complaint that his views on eros and sex regulation are not "realistic." He has anticipated that those complaints would come especially from young men. And so they are his main addressees in this section.

But why should men, and young men in particular, require his attention here? The fact that he speaks to men above all when talking about the need for sexual regulation suggests one obvious conclusion: that he thinks male sexuality is particularly disorderly or in need of regulation. This conclusion is borne out by what the stranger talks about in this section, for he makes clear what erotic "disorders," in his view, men are particularly prone to. The first of these is homosexual sex.

The stranger discusses homosexuality several times, and a legislator does not talk about something, and continue to talk about it, if it is not (in his view) a problem or a potential problem. The stranger would not talk about male homosexuality if he did not think that it was a real attraction to (or danger for) many men. As he notes to Kleinias and Megillus, their very own societies encourage male homosexuality (recall 636b-d). But these societies, while he thinks they are extreme in this respect, only encourage something that the stranger thinks is attractive to men in any society.

The second disorder he dwells on is adultery. Again, he would not bring it up again and again if it were not a problem in his eyes. One should remember that he is the same man who earlier in the *Laws* said that men in particular will have a great desire to marry if they think it will bring them children who will carry on their names. He knows how to make marriage attractive to men. But the fact that he thinks men, in particular, need to be attracted or persuaded into marriage shows that he thinks that they have some ambivalence about it. And this ambivalence reveals itself, most commonly, in adultery.

There is a more general way to view these two disorders. The stranger reveals that in his view homosexual sex is a thwarting of nature. This is, in a sense, obvious. No procreation can come from the sexual union of two men. The sexual union of man and woman is, in this not insignificant respect, the more natural union. As the stranger also puts it, it is the union of male and female—and not male and male—that we can observe all around us all the time in the rest of (non-human) nature. Conversely, in his view, adultery involves the thwarting of divine injunctions. Marriages are sealed with a vow, a vow that is usually made before god. And marriage, as he presents it and as it is still known to this day, is usually seen as being instituted by some divine power. Thus, while adultery may not involve any "unnatural" actions—indeed, it may culminate in the most natural acts—it contravenes the divine power that upholds marriage.

But what makes men prone to thwart nature and the gods, whether in homosexual sex or in adultery? It must be a powerful force to lead them to fight against these two great entities, and, of course, it is. The root cause of the problem is, in the stranger's view, pleasure. Now, people today usually take pleasure, all pleasures, to be a good thing. This stance is not only very common; it has a natural root. Human beings, by nature, seek pleasure and avoid pain. But what distinguishes the stranger from many people today is that he thinks that not all pleasures are created equal. Some pleasures are worthier than others or better than others. And this "worth" or "goodness" is not determined by the power of the pleasure. Some pleasures may be very vehement and yet still not worth pursuing.

The problem, he indicates, with the very powerful pleasures of homosexual sex and adultery is that both are pleasures taken in bodies. The goal of each is to take pleasure in the body of the other, the lover, whether that lover is male or female. But bodily pleasure is not the only pleasure it seems. In fact, the stranger seems to want to curb the lust for bodily pleasure. Why he should want to do that is still a question.

But before going on to address that question, we should remember once more that he singles out men for this lecture about sex. Why not women too? He does not completely exclude women. When he introduces the topic, for example, he does say that the "erotic attraction of women for men and of men for women" must be regulated for the good of the whole community and of the human beings who live there (836a7-b1). It is not as though he is saying that women do not have erotic desires; he acknowledges that they do. But he at least makes it seem as though he thinks women, on the whole, are less subject to the disorders of erotic activity that he is concerned with here—homosexuality and adultery. Again, that does not mean that he does not think there ever have been homosexual unions of women or adulterous wives. He had no doubt heard of Sappho and Clytemnestra. But he does seem to think they are not as great a danger as male homosexuality or male adultery. So why should women not be as much as a problem in regard to these two disorders?

There are at least two possibilities. One is that the stranger thinks that women are less moved by the bodily pleasures than men are. These bodily pleasures are catered to by homosexual sex and adultery. If women are not moved as strongly by these bodily pleasures, then they will not be drawn as urgently towards these activities. A second possibility is that the stranger thinks women are more bound by the powers which those two activities thwart. As said before, homosexual activity thwarts, in one sense, our nature, while adultery thwarts the gods. Maybe the stranger is suggesting that women are more respectful than men are of our sexual, procreative nature and that they are more pious, in general, than men are. The source of female respect for our procreative nature would, it seems, be obvious. The suggestion that women are, in general, more pious than men is one that the stranger makes several places throughout the *Laws*, and is worth following up at another point in our travels.

Let's Be Friends

But let us now return to that previous question: why does the stranger try to dissuade men from pursuing the bodily pleasures enjoyed in homosexual sex or adultery? What is the goal of his erotic legislation?

To answer this question we have to observe that the stranger ends by offering not one but two laws, two competing or contrasting laws, concerning sex. One is the law he says he would like to lay down. The other is the "second-best" law concerning erotic things. The best law, he says, would outlaw any man from touching any free person except his wife and would specifically outlaw adultery and homosexual unions. The second-best law would still outlaw homosexual sex, and would make adultery shameful and dishonorable—if one is caught. Otherwise, as he puts it, "for one to escape notice while doing these things—let it be noble" (841b2-3).

The stranger says that he must offer this "second-best" law because of the complaints of young men. They would see the first law, the "best law," as overly harsh and demanding. But, from today's more permissive perspective, one could ask, Why have even that "second-best" law? Why push consensual adultery in the closet? Why make homosexuality illegal? Why try to lead men away from pursuing these bodily pleasures? What is wrong with bodily pleasure?

The stranger clearly thinks that there is a lot wrong with it. Or, to put it conversely, he clearly thinks that there is a lot of good to be done by regulating sex. As he puts it, in a very striking statement (839a6, b2), "Tens of thousands...and many, very many other good things would come about" if the city had such laws. What are some of these things? He says following such laws would "stop erotic wildness and madness" (839a6). He may be thinking here of the way men get worked up about their lovers and their wives. He may especially have in mind the very bloody altercations that can occur over lovers and wives.

The stranger also says that such regulation would help cut down on "much eating and drinking" (839a8). The connection between eating, drinking and sexual license may not be so obvious. But no doubt in ancient Greece as in modern America many sexual liaisons occurred because the participants did too much drinking. And people usually drink too much while eating too much. Likewise, debauchery is often followed by lots of eating and drinking. It is as though firing up one of those three profound needs or desires stokes the fires of the other two as well. Finally, in this section (839a), the stranger says that such regulation will make men "more familiar and dear to their wives" (839b1). With such laws, women will be able to live less worried that their husbands are dallying with the girl—or guy—next door.

However, there is one further, significant good that the stranger may have in mind as resulting from this somewhat rigorous sexual regulation. He describes two kinds of friendship of love: the attraction between similar and equals "in respect to virtue" and the attraction between those who are unlike or unequal (837a6-7). The first he calls gentle and mutual and lifelong. The second he calls terrible, savage, and seldom mutual. And these two forms can mix together. Then they form an attraction in which a man wants to "pick the bloom" of a youth and have sex with him (837b8), yet also wants to let that young boy's soul develop and become a mature and mutual friend. The stranger clearly wants to encourage that latter desire. For then, he says, law can encourage the friendship that "is of virtue and desires that the young person become as excellent as possible" (837d5).

So here is a further reason for regulating sexual life: for the promotion of a certain type of friendship. His fear seems to be that if sexual life is unregulated—if men pursue their desires unchecked—the prospects for this friendship of virtue will be very slim. One begins to see here the possibility, then, of a pleasure that goes beyond the satisfaction of bodily lusts, a pleasure based on a friendship of two similarly virtuous individuals. It is to shelter this gentle and tender growth that the Stranger uses the sometimes violent power of law to restrain sexual desire. It is a choice he makes. Those of us living today have to wonder whether by choosing differently, we make the development of such friendships, especially but not only between the sexes, all the harder or even impossible.

Putting Love and War to Bed

We have already seen that the stranger focuses much too intently on the good of the community as a whole to serve as a popular "relationship-counselor" of the John Gray type. One need not imagine, he himself admits, that advice such as "marry someone unlike yourself" in wealth or disposition, would not win him many clients or referrals. Nor would his wary words about bodily pleasure win him many adoring fans in any place or time.

But of course it is his focus on the principles of politics and the human soul that make the stranger more worthy of attention than fad-mongers. Book Eight of the *Laws* extends the regulation that his proposed city would cast, like a net, over the lives of its citizens. It shows further how steadfastly that regulation aims at their preparation for war. These citizens could never forget the large place of Ares in their lives.

But, the stranger reveals, the best preparation for war, in his view, is not to make bloodthirsty citizens. Such an education would no doubt threaten the city's own existence, to speak nothing of the citizens' own souls and happiness. As martial as they may be, these citizens, or at least the best among them, should not become devotees of Ares. As he has suggested before (recall Book Five), the stranger wants to moderate their anger, their desire to punish, their thirst for revenge. They should devote themselves to God, but to a God who would never deign to mix himself in battle with human beings or even other gods.

Just as the stranger reigns in Ares, he also pours some cold water on Aphrodite. We have already seen the many ways he encourages marriage but at the same time weakens familial bonds. He does not—he says he cannot—entirely subsume private erotic desire for the public good. But he tries to do so as much as possible. Still, such subsumption is not only for the public good. In this case the public good and the private good are not exclusive. The moderation of sexual passion preserves, in his view, the possibility of something more lasting and worthwhile than physical coupling: the friendship of virtue. Here too, a God who cares for excellence, even super-human excellence, offers a better model than one who delights in lovemaking.

In Homer's tale, while they watch Ares and Aphrodite trapped in their adulterous bed, most of the assembled gods tut-tut and claim that they would never want to be caught in such a shameful position. Only Hermes, a deity known for his guile, fesses up to his willingness to pay any price to have sex with Aphrodite. One can imagine the stranger deprecating Homer's poetry in this case. In this light, perhaps, for all the differences between high art and low hucksterism, Homer and John Gray share something in common.

Note

[1] For further testimony on hunting's value in preparing for warfare, see Plutarch, *Philopoemen* 4, and Machiavelli's *Prince* XIV (Mansfield 59).

Chapter Nine:
Doctor of Philosophy

Missing Socrates

A tour through any one of Plato's dialogues, including this one, is usually organized under the general auspices of one particular discipline: philosophy. Plato is, after all, known as a philosopher. But so far, what philosophical sights have we seen? Our travels have taken us through many topics of political importance, some dealing even with the principles of politics itself. This survey could be said to treat politics philosophically, as an object of wonder and contemplation. But to say this would be to assume that we know what philosophy is, or that we know what Plato understood philosophy to be. Yet, through two-thirds of this book, we have traveled without once seeing a platonic presentation of philosophy.

The two explicit appearances of philosophy in the *Laws* stand out by their rarity. They are also conspicuous for the negative tone that they take towards philosophy. In the second case, in Book Twelve, philosophy is mentioned only to be insulted and condemned (967c). But the first reference to philosophy occurs in Book Nine, at 857c-e. Though it too hardly endorses philosophy, it is worth studying for what light it may shed on Plato's understanding of his own endeavor, the endeavor that guides the writing, if not the conversation itself, of the *Laws*.

This passage concerns the "slavish" and "free" doctors that the stranger first discussed long before in Book Four. He goes on to say here,

> One should know well this very thing: if a certain one of those doctors who sets his hand to medicine on the basis of experience and without reason [a slavish doctor] should ever come upon a free doctor in dialogue with a free man who is sick, a doctor who uses arguments that come near to philosophizing and who grabs hold of the disease from its source, going back up to the whole nature of bodies, he would quickly and readily laugh and would say that sorts of things that are always thrown about concerning such things by most so-called doctors. He would exclaim, "Fool! You are

not doctoring the sick man but practically educating him, as though he needed to become a doctor and not well" (857c6-e1).

Kleinias then responds, "Well, wouldn't he be speaking correctly when he said such things?" (857e2) And the Athenian replies, "Perhaps—if he at least went on to recognize that whoever goes through laws in the way we're now going through them is educating the citizens but not legislating" (857e3-5).

Again, this is the first of only two mentions of philosophy in the whole of this enormous book, Plato's *Laws*. And, like the second, this passage does not offer a positive picture of philosophy. The slavish doctor upbraids the free one, to whom the philosopher is compared. And the interlocutors appear to support the slavish doctor's judgment.

Recognizing the near uniqueness of this passage, and its tone, allows one to make a certain characterization of the *Laws*. Philosophy itself is barely present in the *Laws*. It exists only on the horizon, so to speak, and it seems unwilling to show its face. It lurks only in the shadows or on the very edges of the discussion.

There is one other strong sign of this fact. A reader who has persevered thus far in the book may continue to wonder who this Athenian stranger is. (On this topic, recall Chapter One). It is, after all, very odd that Plato would make the main character of his longest dialogue a stranger. As seen, in his *Politics* Aristotle refers to the main character as Socrates, the famous teacher of Plato. To Aristotle, the Athenian stranger is Socrates, and, no doubt, Aristotle was in a good position to know about these things. A sign that Aristotle is right is that this Athenian stranger uses many arguments that are exactly the same as arguments that Socrates uses in other platonic dialogues.[1] And this Athenian stranger engages in a dialogue, as Socrates always does. That is, the Athenian stranger sounds just like Socrates.

Such evidence is not ironclad. But it does seem as though the Athenian stranger is Socrates or a Socratic. So why did Plato not just skip all the trouble and mystery and make Socrates the explicit main character of this dialogue, as he is the main character of every other platonic dialogue? Why go through the trouble of hiding Socrates behind the guise of an "Athenian stranger"? A likely reason is that Socrates, in all those other dialogues, represents the philosophical life. Socrates is the philosopher, par excellence. Wherever Socrates is present, philosophy is in the reader's face. But, in the *Laws*, philosophy lurks only at the very horizon of the conversation. In the *Laws*, philosophy travels in disguise, *incognito*. In the *Laws*, the conversation and the readers never reach philosophy itself.

Does that mean that the *Laws*, a book many readers may have picked up thinking that it is philosophical, is far from being the real article? Is this a platonic bait-and-switch? Not at all. This odd characteristic, the near-absence of philosophy, is the beauty of the *Laws*. The *Laws* does not throw philosophy in the reader's face. Instead, it starts and stays very close to regular people and to regular concerns. For the very great majority of human beings are not philosophers. The *Laws* stays the closest of any of Plato's dialogues to the non-philosophic "everyday" sort of life—the life that most people live. It does not take philosophy or an interest in philosophy for granted.

Medicine

The book does, of course, raise profound political questions, such as, "Who should rule?" "What is justice?" "What is true equality?" "What is education?" The necessity of these questions, the practical necessity of them, forces thoughtful people to turn to an inquiry that can be called "philosophic." It is appropriate, then, at this point in one's reading, in a way that it would not have been appropriate upon picking up the *Laws*, for one to begin to ask what philosophy looks like. To begin to do that one must study this image that the stranger uses to introduce philosophy: the image of the slavish and free doctors.

These two are, as he mentions, the two doctors that he first referred to in Book Four (720a-e). He first mentioned these two doctors in order to help Kleinias understand what law is. Here he returns to these doctors to better convey his understanding of legislation and philosophy. The free doctor is the one who knows the medical art on the basis not only of observation and experience, but on the basis of reasoning. He knows why people get sick and why certain medicines or regimens cure them. The slavish doctor "knows" about medicine only on the basis of experience—from seeing some treatments succeed and other treatments fail. He does not know why one treatment works better than another.

So what does this image of the two doctors teach us about philosophy and legislation? Clearly, the stranger likens the free doctor to the philosopher, but he does not equate the two. The free doctor is not the philosopher or vice-versa; the free doctor is only like a philosopher. Likewise, the slavish doctor is like a legislator and vice-versa—the legislator is like a slavish doctor.

By itself this analogy is already quite surprising. Kleinias, Megillus, and the readers had been led to believe, through almost this entire conversation, that legislation is a very impressive task. Back in Book Four, when contemplating the great difficulty of legislation, the stranger himself had exclaimed, "It really is the case that lawgiving and the founding of cities is the most perfect test of the virtue of men" (708d6-7) Kleinias, who is a legislator, readily agrees. The only note of discord the stranger has sounded occurred in the middle of Book Seven. (See Chapter Eight.) But now the stranger clearly asserts that, in some decisive sense, legislation is inferior to philosophy. The legislator is to the philosopher as the slavish doctor is to the free doctor. Or, in other words, the stranger hints that the "manly virtue" required for legislation is not the height of human virtue.

The free doctor, the stranger says, "dialogues" with the free man who is sick. That dialogue or conversation concerns the sickness, which the free doctor tracks up to its source, and then he shows the free man how the disease is rooted in the "whole nature of bodies." This is similar to something the stranger says in Book Four about the free doctor. In that book, the stranger says that the free doctor investigates illnesses from their beginning and according to nature.

The dialogue of the free doctor with his patient concerns nature. Nature is the main concern or object of investigation of the free doctor. It is because he knows about nature—about the nature of bodies, to be precise—that the free doctor knows why certain diseases occur or why certain cures or regimens counteract them. Knowledge of nature answers the question "why," the question of the cause of disease or illness. The slavish doctor, by contrast, does not dialogue about nature. He issues commands. He does not seem to know about nature at all. He "knows" only what his necessarily limited experience has taught him; he "knows" certain customs—customary ailments and customary cures.

To complete the analogy with philosophy and legislation, the main concern or object of investigation of the philosopher is also nature. But the philosopher is interested not simply in the nature of bodies, but in nature itself, nature in the broadest sense. And so the philosopher's knowledge of nature allows him to answer the question "why?" in the broadest sense; it gives him knowledge of the most comprehensive causes. In contrast, the legislator as legislator—the legislator who does not partake at all in philosophy—does not possess this knowledge of nature or knowledge of the causes of things. His experience may be very broad and helpful. But he is chained to that experience. He does not know anything that goes beyond his necessarily limited experience, his customary experience. And it is on the basis of that experience that he issues commands. The legislator, unlike the philosopher, is not an inquirer or a conversationalist—he is a commander.[2]

So far, the stranger's image has taught two things: that in his view the philosopher is, in one important sense at least, superior to the legislator. And what is that sense? The philosopher, unlike the legislator, is a knower of and inquirer into nature, not a commander on the basis of experience. A third point follows from this second one. One learns, in the image, that what the free doctor does is to educate his patient. This is what the slavish doctor accuses him of: "You're teaching your patient to be a doctor!" The free doctor's goal seems to be to remove the sick man's ignorance about bodily things and to replace that ignorance with knowledge of bodily nature. The slavish doctor, in contrast, tries only to heal his patient, not to make him know medical matters. After all, the slavish doctor does not know such things himself. The goal of the slavish doctor is to remove the sick man's disease and to replace it with health. This is a surprising description: the free doctor tries to teach, the slavish doctor tries to cure. But it is one both Kleinias and the stranger agree on.

A qualification is needed here. Surely the free doctor also wants to cure his patient. But to do that he must do something more than teach, it seems. One can see this point if one recalls the discussion in Book Four for a moment. There the stranger first talks about the free doctor, and he says, "The free doctor doesn't give orders until he has in some sense persuaded; when he has on each occasion prepared and tamed the sick person with persuasion, he attempts to succeed in leading him back to health" (720d6-e2). The free doctor does issue commands as well, as the slavish doctor does. But he does so only after trying to teach the patient all he can about the illness and about the nature of bodies. Still, the command is necessary if the patient is to be cured. In other words, the free doctor has to adopt the practices of the slavish doctor if he is to succeed in curing anyone, besides just teaching people medical things. Knowing about the nature of bodies in general is not enough if you are sick. You must also be told what to do and sometimes, because of your diseased state, even forced to do it.

So what are we to conclude from all this about the philosopher and the legislator? The conclusion would seem to be that, vis-a-vis other people, the philosopher educates them, educates them about nature in the broadest sense. But, if he is like the free doctor who primarily educates people and does not heal them, then we would have to say that the philosopher educates people but does not necessarily make them good or make them better. It is the legislator, in contrast, who is analogous to the slavish doctor. And so, just as the slavish doctor replaces people's illnesses with health, so too, one should say, the legislator replaces people's badness or unruliness with goodness or lawfulness. The philosopher teaches; the legislator betters.

Or, to put all this a slightly different way: as observed, the free doctor, in order to cure people, must eventually adopt the methods of the slavish doctor and issue commands. But that is not who the free doctor essentially is; he is not a commander. Similarly, if the philosopher is to better people he must become a legislator, a commander. Nonetheless, the success of the free doctor as a doctor depends upon the activity of the slavish doctor. If the free doctor is to heal anyone, he must do as the slavish doctor does and issue commands. Similarly—and this is the critical point—the activity of the philosopher depends on the activity of the legislator. Philosophy, to better the community, depends on legislation.

This dependence takes two forms. First, the flourishing of philosophy depends on the existence and authority of a certain kind of legislation, the kind of legislation that instills lawfulness and moral goodness. Without the existence and authority of this kind of legislation, it will be very difficult or even impossible for philosophy to come about or to thrive for very long—philosophers and other contemplators do not flourish in civil wars. It is in the light of this kind of dependence that we can begin, at least in part, to understand the importance of Plato's *Laws*, and why Plato must have spent so much time to write this book. In the *Laws* we get a glimpse of what this "certain kind" of legislation might look like, a legislation that sets a foundation for philosophy.

But philosophy's dependence upon legislation also take a second, less self-interested form, one that becomes apparent if we continue to take seriously the metaphor of the two doctors. The slavish doctor criticizes the free doctor for appearing only to educate, rather than to cure, his patient. The criticism makes sense, if education is all the free doctor undertook to do. But, as mentioned, the free doctor, as a doctor, does wish to cure his patient. And so he must adopt some of the manners of the slavish doctor, teaching but also if necessary commanding. If the analogy holds, the philosopher may be said to care for the betterment of the souls of those around him. Some souls respond to teaching, instruction, and are bettered thereby. But others need commands, precisely in order to begin to build the habits of living freely. Just as it would be a strange doctor who wished to lecture and never cure, so it would be a strange teacher who wished only to teach and not to better his fellow man. The philosopher depends upon the modes of the legislator to accomplish this essential part of his own vocation. Far from being opposed, upon analysis the two activities appear closely conjoined.

One more qualification to this discussion is needed. Shortly after this discussion of the two doctors, the stranger says to his two interlocutors: "We are becoming lawgivers but we aren't yet lawgivers, though probably we may be" (859c2-3). This statement is odd and seems paradoxical. But, if one reads it in the light of the previous image, its meaning may become clearer. The three of them are not legislators. They may be legislators in the future, but that is an open question. Right now they are just talking about the nature of regimes. They are not issuing commands. Even by the end of the dialogue they have not instituted any actual legislation. This is all conversation, all talk.

What they are doing is trying to learn from and teach each other. That is, even though this book is called the *Laws*, and even though it is stuffed full of concrete political proposals, the conversational activity of the characters points more towards philosophy (dialogue) than towards legislation (commands). That being said, every moment of their conversation also reminds the reader of how fundamentally important is that legislation which would support the philosophizing towards which their conversation quietly points. Its importance becomes only clearer as we expand our attention to the rest of Book Nine.

Shameful Justice

Our eagerness to view this rare appearance of philosophy should not keep us from surveying the whole of Book Nine. This book presents what has been called the *Laws'* "penology," namely, its discussion of punishment.[3] Punishment occupies a curious place in the *Laws*. Punishment is obviously a large concern of these would-be lawgivers. Their discussion of punishment occupies more than an entire book. But it is not their first concern. Their discussion of punishment is postponed; it comes late in their conversation.

Also, as the stranger admits, there is something unsavory or even "shameful" (*aischra*) about discussing and enacting punishment (853b4). It is shameful to think that some of the citizens of the would-be city—a city with better laws than any other city has ever had or ever will have— would need to be punished in the manners described in Book Nine. It is shameful, the stranger says, to think that some of the citizens would ever commit such crimes. But the discussion of punishment is no mere afterthought. It is, after all, the place where philosophy is first mentioned. Also, as the stranger makes clear late in the book, part of the purpose of laws about punishment is to "teach the people a certain way in which they might mingle with one another and dwell in friendship" (880d8-e1). That is, laws about punishment may have an educational effect. The discussion of punishment—as shameful and as postponed as it is—continues the education offered in Plato's *Laws*, and continues it in essential ways.

There is, nonetheless, something problematic about punishment in the stranger's eyes. Or, to be more precise, punishment raises a certain problem. It is necessary to make clear what that problem is, what is the stranger's response to it, and what that response teaches us about ourselves. For his reaction to this problem is both odd and illuminating.

The problem that punishment raises, according to the stranger, is something like this. Punishment, he says, and his interlocutors agree, is something just (859c ff.). Punishment—as opposed to random violence or even angry vengeance—gives the wrongdoer what he deserves. Punishment is one of the natural consequences of justice. However, the stranger says, and again his interlocutors agree, punishment is also something shameful or ugly. It takes notice of wrongdoing and expresses disapproval of that wrongdoing. Both the public notice of the wrongdoing and the punishment of the wrongdoing involve shame. The workings of the criminal justice system, as one might call it today, are necessary, but ugly. So the stranger draws this partial conclusion: Punishment is agreed to be one of the just things. But punishment is also agreed to be one of the shameful things. Thus, in the case of punishment at least, people learn that the just things can be ugly.

What is the problem with that? There would not be a problem, except for this additional point: In this same argument the stranger asks his interlocutors whether justice is something noble or shameful. Kleinias strongly affirms that justice and "all the just things" are noble (859e6-10). Justice as a whole is noble. But, by looking at punishment, they have concluded that the just things, at least in the case of punishments, are ugly. In Greek as well as in English, "noble" is opposed to "shameful" or "ugly." Nothing can be both noble and ugly in the same respect. So the problem that punishment raises is a problem concerning justice. It raises the question of whether justice truly is noble or ugly or somehow both. It cannot be both in the same respect. So it also raises the problem of whether justice is one thing or whether it is essentially divided against itself.

Obiter Dicta

Before considering the stranger's resolution of this problem, it is important to observe some of the paths he does not take. He faces the seeming contradiction that justice is always beautiful or noble, but just punishment is ugly and shameful.

One approach to this problem that he could have taken would involve distinguishing two aspects of punishment: active and passive. That is, it would involve saying that what the criminal suffers is ugly but what the punisher does is beautiful. The stranger does not try to defend the beauty of justice by taking this approach. He does not say that suffering punishment is shameful but inflicting it is noble. For, if he had, someone could reply that, since justice is always beautiful, but suffering punishment is ugly, then suffering punishment must not be just. But clearly it can be, or must be, especially if one insists that exacting punishment is just. One may view punishment from various directions; but it must retain moral unity.

Nor does the stranger defend justice's nobility or beauty by denying that a justly ordered punishment is shameful or ugly. Such a denial does not, by itself, contain the contradictions of saying that suffering punishment is ugly but inflicting punishment is beautiful. But to deny that suffering punishment is shameful, to claim instead that it is indifferent or even noble leads to surprising results. This claim would imply that the greater the suffering the greater the nobility. It would put those who have endured the greatest punishments on a plane of nobility similar to that occupied by those who have done the finest deeds.

Still, one can defend this claim, surprising as are these consequences. First, the nobility belongs to accepting the punishment and enduring it. It does not attach to the crime that brought on the punishment. Thus this view of punishment demands seeing the recipient of the punishment as voluntary—as one who accepts the pain he must suffer. It recognizes this "noble punishment" as the public face of penitence. And this view finds popular expression in the assertion that criminals who have served their term of punishment have, at least in part, "repaid their debt" to society. But repaying what is owed is one form of justice.

Of course, the existence of prison walls, watchtowers, and barbed wire indicate that few of the punished are voluntary or see themselves as freely paying a debt owed. Few criminals will make their punishment noble. That does not mean that such a view of punishment is illogical or impossible. But, again, the stranger does not take this approach.

Unjust, Unfree

To put it most succinctly, the solution that the stranger offers to this problem begins in his claim that injustice is always involuntary (see 860d-e). No one, he argues, ever does injustice voluntarily. Because wrong is never voluntary, punishment must transform itself into correction or curing: the lawgiver should not aim to cause pain to the criminal, but to correct the harm he has done and to cure, if possible, the criminal's involuntarily bad state (862b-c). At the worst, if the criminal is incurable, he must be killed. Even "capital punishment," then, does not seek to punish the criminal, but rather to remove him from a life he cannot live well, and to protect the rest of the city from his actions and example (862e).

Obviously these are very odd statements. They are in fact

opposed to what most people think about themselves and others. So they require some explanation. The stranger does not here explain his claim that all injustice is involuntary, but refers back to a previous discussion (860c). That discussion is in Book Five (731b-d). It is there that he hints at his argument that injustice is always involuntary. So it is to there that we must, for the moment, return.

There the stranger makes the following very important statement:

> Of all the injustices that people do, in regard to the curable ones, one must first understand that every unjust man is involuntarily unjust. For no one—no where—ever would voluntarily acquire any of the greatest evils—and least of all when the evil afflicts his most honored possessions. But the soul, as we said, is truly the most honored thing for everyone; therefore, no one would ever voluntarily take the greatest evil into his most honored possession and live, through the whole of life, possessing it. So the unjust man, like the man who possesses evil things, is altogether pitiable (731c1-8).

What is the stranger saying here? First, one must observe that he focuses on the harm that the unjust man does to himself. The stranger's focus is not on the harm that his injustice may do to other people. Primarily, the stranger is saying here that the unjust man hurts himself. But how? How does injustice harm oneself? Clearly, injustice does not necessarily harm the body of the unjust man. The unjust man may be strong, handsome, healthy, and rich. Indeed, it may even be claimed that being unjust will improve one's bodily state by bringing riches and certain bodily pleasures. So, the stranger makes clear that injustice harms the soul of the unjust man. Injustice, it seems, involves taking the "greatest evil" into the soul. It involves making that evil abide in the soul, for life. And, most importantly, the soul is the best part of your self. So what the unjust man does is to take the greatest evil into his best part for the longest time.

From the stranger's description, it sounds as though the unjust man is acting similar to someone who purposely injects himself with the Ebola virus or the like. Except that injustice is far more destructive. The Ebola virus affects only the body, and the suffering it causes is rather short-lived. Injustice harms the soul and its harm can last for many years. Again, the stranger's main point is that the unjust person harms himself. He makes himself worse in his best part. The unjust person does himself the greatest badness.

Just, Unfree?

This claim has some plausibility. To be sure, one would have to know what exactly is the "evil" that the unjust man "acquires" in his soul by doing injustice. But let us leave aside this question for the moment. Let us assume that the stranger is right, that the unjust man harms himself with the greatest harm. How does that observation justify his claim that all injustice is involuntary? Clearly, there is an unspoken premise lurking here. The stranger's unspoken premise is that no one would voluntarily harm himself, that is, no one would seek to harm himself. Rather, everyone seeks to avoid harm. So, since the wicked man harms himself, he must do so involuntarily.

But why then do so many people do themselves the "harm" of injustice? And how does this premise, this line of argument, then resolve the stranger's original problem, that justice itself, in the case of punishment, looks both noble and shameful? Strauss (followed by Pangle 497-502) argues that "only if virtue is knowledge can just punishment be seriously reduced to education and thus be as noble as any other just thing. One might say that Plato here, as elsewhere, indicates the conditions which would have to be fulfilled if there were to be a truly gentle penal law but which cannot be fulfilled" (*Argument and Action* 133).

In this way Strauss argues that the stranger, or Plato, here hints that a true resolution of the problem would require viewing vice as involuntary in the sense of due to ignorance. But both Strauss and Pangle also suggest that the "spirited passions" or "*thumotic* 'cords'" within the great majority of the populace keep the stranger from fully incorporating this view of vice into his proposed law code (see Pangle 500). The best he can do is to surround the penal laws, laws which at times do treat the criminals as responsible, with speeches about the involuntary nature of injustice.

This interpretation, if correct, would begin to eliminate the contradiction between justice and punishment by explaining justice as knowledge and punishment as education. As Strauss and Pangle note, the stranger comes close to such an explanation when, in Book Nine, he defines justice and injustice:

> Now, in fact, I would clearly define for you the just and the unjust, as I at least understand them, without qualification. The tyranny in the soul of spiritedness and fear and pleasure and pain and envy and desires, whether it does some injury or not [that is, some injury to other people], I pronounce to be total injustice. But the opinion of what's best, in whatever

> way a city or private people believe that these things will be,
> if it does rule in souls and order every man, even if it is in
> some respect mistaken, one must declare to be altogether just
> whatever is done through this opinion and whatever part of
> each man becomes obedient to such rule—and best for the
> whole of human life (863e5-864a6).

Injustice, then, is the rule of certain passions in the soul, above all spiritedness and desire, even if they cause no harm to anyone else. Justice, in contrast, is the rule in the soul of a certain opinion, a certain understanding, about what is best. Injustice or vice is ignorance of this "best." Again, the unjust man thus becomes an object not of anger but of pity and care. He needs education not punishment. At the worst he must die—for the good of others, but also to minimize his own further harm.

Does the stranger thus resolve the problem by showing that both justice and punishment—understood in this rarified manner as knowledge and education—are noble? Not exactly, according to this interpretation. According to Pangle and Strauss, the great obstacle to a reasonable understanding of justice and punishment is *thymos* or anger. The great response to that obstacle is to show that the unjust man acts involuntarily, ultimately due to ignorance. But what are the roots of that ignorance?

The roots, they claim, concern the good (see Pangle 502 and Strauss, *Argument and Action* 133). The stranger has already claimed that all men seek to avoid harm to themselves (recall 731c). This interpretation, in its fullest extent, requires that one transform this principle into a related one: that all men not only seek to avoid harm but also desire to acquire good for themselves.[4] But if everyone seeks his own good, then in this respect the unjust man and the just man are exactly the same. Both the unjust man and the just man have the same fundamental intention. Both the unjust man and the just man are seeking their own good.

What then is the difference between the two? The difference concerns knowledge or understanding. The just man seeks what is truly good for himself. The just man has a clear moral eyesight, so to speak. He has a clear vision of the good. The unjust man, in contrast, does not possess knowledge or true understanding of what is good. The unjust man seeks a warped phantasm of the good. The unjust man imagines that he is pursuing what is truly good. But in fact he is chasing a chimera, an image of the good that masks great badness.[5]

But this is the decisive point: in their intention, the two are the same. The just and unjust men are the same. Both seek their own good. Or, to put it even more disturbingly: neither the just man nor the unjust man chooses to pursue what he thinks is good. Each of them does that without choice. There is no choice about pursuing the good—the good that one thinks is good. One does not choose one's moral vision. Whether one is born with a certain moral vision or one is given it over time by parents and teachers—this is not clear. But what the stranger implies, according to this interpretation, is that human beings do not choose that moral vision, that image of the good that they pursue. And they must pursue it. They do not get to choose about that either. Fundamentally, then, human choice would be circumscribed by the involuntary. People may make certain choices of actions. But those choices would be circumscribed by a certain moral vision or thoughts about the good that they do not get to choose. This moral vision, or their unchosen knowledge or ignorance about the true good, would separate the just and unjust men—not their choices.

In this interpretation, this conclusion—that, fundamentally, human choices about actions are circumscribed by a certain unchosen or involuntary moral vision—is the basis for the stranger's resolution of his original problem. The original problem concerned whether justice is noble or shameful. Whatever they are, both nobility and shame presuppose choice. To be seen as noble, one must choose to do the noble deed as noble. Conversely, to be ashamed, one must be caught choosing to do the shameful deed even though one knows that it is shameful. But according to this view, justice and injustice are not matters of choice. Ultimately, human beings do not have choice about such matters. Everyone seeks what he thinks is good. And, in the end, people do not have a choice about our "vision" of this good. Reversing the apparent agreement between the stranger and his interlocutors, Pangle and Strauss would conclude that justice is not noble, nor is anything else, unless one understands "noble" as good for oneself.

Seeking the Good

Even before it was revived by 20th century readers, Aristotle dismissed the interpretation sketched above by observing that it would destroy the difference between virtue and vice.[6] We should also raise questions about it, questions which may help us better understand the stranger's true position.

First, our main concern must be the unspoken premise that all human beings not only seek to avoid harm but also desire good for themselves. If this premise means that all human beings are selfish at least some of the time, it expresses the obvious; if it means that all human beings put themselves first in all of their choices and actions, then it begs for support. Many other modern philosophers such as Hobbes, Locke, Rousseau posit self-preservation as the first precept of the human heart. But even they disagree with one another about how thoroughly this precept operates in human life, and whether it operates unchallenged.

Indeed, as Aristotle warns, to hold this premise in the way the previous argument demands requires interpreting all seemingly selfless or noble actions as illusory. It requires that the would-be philosopher claim that the moral individual is lying to himself, caught in the contradiction of seeking selflessly to benefit himself. It requires that this philosopher claim to know the moral individual better than that person knows himself. But such presumption opens this philosopher to easy rebuttals by the lover of the noble: "Of course," he may reply, "I am willing to sacrifice. But my desire is not for the sacrifice; I do not love it. What I love is the good, the good common to us all, that such a sacrifice, if needed, may bring about." The moral individual need not accede to this interpretation's mechanical scheme for undoing him.

This example reveals that this interpretation also requires understanding "nobility" and the "good" in strikingly narrow and exclusive ways: the first as self-sacrifice and the latter as personal benefit. But what is the justification for such renderings? Some philosophers, such as Kant, propose something like such definitions; but common speech, as often reflected in Plato's own work, acknowledges that these terms have much broader meanings. "Nobility," in particular, nowhere betrays so austere or selfless a guise in Plato's work. Aristotle, likewise, throughout his *Nicomachean Ethics*, unites moral excellence and happiness. And the Christian philosophical tradition which, in part, grew out of these Greeks' thoughts also teaches that obligation or duty, "the noble," holds a privileged place in happiness (see FitzGibbon).

Finally, Plato's own text underscores the tenuous character of this approach. In a passage already referred to, *Apology* 25d, Socrates asks Meletus if people prefer to be harmed or to be benefited (25d1). He then rephrases the question, "Does anyone wish to be harmed?" (25d2) Of course, Socrates does not have the luxury of truly dialoguing with his interlocutor here. They cannot explore the consequences of each alternative. But even in this constrained situation, Socrates' words seem to indicate the difference between avoiding harm and seeking benefit. We should also observe that Socrates poses these precepts in a question, and does not offer his own view. Meletus, not he, claims that no man wishes to be harmed.

Though he has very little room to maneuver, one could see Socrates here, even at his trial, acting as a teacher, not dispensing doctrine, but encouraging his more sympathetic audience to think about the variety of goods in human life; not to ignore the presence of selfishness, but not to reduce all goods to the form of selfish benefit. After all, explicitly in other dialogues (such as the *Alcibiades I*), and implicitly in the *Apology* itself, when he speaks about the mystery of death, Socrates expresses his own ignorance about what "the self" really is (29a-b). But surely a man so doubtful about the meaning of "the self" could hardly espouse a philosophy that makes selfishness supreme?

Wielding the Cadeuceus

If such criticisms hold fast, then what the stranger actually proposes in Book Nine begins to make more sense. The stranger himself avers that people do some injustices involuntarily, other voluntarily (861e). He proposes that ignorance causes injustice (863c), but that anger and pleasure—voluntary forces—do so as well (863b). As seen, he then identifies the tyranny in the soul of these powers (not only ignorance) as injustice, and the rule of "the opinion of what's best" as justice (863e-864a). He does not identify "what's best" with what is most beneficial. And the penal laws that follow, many of which work upon criminals' habits and not only upon their understandings, imply that he believes that people construct their opinions through their own efforts, in an active and voluntary way, and do not simply receive them from an inborn "vision."

Punishment, therefore, may become something noble, in the stranger's view, something truly noble, even without turning into an education in virtue as knowledge. This claim does not mean that all punishment is noble. It is hard to see the nobility in "punishing" stones or brute animals (see 873e-874a). Even in a very good city, the laws may, as Strauss and Pangle observe, become infected with spirited anger and ignorance. But on the whole the stranger's penal laws attempt to teach the citizens less by precept than by example, seeking to change not only their minds but also their habits. As the stranger is acutely aware, the laws cannot make citizens good, by force or by logic; they must encourage citizens to choose the good freely. In some men, the scaffold may bring out the finest things.

It has been necessary to pay such close attention to the stranger's thoughts on punishment, and the controversy over those thoughts, in order to better understand the so-to-speak medicinal role of philosophy in the *Laws*. As mentioned earlier, the philosopher, in the stranger's image, depends upon the legislative art the way the free doctor must rely upon some of the practices of the slavish one. If a philosopher believed that all men pursue only their self-interest, that there was no sound moral difference between the just and the unjust, then his desire to "cure" his fellows—beyond his wish to avoid harm from them—would make no sense. But Plato's repeated comparison of philosophers with doctors, in this dialogue and others, even in the absence of such arguments as the above, should keep us from such a view.

The stranger's discussion of punishment reveals that the legislative challenges the philosopher faces in this task are various. Men do not live by reason alone—indeed, the law acknowledges that reason may play a very small part in most men's lives. The law may educate some. But in most citizens it must encourage the development of healthy habits: active conditions which the citizens choose—they choose their formation in every action they make—but whose roots and full consequences they may not understand. The philosopher remains primarily a teacher, as the *Laws* itself remains a discussion about laws and not a law code. But, whatever history may say, as far as Plato was concerned, Rousseau was not far off, and was not posing a paradox, when he agreed, "Greece owed its morals and its laws to Philosophers and to Legislators."[7]

Notes

[1] For one of the most famous, see the discussion in the latter half of this chapter.

[2] Cf. Nietzsche, *Beyond Good and Evil* section 211: "Genuine philosophers...are commanders and legislators" (Kauffman 136). Compare as well Kant, who makes clear in his *Prolegomena to Any Future Metaphysics* that the philosopher seeks to understand nature, but, as well, that every human being "legislates" the very laws of nature in the conditions for his understanding. It is precisely as a maker of law, a legislator, that the Kantian philosopher knows nature or any other condition of possible experience. On this final point, see Lachterman.

[3] See Strauss, *Argument and Action* 126 ff.

[4] For a similar equivocation, by Socrates, see *Apology* 25d.

[5] Aristotle inserts this argument, not in his own voice but in the voice of a hypothetical objector, into *Nicomachean Ethics* III.v.

[6] In his translation of Aristotle's *Ethics*, Joseph Sachs deftly deals with this hypothetical objection and the attraction that many interpreters have felt towards it (47 note 59).

[7] In his "Last Reply" to objectors to his *First Discourse*. See Gourevitch 72.

Chapter Ten:
The Blessings of Intolerance

Atheism is a Religion?

In July 1999 the US Eleventh Circuit Court of Appeals ruled in a case then known as *Chandler v. James*. The case concerned an Alabama state law that allowed students, on their own initiative, to lead prayers at public school events—even if the school compelled all students to be present at the events. In 1997 a district court judge (the unfortunately named Ira DeMent) had ruled the law unconstitutional, as violating "the separation between church and state," and permanently enjoined its enforcement.

The Circuit Court overturned Judge DeMent's injunction, in what was then considered a surprising setback for advocates against school prayer. Even more surprising, however, was the Circuit Court's reasoning. The court observed, as many others have done, the large role that non-sectarian prayers or religious symbols play in the public life of the United States, including its educational system. It held, as some have done, that an action's causing offense to one or more people does not make it unconstitutional. It also argued, against the petitioners, that student speech at school, *per se*, is not state-supported speech; the Establishment Clause does not require, then, the state to censor student speech for religious content.

But most surprising of all was the Circuit Court's claim that "'Cleansing' our public schools of all religious expression…inevitably results in the 'establishment' of disbelief—atheism—as the State's religion. Since the Constitution requires neutrality, it cannot be the case that government may prefer disbelief over religion."[1] This pronouncement, that public secularism promotes atheism, and that atheism is a sort of religion, drew considerable attention. Some observers welcomed this turn of events. For example, the conservative *Massachusetts News* editorialized (April 2000) that rigid secularism is a branch of "the Humanist religion," and so outside the pale of constitutional protection.[2] Many professed atheists reacted (one might say characteristically) with disbelief. "Atheism is as much a religion, as disease is a form of health; black is a type of color; or bald is a type of hairstyle," were and are some of their most prominent refrains. However, other atheists praised the decision, arguing that it will force the state to tolerate any and all of those who would make religious expressions or hold religious gatherings in the public square, "regardless of how many gods they believe in, or if they believe in no gods at all."[3]

That a prominent court could, with good conscience, and in a most public document, describe atheism as a form of religion indicates how distant, in the public mind, contemporary atheism is from its older, militantly anti-religious forms. That atheists themselves should agree with the court's assessment only confirms that public opinion. In the Age of Reason nothing looked more reasonable, more scientific, than to deny the existence of God. Now, in the wake of postmodernism, the theists have become humanists and the atheists have found religion.

No doubt some people still publicly identify themselves as atheists, but does their defense of their position go far beyond catchy slogans? Are they the most advanced and respected of the scientific minds among us? Or are they clutching to a "scientific" promise, a rationalistic dream, which has long since been dispelled? Does contemporary science, which posits the possibility that matter may pop in and out of existence inexplicably, offer conscientious atheists with any reason to reject even the most grotesque "miracles"?

Though one might suspect that the answer is no, the court's decision also poses tough questions for traditional religious groups, which largely gave the decision a warm reception. Even if one allows that the atheist only "believes" that god does not exist, does any belief about god—or, for that matter, anything at all—amount to a religion? Can one be religious without positive claims about transcendence, and without a corresponding code of ethics? Neo-Pagans, Raelians, and various humanist groups may say yes. But what reason is there for traditional religious believers to subject their definition of "religion" to the standards of these novel sects?

The Eleventh Circuit Court's decision in *Chandler v. James*, if one agrees with it, would certainly bolster the often repeated claim that America is the most religious nation on earth. By the *Chandler* standard, the population must, logically, be 100% religious. Likewise, this case and others like it remind us that the debate about what place religion should hold in public life—or even what constitutes a religion—is still alive, and maybe even growing stronger, in contemporary America. But the court's decision, and the reactions to it, also suggest that the main participants in this debate may be losing their bearings about the fundamental matters. Regaining such bearings is, paradoxically, sometimes the major benefit of foreign travel, such as is attempted in this book.

Washington and Tehran

One thing that we have consistently observed while studying Plato's *Laws* is how different the stranger's recommendations often are from present-day laws and practices. This is, after all, perhaps the greatest benefit of travel, including intellectual travel: the chance to see one's own ways in new light and so understand them better. The stranger's proposals give readers a most different perspective from which to view their own communities.

There is probably no place, however, where the stranger's laws differ from contemporary Western law more than in matters of what is today called religion. As seen already, the stranger proposes that in the new city there be constant civic festivals—festivals that the entire citizen-body will attend—and at the heart of these festivals will be sacrifices, holy sacrifices, sacrifices to the gods (828b). Civic life, in other words, will be centered on religious devotion. Second, the stranger proposes that priests be governmental officials in this city (759a-e). And now, in Book Ten, he announces that he would institute laws against impiety, laws that will punish unbelief when it manifests itself either in word or deed. Nothing seems farther from the American way.

To be fair to the stranger, one must note that in his governmental scheme the priests hold a very low rank; they are among the weakest civic officials; they are certainly not in charge. This city in speech would be no theocracy, as that term is usually understood. Also, as seen in Book Eight, the daily religious festivals are not the highest activity in this city. They exist for the sake of military training (829b). And even military training is not the highest—though it is the most widespread—form of education that the stranger proposes. Nonetheless, the stranger does continually bring in gods and religion as the foundation of his laws—whether it is the goddess who is said to rule the ancestral farm, or the twelve gods who rule over the months, or the Muses and Apollo who rule the dances and songs. The gods almost seem almost the very ground from which his city would spring.

Again, nothing would seem to be farther from the way of modern democracy. Recent American jurisprudence has strictly limited the role of religion in public. In 2000, the United States Supreme Court decided that prayer even at school football games is too great a religious intrusion upon public life. This decision has followed many others, all of which appeal ultimately to the First Amendment to the Constitution, which reads in part that "Congress shall make no law respecting the establishment of a religion or prohibiting the free exercise thereof." This amendment has been interpreted to mean that no governmental body in the United States, not only the Congress, shall favor any religion in its actions. Thus American citizens and their religious practices are ruled by phrases such as "the strict separation of church and state," or the "wall" between church and state, or the transcendent importance of "religious liberty."

To be sure, religion is far from absent from present-day public life. The United States Congress opens each session with a prayer to God. Currency and public buildings are often inscribed with mentions of God. The unofficial national anthem sings "God Bless America." But these quasi-religious statements are often defended today as part of the cultural heritage of this country, not as binding or authoritative religious decrees. They do not "establish," that is, give authority to any particular religious view nor do they force any citizen to profess any particular belief. If they do, they are protested against and ultimately repudiated.

Religious liberalism, or freedom from religious authority in public life, seems as unquestionable to contemporary Americans as the air they breathe. It sets us apart from, and even at odds with, some of the other most important nations in the world today, such as Iran, Saudia Arabia, and Malaysia. The case is entirely different in the *Laws*. Yet the stranger was a very thoughtful person. He must have had some reasons for making these recommendations. Understanding his reasons may then help us understand better our very different way of treating these matters today.

Teaching, not Preaching

One must keep in mind, to begin with, that the stranger did not need to do what he does in Book Ten. He could have left well enough alone. He could have kept devotion to the established gods at the center of the civic life. He could have outlawed impiety—the expression of disbelief in word or deed. He could have laid down harsh punishments for the impious, up to and including death. That is all that Kleinias wants. As Kleinias makes clear at the beginning of Book Ten, he cannot understand why anyone would be gentle towards the impious. "Why bother talking to unbelievers?" seems to be his attitude (885c).

The Athenian could have just played along. Kleinias' attitude was entirely respectable, after all; it was one shared by most of the people and all of the cities of that time, including the stranger's home city of Athens. Athens was known in the ancient world as the least conservative of cities, as the one most open to new ways and unorthodox ideas. Nonetheless, Athens had laws against impiety and the Athenians prosecuted unbelievers. They killed the philosopher Socrates himself in the suspicion that he did not believe in the city's gods. The stranger could have leveled stern and simple laws against impiety and no one would have batted an eye.

But instead, in Book Ten, he offers long arguments to the possibly impious person. In effect, he proposes that a considerable portion of the law-code read as a dialogue about gods. It is an amazing thing to do. Why does he do it? He reveals part of his purpose in this way: "in gentle arguments, while admonishing, at the same time to teach the unbelievers about the gods—first that they exist" (888a1-2). Also, he says that they, the lawgivers, should speak "without spiritedness" (888a5) to the unbelievers, and "argue gently, quenching spiritedness, as if we were in dialogue with one such man" (888a6-7).

In other words, Book Ten does not simply lay down laws about impiety. That is really only a secondary goal. The primary goal is to teach the citizens about the gods, and especially to teach those who have doubts. And the stranger seeks to teach them without spiritedness, without anger. He offers them, as best he can in this setting, an introduction into divine science.

Soul's Almighty

First the stranger does a surprising thing. He first presents the contrary argument, the argument that gods do not exist. Again, he did not have to do this. Now, by doing so, he makes this very argument—the impious, atheistic argument—an official part of the proposed law-code. He contributes, one could say, to the possible corruption of the future citizens. After all, Kleinias had no idea that such arguments exist; he had no idea that someone could be a thoughtful atheist (see 885e-886b). The stranger is taking quite a risk by giving the thoughtful atheistic argument a major place among the proposed laws.

The atheistic argument that he cites can be summarized in the following way (see 886c-890b). The atheist argues about the beginning of things. He says that there are three causes of things in the world: nature, art, and chance. "What is first?" he asks. Chance is his answer. The big bang is chance. It is chance that there are various particles, such as protons, neutrons, and electrons. It is chance that there are 109 or so elements rather than 59 or 209. It is chance that the gravitational force attracts rather than repels matter. Who knows why there are such laws—such as the law of gravity—and not others? There is no reason, says the atheist. The answer is just chance.

So chance determines the origins of all things. Once chance determines all these things, such as the elements and the laws of physics, then the "system," as one might say, starts chugging away on its own. That is what people then call nature: the work of this system. This system of elements and laws gives rise to more complex forms—molecules, planets, organic beings, plants, animals, and eventually man. Chance and its offspring nature build up all these things. And once humanity exists, people begin to make things on their own. That is art. Man makes tools, and huts, and friends, and families, and clans, and eventually political communities. All these are artificial. Above all, man makes gods. The gods themselves are the products of human art. The gods are make-believe. For whatever purposes human beings makes them—whether to console themselves or to frighten each other—the gods are the product of human art. They do not exist except as human creations.

This is, more or less, the thoughtful atheistic argument that the stranger cites. The premise of this argument is clear: chance is first and inorganic nature—elements and physical laws—comes second. Everything else is derived from these things. What else could there be?

The great alternative—and the one the stranger cites—is soul. "Where does soul fit in this scheme?" he asks (892a). It seems, according to the thoughtful atheist, that the soul is a by-product of matter (and hence a by-product of chance). Soul is just one of many constructs down the line, a product of DNA or hormones or the like. This is the point that the stranger challenges. He sets out to demonstrate that, in fact, soul is primary, soul is first of all things (892c). This demonstration, it turns out, will be the key to his argument that gods exist and are not merely human inventions.

At this point we have climbed our way to the most difficult part of the stranger's argument (see 892d-899c). This most difficult part concerns motion. The stranger begins with a very moderate premise, something that seems obvious: some things move; other things are at rest. Though such pre-Socratics as Parmenides and Heraclitus hotly debated it, this observation seems a modest starting point. The stranger then considers the things in motion. He sets forth a list of ten types of motion that do not need to be considered individually, but which do seem sensible. They are not abstract motions (up, down, left, right, back, and forward) but motion such as human beings experience it in everyday life. Suffice it to say that the most important of the ten motions is the tenth: the motion that both moves itself and moves other things.

This is a motion that all people are familiar with. It is the motion that any living thing feels when it desires something or seeks to run away from something. All human beings are familiar with moving themselves, with not merely being puppets. But, as the stranger points out, this tenth motion is a very different sort of motion from the others. The stranger asks, implicitly, where did all these motions come from. If most motions merely move other things, what moved them? There could be a chain of motion, one thing moving another thing and so on, but what causes this chain of motion in the first place? The answer, the stranger says, is this motion that moves itself and moves other things. Since there are later motions, there has to be a first motion, he implies. And that first motion—since it is not moved by something else—can only have moved itself. So this particular type of motion—self-motion—must be first and oldest.

This is one important conclusion. Then the stranger asks about names. What do people call the motion that moves itself? As hinted at earlier, this is a type of motion that every living thing is familiar with. Stones are not familiar with it; stones do not move themselves. Only living things do. The motion that moves itself is called living. So, the stranger says, this motion is soul. This is the definition of soul: self-motion. And, since this self-motion must be first and oldest, that means that soul must be first and oldest.

To expand on this point: the stuff that moves only other things and not itself is called body—stones or molecules or the like. Thus the argument shows that soul must precede body. That means that soul precedes all body. Soul must then be the cause of all bodies. That means, for example, that soul causes and moves the entire world, including the heavens. Soul is everywhere.

And there is one final step in the stranger's argument: since soul is first and pervasive, the things that go with soul are possibly everywhere. The things that go with soul, he says, are such things as opinion, character, ignorance, and intelligence. But, the stranger adds, it is possible that there are a couple or many souls causing motion in the world. There may be intelligent souls moving things or there may be stupid souls moving things. But which kind rules above all? The stranger responds: look at the world. Does it seem orderly to you? Do the heavens seem to move in order? The heavenly bodies seem to move in generally regular fashion. There seems to be amazing order in the world. So, he concludes, the intelligent soul or intelligent souls are highest. They move the heavens, at least. And what should we call these intelligent souls that move the heavens, if not gods? In this way the argument concludes that gods exist.

And the stranger lays down a challenge to his listeners and to Plato's readers: if you accept all the steps in this argument, then do you not agree that gods exist? If you accept all the steps, must you not believe? And if you do not believe, do you not have to show some error in the reasoning? That is the challenge that we face after this brilliant tour-de-force.[4]

The Divine Architect

The second form of impiety that the stranger addresses in Book Ten is the belief that the gods do not care about human beings and human affairs (see 899d-900c). What are the gods to someone who holds this belief? They are so lofty that they care for humans no more than humans care about dust-mites or amoebae. They are entirely ignorant of or indifferent to human beings. People are born, struggle, die, and the gods take no notice of their joys or tears. All their prayers and pleas are directed at a heaven that does not listen. It is a sad view.

At the beginning of discussing this impious view, the stranger talks about the source of this view. He spoke similarly when dealing with the first impious belief, the belief that the gods do not even exist. In that, earlier, discussion he implies that the belief that the gods do not exist may be due, in part, to youth; that it is a belief that young people are especially prone to (888a-c). But most young people do not fall into this belief on their own; they find their way to it through reading certain works or poetry or prose (890a). The proximate cause of the belief that there are no gods, then, are certain observations followed by arguments and conclusions.

The source of the second impious belief, the belief that the gods exist but do not care about human beings, differs. The stranger implies that this impious belief is due to certain judgments that are very common. The impious young man has seen praise given to men he considers unjust, praise that says that these unjust men are most happy. For example, the claim that Stalin or any other tyrant could live happily and die peacefully after murdering and pillaging his subjects. Or this impious fellow has seen other people commit what he considers to be the greatest injustice and then live lives full of honors and riches. For example, generations of Europeans grew up believing that Napoleon—one of the greatest tyrants of modern times—was a god among men.

So, the belief that the gods do not care derives ultimately from certain observations or, more precisely, certain judgments: it derives ultimately from the judgment that injustice sometimes flourishes and is rewarded. That is probably why this particular belief—that the gods do not care—can last, as the stranger observes, through one's entire life (888c). He says, in contrast, that no one grows old believing that there are no gods whatsoever. It is, after all, hard to determine whether or not gods exist. It is not something that can be easily observed. That makes it easy for human beings to vacillate, throughout their lives, over whether the gods exist or not. But, in contrast, the belief that the gods do not care can stick throughout life because these judgments about injustice are very easy to make. Just look around. It is easy—if one believes passionately in justice—to get very angry, and then to despair, at all the injustice that flourishes in human society. Still, this second point of view is a believing point of view. The people who believe that the gods do not care about human things still, at least, believe that there are gods. Their slander against the gods derives from their happy kinship with or insight into the divine order (see 900a).

How does the stranger prove that the gods do care about human beings? First, he takes a premise from his first argument, the one that shows that the gods exist. He says that one must begin by remembering that it has been proven that the gods are wise or intelligent souls (900d). Then, he says, since they are wise, they are good. Intelligence, after all, is the leader of all the virtues. And since they are good, they possess all the virtues and all the noble qualities (900e). Now, carelessness and laziness are not noble qualities; everyone would agree to that. Conversely, their opposites, carefulness and energy, are noble qualities. So, since the gods possess all the virtues and all noble qualities, the gods must be careful and energetic, not careless and lazy. The gods are not like "drones," sucking up the honey of the world without doing any work (901a). So, since the gods are careful and energetic, they must exercise supervisory care over all things great and small. And among these small things that they care about are human beings. This is the stranger's major conclusion (901a-903a). He moves from the premise that the gods are wise souls to the conclusion that they must care about all things, even human beings.

Now, before going on, one should observe an important feature of his argument thus far, a feature that may be surprising. The stranger's argument does agree with the impious view in one very important respect: they both agree that human affairs and human beings are puny matters. Men really are, in comparison to the gods, small potatoes. The stranger's argument does not try to prove that the gods care about human beings because humans are so special or so great. His argument does not show that human beings are exceptional beings in the world. He does not rely upon positing that human beings have a special connection to gods. He does not assert, for example, that human beings are made in the image of god or that they are the children of gods. Instead, as noted, he seems to agree with the impious person that human beings are puny, little, next-to-nothings.

And, in fact, this has been his view for some time. One could recall the middle of Book Seven (803a-804b), where the stranger had his amazing outburst. In that outburst he said to Kleinias and Megillus that human things are not worthy of great seriousness, that human beings are nothing but "puppets" of the gods, and that humans share but in small portions of the truth. Megillus rebelled and rebuked the stranger for running down the human race. But this is, it seems, the stranger's view: that human beings are puny. He does not soften that harsh view in order to prove that the gods care. Instead, his emphasis upon the littleness of man, one might even say man's unworthiness, lays bare a possible contributory source of the objector's question: why should the gods care about such insignificant beings?

But, to return to his argument: what has been seen thus far is that he shows, by starting from the premise, taken from his first argument, that the gods are wise or intelligent souls, that the gods must care about all things, great and small, including human things. But then the stranger does something else that is unexpected. To round out this argument, he considers all the possible opposing views and tries to respond to them. It is though he asked himself, "Why would the gods not care about us?" And to each complaint he offers a response.

For example, to those who would say that the gods are lazy (901c), he responds that he has shown that they could not be lazy; they are too noble for that. But perhaps, a second person might say, the gods are ignorant of human being—they just do not see humans—just as people do not even know how many ants or amoebas they trod on with every step (901d). The stranger responds that all people agree that the gods see everything and know everything. Their perceptions and knowledge far outstrip human perceptions and knowledge. It is not fair even to make the comparison. But, someone else may say, the gods cannot care about human beings because they are not strong enough—they use all their energy taking care of the stars or the like; they cannot spare energy taking care of humans (901d). Again, the stranger would respond, everyone agrees that the gods are super-powerful. They are the souls who cause the existence of all things. How could they not be powerful enough to take care of the big things and the little things?

Well, a fourth person may say, human beings are nothing to the gods—neither good nor bad—so why should they care about humans (902b)? Here the stranger responds, essentially, "Does not everyone agree that human beings—all things in fact—are possessions of the gods? And as possessions, human beings are something to them. Just as any person cares about his possessions, even his little possessions, so too do the gods, our masters, care about us, their possessions." Finally, someone else might say that perhaps the gods care only about the really big things—the planets and pulsars and the like—and not the little things, because the little things are beneath their dignity (902c). They are too noble and lofty to take notice of little stuff like men. Here the stranger responds with the example of artisans, such as builders and doctors. Human artisans, he points out, take notice of the big and little things, for, as people say, the "devil's in the details." If one does not pay attention to the little things, the big things suffer. So, are the gods even sloppier than human artisans are? Of course not. They must pay attention to both the big and the little things. That, it seems, exhausts all the possible objections, all the claims that the gods may not care about us. And so the argument concludes: the gods do care (903a).

But just when one might think that he was done, the stranger takes one more unexpected turn. When this argument is over, the stranger does not stop. Instead, he proposes, he should add certain "mythic songs" that sing the same lesson as the argument, the lesson that the gods do care (903b1). That is, he adds a myth to the proof. This is odd. He did not do this with the first argument, the argument that the gods exist. Certainly there are many myths that propose that the gods exist. But he did not add even one to his first argument; he left well enough alone. But here, to the argument that the gods care about human beings, he adds a myth.

Why? Some might say that by including this myth the stranger indicates that the arguments he just offered are insufficient, that the myth adds rhetorical force while pointing out the logical failings of the preceding *logoi*, that it is a politic story designed for the less thoughtful citizens (see Strauss, *Argument and Action* 153). But such a reading seems quite uncharitable to the stranger and Plato. Minds trained by the Enlightenment might hear "myth" and start looking for deceptions. But, precisely if the stranger were of such a mind, then including a myth would be rhetorically self-destructive, not supportive. A myth by itself, or arguments by themselves—that would make sense, if the two categories are opposed. But not both together. It seems much more reasonable to assume that the stranger offers this myth either as an imaginative portrait of the consequences of his arguments or as, in fact, a depiction of an insight that he cannot prove through his arguments, but to which they point.

The myth teaches the listeners that God is the King or Craftsman of the whole—god is the universal craftsman (903b-905c). God is like a builder, and he has put together all the parts of the universe into one whole. And you, the myth teaches, are a part. So, as little as you are, god cares about your task, about your doing your part. You may be as small as one nail is in a three-story house. But the craftsman put that nail there; he wanted it to be there; he put it there for a reason. As long as it is there, as small as it is, it is serving its purpose. So too, as small as you are, you have a purpose in this whole of things. And your purpose is, in general, to contribute to the good of this whole.

The craftsman makes all things, all the parts, with a view to the good of the whole—whether it is the health of a body or the structural integrity of a house. You, the part, exist for the good of the whole. And that means, of course, that no matter how "bad" things look for you, or no matter how tough things are for you, the whole of things is well-ordered, for it has an intelligent God as its maker. So, even if things seem to go badly for you, you can rest content in the belief that you still may do your part for the goodness of the whole. In this way the stranger refashions the place assigned to the "bad souls" in the first argument (cf. Strauss, *Argument and Action* 151). The stranger uses this entire discussion to educate his audience: the myth in the second part represents a theological correction to and advance beyond the arguments of the first part (see Thomas, *Summa Theologica* I.2.3, reply to objection one).

Finally, though not least importantly, the myth teaches that how well you do—how well you persevere for the good of the whole—will determine your place within that whole after your death. Death is not the end for us. Human souls go through transformation after transformation during life and after death. Will you be transformed to a better and more important part? Or will you be demoted within the universal organization? That is up to you, to how well you perform your duty within the whole. The myth teaches that there is a whole of things, that it is well ordered, and that mortal lives, no matter how small, are not insignificant. They have a purpose and are taken note of. Of course, the myth does not promise, nor it seems does the objector demand, that we human beings can or ever will completely understand that purpose.

Again, one might say that this myth works upon the already existent beliefs of this particular disbeliever. This man believes that gods do exist. He denies that they care for human beings. Perhaps then the myth works upon a latent wish within him, a wish that the gods would take care of us, a hope that they might set things right in the end. The very beauty of the myth, a beauty no argument can capture, would serve as the key to tip the heretic from disappointment to happy hope.

But such an explanation assumes that the stranger does not believe the teaching of the myth; it even hints that he may doubt the proofs for the existence of the gods which he offered so vigorously in the first part of this book. While it is clear that he revises and improves upon the education he offers he as he goes on, and while he remarks at the end that he spoke these proofs almost too vigorously (907c-d), these observations can in no way lead us to conclude that the stranger does not offer these arguments in good faith (cf. Pangle 503-504).

The myth of the divine craftsman occupies the center of the stranger's tripartite discussion of theology. In it he pictures the consequences of their agreement that gods, intelligent and all-powerful souls, exist. But the myth speaks not only of the gods but also of the believers. The myth fleshes out the moral state of one who has come to accept these arguments, in a way that arguments alone cannot do. The myth helps the addressee recognize the worthiness of his actions, his sacrifices, his sufferings, and his joys. It provides an imaginative response to the human sense of incompletion, of being a part of a still-mysterious whole. One might just as well conclude that this sense is a gift of god than claim that it conjures up gods. Not the least, the myth reminds the citizen and the legislators that the city itself, as imperfect as it must be, stands as a shining imitation of the cosmopolis.[5]

Sheep Dogs and Wolves

The stranger's third and final argument in Book Ten teaches that the gods are just. This is, at any rate, one way to describe that argument. By describing it this way, one links this argument to an entire tradition of asking the question "Is god just?" This is the tradition of theodicy, speeches about god's justice. But the more precise way to describe this argument would be to say that it is the argument that the gods cannot be appeased (888c, 905d). That is, they cannot be turned from their purposes by gifts or by prayers. As will be seen, this argument about appeasement is closely connected to the question of the gods' justice.

Before looking at the argument itself, one should observe that the very claim that the gods can be appeased implies several things. This claim first implies that the gods do rule over human things. That is why anyone would want to appease them. No one tries to appease something that has no power. No one tries to appease stones or trees. One tries to appease those who could willingly hurt one. This realization leads to a second point: this view—that the gods can be appeased—implies that the gods get angry at human beings and show that anger. The person who tries to appease the gods does so because he is afraid; he is afraid that without appeasement the gods are going to hurt him out of rage. Why would anyone think that? Why would anyone expect someone else, or some god, to get angry at him and hurt him? What the impious person fears is that the gods are punitive, but that means that he thinks that the gods care about punishing and hence that they care about justice, about punishing wrongdoers.

So, the person who holds the impious view that the gods can be appeased believes quite a number of things. He believes, obviously, that the gods exist. He believes that they rule over human things. He believes that they can get angry and take out their anger in the form of punishment. And hence he believes that the gods do care about justice and do tend to punish injustice. A lot is implied in this final impious view.

But have any of these things been shown? Does the impious person have good reasons, in the stranger's arguments, for thinking this way about the gods? In particular, is there good reason for thinking that the gods are prone to anger and punishment? The stranger has proved that gods, of a certain sort, exist. But, in the first argument, he showed that these gods are intelligent souls. They are self-moving beings, who move in a regular, orderly fashion. No mention of anger or punishment occurs there.

In the second argument he showed that the gods must care about all the things in the cosmos and take notice of them. However, he does not show that they get angry and punish people. Even in the myth, which he distinguishes from his second argument proper, he does not speak of angry or punitive gods. The god of his myth is a craftsman who orders the whole of things for some universal good. He aims to build, not destroy or to punish. And even those who do not serve the good of the whole are not spoken of as enduring the wrath or punishment of god. They determine their own place in the whole, by their actions (see 904c). The gods do not seem to take a hand in it. The whole seems to work on its own, with each part settling into place. So, from the beginning, the person who holds the impious view that the gods can be appeased seems to hold premises that the stranger would not, on the basis of his own arguments at least, accept: the premises that the gods can get angry at and do punish human beings.

The stranger begins his argument against this particular impiety in a somewhat curious way. He begins by examining the premise of the one who claims that the gods can be appeased. This is, one could say, a very dialogic way to begin. As the stranger said earlier in Book Ten, one must imagine oneself in dialogue with a young man who makes these impious pronouncements (888a). What one does in a dialogue is try to see, without anger, the opponent's point of view and where it leads. That is what the stranger does here. He takes his opponent's view as the starting point of his argument.

But this is not something he did, strictly speaking, in the first two arguments. In the first argument he presented the atheist's point of view on its own. Then he presented his own argument. His own argument started with a premise that was drawn not from the atheist's point of view but from human experience of everyday life. In his second argument, the stranger began by explaining the opponent's point of view, the view that the gods do not care for us; he explained it by talking about its origins. But when it came to arguing against this point of view the stranger begins by taking, as his premise, the conclusion of the first argument, the conclusion that the gods are intelligent or prudent souls.

So, it is in this third argument that the stranger comes closest to engaging in true dialogue with his impious opponent; only here does he begin by simply taking the impious person's point of view as his starting point. But that also means that this argument starts from premises that are not the stranger's own. He does not vouch for the starting point of this third argument. This argument is closest to his opponent's view; but it may be quite far from the stranger's own view.

The premise that the impious opponent holds is, as has been seen, that the gods are rulers of human beings, rulers who can get angry at human beings (905e). That is why the gods need appeasing, in this impious person's view. This impious person does not claim to be superior to the gods. He knows that he is a small fry compared to these big fish. But he does claim to know what the big guys like to get, and he tries to supply it to them.

So, the stranger asks, in effect, "You think the gods are rulers of human beings? What kind of rulers?" He lists several possibilities taken from human life (905e-906a). Are they like horse-drivers in a race? Are they like pilots of ships? Are they like generals of armies? Are they like doctors, who rule over bodies? Are they like farmers ruling over their crops? Or are they like sheep dogs that rule over flocks of sheep?

It is a comic list. It is, of course, humorous to imagine the gods as horse-drivers or sheep dogs. But it is also funny because the stranger leaves out the most obvious human ruler to whom to analogize the gods: the statesman or legislator. Why not ask whether the gods are like statesman ruling over cities? Maybe because the stranger thinks his opponent would too easily reject this possibility. Statesmen, after all, are supposed to care about justice and lawfulness above all. And that is exactly what the impious person hopes the gods can be swayed from. However, some statesmen are also well known for accepting bribes. Maybe that is another reason why the stranger does not mention them here.

The omission of statesmen from this list also makes clearer another feature of it: it lists "rulers," so to speak, who can all be expected to profit, either directly or indirectly, from their ruling activity. Generals may risk their lives, but they gain great glory from their exploits. Pilots do not want their ships to sink, not only for their passengers' good, but for their own good too. Doctors do not become healthier from curing their patients, but they learn from the experience and may be paid too. And it is obvious that farmers or shepherds benefit from having bountiful crops or flocks. These goods are certainly not all the same, and all these activities demand sacrifices too. But their sacrifices are usually not as stark as the sacrifices of the statesman, who must usually abandon all private life and private interests if he is to pursue, fully, the public good. Perhaps, then, this omission concedes something to the impious person's fear that the gods do look out for their own profit first.

The stranger asks what kind of rulers the impious person thinks the gods are. He then sharpens the issue by stating what "we have agreed"—presumably in the earlier two arguments (see 906a3). He says that they have agreed that heaven is full of good and bad—and more of the bad than the good (906a-c). He thus says that there is a "battle, an immortal one" (906a5), going on in the cosmos. The gods and their henchmen, the demons, are fighting for virtue and justice. The human beings are their possessions, and presumably by their fight for justice they are fostering the cause of justice among us.

So, how does the impious person's view fit in here? Since there is this immortal battle between the just and unjust going on, the impious person is on the other side, the side of the unjust. And he is trying to appease the gods, the defenders of the just. He is like a wolf, trying to buy off the sheep dog that protects the flock of justice.

This is a very questionable step in the stranger's argument. But before questioning it, one should observe this point: by speaking of an immortal battle and then calling the gods guard-dogs, the stranger limits the possibilities of what kind of rulers the gods are to two: they are like generals fighting a battle or like sheep dogs protecting a flock. Now, as mentioned before, each of these two pursues a certain good. But those goods are very different. A general presumably fights for the good of a whole community. If he wins victory, the whole community benefits. If he loses, the whole community suffers. The sheep dog, in contrast, defends the good of the sheep, to a certain degree, but ultimately he serves the good of his master, the shepherd, the owner of the sheep. So the stranger's argument raises these questions: Are human beings the gods' allies? Or are humans their flock? If humans are the gods' flock, and the gods are the sheep dogs, then who is the shepherd?

To return to the argument: this is what the impious person must assert, that the gods are like one of these rulers (e.g., the sheep dogs) who have been bought off by their enemy (the wolves). One then comes to the conclusion of the argument. The conclusion comes about rather easily. The stranger uses what one might call the laughability test. He looks to see if the impious person's assertions lead to laughable results (906e).

He returns to that list of human rulers to whom he had compared the gods. Since the impious person says that the gods are like rulers who have been bought off by their enemies, which bribed rulers exactly does he have in mind? Are they like pilots who have been paid to wreck their own ships? Are they like horse-drivers in a race who have been paid to lose? Or are they like generals, doctors, farmers, shepherds, or sheep dogs that have been paid to fail at their duties?

Certainly, the stranger knows, all these things have happened before. Doctors have been paid to kill patients. Athletes have been paid to throw fights. But all these people, all the people who have been bribed by their opponents to fail, they all look like losers or failures. Indeed, they are losers, failures at their respective duties. But, he says, "we"—the impious person and the stranger—have agreed that the gods are the greatest guards of the greatest things (907a). So, are the gods as bad or worse than human losers? At this point Kleinias comes into the argument: he vehemently denies that the gods could be such losers. He rebels at the notion that the gods could be as bad as or worse than a human being who abandons his duties and gives in to bribes. And so the argument concludes: the gods, as "we" have agreed them to be, cannot be appeased (907b).

There are many complexities in this argument, complexities worth the traveller's personal observation and contemplation. But perhaps one problem deserves extra attention. This third argument, as stated, appears to conflict with the "myth" that the stranger gave earlier, the myth that speaks of god as a craftsman of the whole. Here he describes the gods as great powers, but powers who are fighting even greater powers of injustice. They are not in control of the whole of things. They are certainly not the causes of the whole of things. So, the picture of the gods' place in the whole is vastly different.

Which view is the stranger's own view? It is not easy to say. One must remember that this entire third section proceeds in a dialogic fashion, engaging directly, but also ceding much to, the opinions of the objector. As seen, one of his prominent beliefs is that the gods get angry, that they are spirited. The stranger's reintroduction of the claim that the gods must wage a cosmic battle against evil seems suited to the assumptions of this objector. It also seems a step down from the picture of the myth in part two. The stranger, at any rate, reasserts his own view, from the second part, at the beginning of this third argument, when he recalls that the gods must be rulers, for "they govern the whole heaven without interruption" (905e3). The interruptions, the outright warfare, envisioned by this third objector stand, in fact, as a superficial observation of the craftsmanship described in the second part.

Still, this third objection does push to the fore something not addressed completely by the myth, and perhaps not entirely addressable by any speeches. The myth claims that the gods care for human beings the way a craftsman cares for all the parts or pieces or his work. The objector to the gods' justice also claims that the gods care for human beings, but as sources of bribery. The imagined dialogue between the stranger and this objector, particularly when he speaks of generals and guard-dogs, raises the question of the character of that care.

A general, as mentioned, cares for the common good of a city, but sometimes he must sacrifice the soldiers under his command. A guard-dog does try to protect every sheep, but fosters no common good among them. Perhaps then these examples point to the truth by their very deficiencies. Under the reign of the craftsman god described by the myth, who combines omnipotence and intelligence, no "part" truly is lost. Because he need not sacrifice or lose any "part," this god can care for both the parts and the whole, and sacrifice neither to the other. Nonetheless, the goods, individual and common, enacted by this craftsman remain mysterious, reasonably prompting all these questions.

Illiberal Learning

To return to our own land and *Chandler v. James*, the Alabama case over student-initiated prayer, the Eleventh Circuit's decision was appealed to the US Supreme Court in 1999. The high court remanded the case, by then renamed *Chandler v. Siegelman*, back to the Court of Appeals, for review in light of another Supreme Court school prayer case. The Eleventh Circuit reviewed its prior decision and voted to uphold it in 2002. The Supreme Court refused to consider another appeal, thereby letting the decision stand. Of course, as described before, however settled *Chandler* may be, it presents only an unsettled view of the contemporary debate over faith and secularism.

On the surface, the stranger's proposals would create a much more religiously rigid community. Since the law teaches that the gods support the city, and since they compel religious belief and practice, one can expect that expressions of disbelief would be far rarer than in our polity.

But that does not mean that the stranger envisions an end to questioning faith. Indeed, it should not be surprising that, as seen, the stranger's arguments themselves raise many questions. After the first argument, the argument that the gods exist, the stranger practically begs his listeners to challenge him and to ask questions (899b-d). Now, to be sure, the laws will outlaw the preaching of these impious views. But raising questions in a moderate, private manner is much different than preaching or trying to swindle people.

Indeed, one could say that the stranger does all he can to encourage this moderate inquiry. After all, he is putting all these arguments into his proposed law-code as preludes. That means that he is including the three impious points of view in the law-code too (Pangle 503). This inclusion will get some citizens thinking; it will show them at least both sides of the issue.

For most people, the stranger's arguments that the gods exist, that they care for us, and that they cannot be appeased will be enough. These arguments will satisfy their doubts. But his arguments—and his representation of the opposing views—will spark others to think for themselves. Indeed, his wonderful arguments in Book Ten point to the greatest question of all: What is god? It is fair to say that they, and the *Laws* as a whole, thus point to what he identifies as the highest subject of education, divine science.

It is also fair to say that this book poses at least one other question for those of us who live in a much more religiously liberal community: Could the stranger's laws so deftly spark thought about God, could they so strongly encourage the pursuit of divine science, did they not impose some restrictions upon religious liberty? That is, if the law remains silent about divine matters, or if it consciously treats such matters as outside its serious consideration, does it thereby discourage, or even stifle, such thoughts? The debate around *Chandler*, the larger debate about the public status of religion in America, offers little reassurance in the face of such queries. Yet, if the stranger is correct, these are questions that we ignore at the peril of our souls.

Appendix A

Possible Questions about the Argument that the Gods Exist
1. Must there be an oldest motion? What is the alternative? Is it comprehensible? (See Kreeft 65-66.)
2. Even if self-motion is first, is self-motion the same as soul? Does it include all that is psychic?
3. Even if self-motion must be first, does it need to continue to the present day? Is it eternal? Can it cease?
4. How would soul relate to body? (Consider the example the stranger gives, of the sun.)
5. The claim that intelligent souls rule all is based on observation of the world's order. Are that observation and that order complete?

Appendix B

Possible Questions about the Argument that the Gods Care about Human Beings

1. Why must intelligence include or be the same as moral goodness or care for others?

2. How can the gods—who are eternal—know what is always changing (e.g., human beings)?
3. What is the good that the godly craftsman aims at?
4. Do the possibility of multiple gods or stupid souls threaten the good order of the whole? That is, does this argument and its myth logically demand monotheism?

Notes

[1] Opinion reproduced at <http://www.law.emory.edu/11circuit/july99/97-6898.man.html.>

[2] Editorial reproduced at
<http://www.massnews.com/past_issues/2000/4_April/400ed.htm.>

[3] See the article by Blair Scott in *SecularSouth* 2002, "The Good News Club and Alabama Prayer: Good or Bad?"
<http://secularsouth.org/show.php?column=bible_belt&story_id=12.> With this liberal defense of atheism as a religion, one might compare John Locke's argument, in the *Letter on Toleration*, that atheism is one of the few beliefs that should *not* be tolerated, because the atheist denies the foundation of the natural law, itself the template of all justice, private and public.

[4] For possible questions about this argument, see Appendix A at the end of the chapter.

[5] For possible questions about this argument and its myth, see Appendix B at the end of the chapter.

Chapter Eleven:
Testaments

Land or Hut?

In the famous fifth chapter of his *Second Treatise of Government*, the English philosopher John Locke explains the invention of property in the state of nature. Property begins with our own persons: each man has original property in himself. But that original property quickly extends. Because a man has property in his person, he has property in the working of his person, his labor. And because he owns his labor, he also owns the products of his work, the product into which he has mixed his labor. Above all, natural man comes to possess land, into which he has mixed his labor year after year in the raising of crops, fruits sown and reaped for his own subsistence and benefit (Macpherson 18-21).

The French philosopher Rousseau offers, characteristically, a much different picture of the birth of property, in his *Discourse on the Origins of Inequality Among Men*. He agrees with such thinkers as Locke or Hobbes that man, in the original state of nature, lived a solitary life. He even must admit that these solitary men, or ape-men, must have eaten the fruits of the forests and even must have made use of the natural tools around them, sticks, stones, skins. But for Rousseau, it is the "first revolution," the first major change, in the original state of nature that brings about "a sort of property": namely, the decision of the human beings in that state to cease to wander alone or in small groups, to fix themselves a place to live, and to build "huts" or "cabins" from rude materials in which to live—together (Gourevitch, 173).

Property thus arises together with the differentiation into families. And, in Rousseau's eyes, the property, the hut, continues and strengthens that differentiation. Indeed, it is in the hut that humankind learns the "moral aspect" of love: "The first developments of the heart were the effect of a new situation that brought husbands and Wives, Fathers and Children together in a common dwelling; the habit of living together gave rise to the sweetest sentiments known to man, conjugal love and Paternal love" (Gourevitch, 173-174). It is in the hut that mankind develops a heart.

When considering property, its origins and its importance, one faces a choice between, to put it fancifully, Locke and Rousseau. Does property arise out of our neediness, our individuality, our desperate pursuit of preservation? Or does it arise out of our generosity, our desire to share ourselves with others, our love? In the following chapter, which considers some elements of the stranger's discussion of property, we will see that while he does not scant Lockean considerations, he himself demands that we understand property in a way much more similar to Rousseau's. And that understanding will extend itself to matters far beyond property itself.

Family Business

The subject of the second-to-last book of Plato's *Laws*, Book Eleven, is "business transactions" (913a1). In it the stranger talks about how the prospective citizens should conduct purchases and sales, buy or return slaves; what they should do about cheating merchants; how they should handle retail trade; how craftsmen should conduct themselves; and, toward the latter half of the book, he deals with all the many things that can disrupt people's exchanges with one another.

In today's world, many of these matters fall under the rubric of private business. The stranger has certainly not hesitated in the past to regulate things that people today would call "private," but why spend so much time on business in particular? The reason is that business transactions are absolutely necessary for any lawgiver to consider. Without exchanges of goods and services there cannot be cities. The stranger would never say that the business of a good city is business. But without business there cannot be cities, bad or good.

However, the particular matters that the stranger discusses under the heading of "business transactions" are quite broad and may go well beyond what most people today would consider as "business." In particular, the stranger continually returns to various familial matters and their regulation. For example, he talks about how wills should be written, how guardians of orphans should be appointed, and how discord within the family—discord between parents and children as well as between spouses—should be alleviated.

These are not matters that most contemporary westerners usually think about when they think about "business transactions." But maybe such surprise merely shows the narrowness of the usual thoughts about business. After all, today just as in ancient Greece, business profits are still pursued for the sake of people's families. For many people, business and family are inextricable. And certainly, in modern America, the laws concerning private business or private property and the laws concerning private families are closely related. The stranger's discussion of "business transactions" thus tries to acknowledge the richness of this part of human life.

Termini

Before turning to this subject, however, we should make one observation that is both retrospective and prospective. The subject of the book previous to this one is piety. It may seem very strange that the stranger moves suddenly from that lofty subject—the divine things—to business transactions. But if one looks closely, the movement is not so abrupt.

At the beginning of Book Eleven, the first subject the stranger takes up is, one could say, the inviolability or untouchability of private property. The law here is "Do not move the immovable" (913b9). Do not move property lines. Do not pick up what you did not set down. Even if you discover buried treasure, if you did not bury it, you should not remove it. Private property is, so to speak, sacred. This adjective is used advisedly. For, if one then looks back to the beginning of Book Ten, one finds that the stranger says there, "No one is to carry or drive away anything belonging to others, or, in turn, use anything of his neighbor's, unless he has persuaded the owner" (884a2-4). His subject there was violence. No citizen should take what does not belong to him. This subject arose from Book Nine, whose main concern was murder and violence. Book Ten begins, in other words, with a pronouncement about the inviolability of property.

So, the subject that the stranger began to discuss at the beginning of Book Ten, the inviolability of property, is the same one that he returns to and completes at the beginning of Book Eleven. The discussion of impiety, in other words, comes in the middle of a discussion of property (Strauss, *Argument and Action* 157). The stranger did not have to do this, of course, to nestle the discussion of the impiety in the middle of a discussion of property. Why does he? Perhaps the subject at hand—property and especially parental interest in property—will shed some light on the matter. At least one can say this: talking about the necessity of respecting property makes the stranger think of the necessity of respecting the gods.

No Free Will

Deep within Book Eleven—after covering the discovery of lost property, fair trade, retail regulations, and employment rules—the stranger says, "The greatest business transactions—all those that human beings transact with one another—except those that have to do with orphans and their care and raising, have been pretty much arranged by us" (922a16-8). The most important business transactions, in other words, find their summit in the care for children that one leaves behind when one dies. Who will care for them? What property will they inherit? The laws points to these questions as the most important for citizens to think about when engaged in their business pursuits.

So the stranger must talk about wills, about human beings' disposal of their own property and of their children after they die. The problem, he says, is that most people are very "difficult" when they are about to die (922c7). Dying people are usually sick, weak, and not in their right mind. They are particularly "difficult," he says, because people who are about to die often become "angry" (922d1). And in their anger they claim the right to dispose of their property however they wish and to whomever they wish, whether to all their children or to some of their children or to other, unrelated people. In the face of such vehemence, lawgivers tend to allow dying people to dispose of their property however they wish, the stranger observes.[1] But the stranger condemns these laws. He says that the lawgivers who set them up long ago were "soft" and careless in making such laws; i.e., that they were stupid and cowardly (922e1).

The stranger's laws, in contrast, tell the dying man that he must not be so angry (see 923a-c). He must realize the own insignificance of his life, which lasts for "but a day" (923a3). The dying man must realize that, in truth, he himself and all that belongs to him belongs to the city. So the city will show him how to dispose of what he thinks of as "his" property. And he should be happy for such instruction, since the city's law will consider what is best for all involved, what is best for his family and for the city as a whole.

This is, in summary form, the prelude that the stranger's law would sing to the dying man. The law itself follows (923c-924a): the dying parent must choose one son to inherit his family's allotment. He can put aside some property for other children, if they are yet unmarried, but the main thing is to transfer the allotment to one son. Daughters must be married into other families. And as for other, so to speak, excess sons, if another father does not adopt them, they must eventually leave the city to join a colony. There can be no divvying up of one's property among all one's relatives. No showering gifts upon life-long friends. The goal of the law is to preserve the number of allotments and the number of families, whatever the dying parent or the hopeful children may wish.

Obviously, the stranger's proposal differs not only from some of the current laws of his times, but also from the laws of the present. That is not to say that present-day laws allow dying people to do anything they wish with their property. For example, in the United States, a dying husband cannot disinherit his wife. A surviving spouse can claim a right to most if not all of the dying spouse's property. Some states also have laws concerning inheritance by children, demanding that if one has children, they must all inherit equal shares of the estate. One cannot choose to give more to some and less, or none, to others. In particular, the estate cannot go to the oldest son alone.

These laws act as bulwarks against the accumulation of property in the hands of eldest sons and the reemergence of a sort of aristocracy. Still, these restrictions are meager in comparison with the stranger's proposal. For the most part, today's laws would agree with the "current laws" that the stranger condemns, the laws that allow the dying person to distribute his property simply as he wishes. And it is likely that most people today would say, along with the stranger's contemporaries, "Is that not fair? Is it not right to grant dying people that final wish?" In other words, most people would agree with the old Kleinias, who cannot believe what he hears the stranger saying about restricting the wishes of dying people with regard to their property.

Acts of Desperation

But why do people think that way? Why do they think that the fair or just thing is for dying people to be able to dispose of their property as they wish, as they see fit? What does the stranger think is wrong with that very common view?

To answer this question, one has to think about what is going on in the mind of the dying person. This is obviously a very difficult thing to do, but we must try to do it, turning to the book when help is needed. The first thing to observe is some of the things that are not likely to be going through the dying person's mind. At least these are not the most serious reasons for why the dying person insists upon the right to dispose his property as he wishes, and so they are not the most serious reasons why others try to uphold the dying person's wish.

First, no dying person insists on being able to distribute his property as he wishes because he thinks it will bring him some benefit. A father does not leave his son a gold watch because he thinks it will keep good time for himself, for the father. A friend does not leave his friend his favorite book because he, the dying friend, hopes to profit from re-reading it. It is necessary to mention this fact because this is the way people usually think about property: property is something that benefits its owner. The father buys a watch because it will tell time for him. Or the friend buys the book in order to learn something from it. Property is meant to be good for the owner. If it is not good, it is trash or some other liability, something to be gotten rid of. But, outside of ancient Egypt, most people believe that for the dead nothing material at least is good. The dead cannot use a watch or read a book. So people do not insist on willing their property as they wish for such obviously selfish reasons.

So, one might say, people insist on distributing their property as they wish because they worked hard for it. A man sweats over a field or builds a house or grows a business. Thus he claims to be able to give this field, or house, or business, to whomever he wishes. This is an important reason, or beginning of a reason, for why people claim the right to own and use what they have worked for. But this claim is not a sufficient explanation for why people insist on the right to dispose of all their property as they wish. For people claim this right even over property they did not work for. The man who inherits a watch claims just as much right to leave it to whomever he wishes as the man who worked for the watch.

So, if these two suggestions do not explain the matter, what does the stranger say? His words are helpful, for he gives us a speech by the dying man. The dying man would complain, according to the stranger:

> It's terrible, O Gods, if in no way I'm allowed to give my things to whomever I wish or not, and more to one and less to another, of all those who have been evidently wretched or good to me, after testing each in sickness, others in old age, and in all sorts of fortunes! (922d4-8)

Kleinias thinks the dying man is right. But what justifies his complaint? One explanation could proceed this way (see Strauss, *Argument and Action* 162). The dying man clearly sees himself as a judge of sorts. He judges those around him, whether his children or others. He has a whole life of evidence before him, a life of "testing." He knows who has respected him and cared for him or who has disrespected him and ignored him. And so his will is not just a distribution of property but a judgment that hands down justice. Those who are good will be rewarded. Those who are bad will be punished. It is no mistake that the English language calls a will a "will." The will summarizes a person's judgment about his life and about those around him and expresses this judgment, expresses his will. And the dying person demands from the law that it makes sure that his will be done.

In other words, according to this line of argument, people demand to be able to make wills as they see fit—not in order to distribute property in a way that they, personally, would enjoy from its use, nor simply because they worked for the property—but rather because they claim the right to exercise a final judgment through their wills and through the grants of property that they make or withhold. But why do they make this claim? Why do they claim the right to exercise this final judgment? Why do they imagine that in the final moments of their lives or even after their deaths they should have the right to act as judges in this manner?

One reason could be found in the stranger's first discussion of marriage, back in Book Four. In that book the stranger tries to encourage young men to marry by saying that by marrying and by having children they will ensure themselves heirs who will remember them after they are dead (721b-c). But, one could ask, what will they remember their fathers or ancestors as? Clearly, the young men he is speaking to want to be remembered well. Most people do not want to be remembered as scoundrels. The will, the final distribution of property, the final judgment that a parent makes establishes his legacy. This legacy is one of property itself, but, more broadly, the will establishes the legacy of memory. Will a man's legacy be one of riches that he left to his son? Or will his legacy be of debts? Or will it be of bounty given to his illicit girlfriend? He chooses how he will be remembered. According to this interpretation, the thought of being remembered well attracts people as a salve to the painful thought of being dead.

But even the thought of legacy—which looms large in every parent's mind—cannot totally explain why human beings, parents or not, claim the right to make this final judgment. For further insight, in line with this interpretation, one must turn one last time to the passage. Of the dying person, the stranger says, "Seeking authority over everything, he tends to speak with anger" (922d1-2). This is a curious statement, that the dying person seeks authority over everything. The stranger could just mean that he seeks to have authority over all his property and over his family. But then, why would that make him angry? Is he angry that he cannot enjoy this property or this family any more?

Perhaps, but this frustration, it is claimed, points to a deeper source of anger. The dying man, as dying, seeks to have authority over everything in the largest sense, over his life, and over his death, over his living and his dying, over the fact that he must die. Of course he cannot avoid his inevitable death. But he wishes he could. He wishes he had the authority to avert the end. The dying person seeks the greatest authority, the authority over life and death. He seeks, in other words, to be a god, a being above life and death.[2] He seeks to avoid the end. And so he tries to live on, in his judgment, in his judging of his living fellows, in his "will," in his distribution of his goods. But part of him knows that this dream is impossible, that he is not a god, that he must die, and that even this final judgment will not save him from death. His search for authority must fail. And so he gets angry.

Acts of Love

To return to the main argument, we have observed that the stranger's law would strictly regulate the disposition of property at death, in contrast with most testamentary law past and present. Kleinias and the stranger recognize that dying people will complain about such strict regulation. We asked why. The interpretation sketched above finds the answer in the dying person's desperation in the face of death. The dying person rebels at death. He wishes to continue to live, to master himself and the world in such a way as to overcome death. He cannot literally become immortal. So he uses his final act, his "will," to establish a legacy for himself. This legacy will reflect his judgment on those who live on, his judgment of right and wrong. Through his legacy he finds at least a certain way to conquer death. But his underlying hope—to conquer death, to become a sort of god—must appear confused, even deluded. If the stranger thinks that such desperate thoughts do animate the dying man, then his strict regulation of the will becomes unsurprising.

But this interpretation paints hardly a flattering picture of the dying person. Not that we must seek a flattering portrait; the stranger's words are hard. Yet the stranger manages to convince Kleinias, himself an aged man, that his proposal makes sense. It is hard to imagine Kleinias agreeing to an interpretation that treats dying people as desperate, fearful, fools who imagine themselves gods. Furthermore, while this interpretation may appear to fit with the family discord and quarrels the stranger addresses later in the book (see 928d-932d and below), such a cynical interpretation of parental desires is at odds with the picture of parents that the stranger draws in the very next section of the book. There he encourages guardians to take care of orphans, for fear that the caring and watchful ghosts of parents not exact some vengeance. How can one go from being a selfish and desperate tyrant on one's deathbed to, moments later, a caring and watchful ghost?

Let us reconsider what the stranger says about the dying person's state of mind. The dying person seeks to make gifts, in his will, in line with his life of "testing" those around him, seeing who are his true friends and not, and, presumably, in line with his judgment about who truly needs his gifts. The stranger also says that the dying person becomes "angry" in the face of death and seeks to have authority over everything. We should also not forget that the context of this discussion of wills is a larger discussion of orphans, the treatment of the children of the dead. The dying, then, appear here primarily in their role as parents.

From that standpoint, the standpoint of a parent, it is not hard to understand the dying person's anger in a less cynical manner. The dying person does try to extend his will past the bourne of death by use of a "will," his legal testament. But he does not do so simply in order to be remembered, though he may be remembered (for a time) for his will and he may even reflect upon that fact before dying.

The point is that we need not understand the dying person as focused simply upon himself, his illness, his death. Indeed, his words focus on others around him, his friends and family. A dying parent does dwell upon loss. But he dwells less—if at all—upon any loss he will suffer by dying. Rather, he dwells upon the loss his spouse, children, friends will suffer by his death. He dwells upon what he could have done for them if he had lived. Even if he saddens himself with the thought that he can spend no more time with his loved ones, this apparent selfish thought proves the opposite. For time with them surely means opportunities to benefit them, not simply to win benefits from them.

The will allows the dying man to extend benefits to his loved ones even after he has passed away. It also allows him to create a "legacy," in the sense of a memory of himself. But, again, this memory must not be understood selfishly. The dying parent does not seek simply to "live on," for himself, in this memory. Instead, he reflects that his child or spouse will no longer have him present as a father or husband. This is a true loss for them. But they may have his memory, in the best form that he can leave it to them. This memory cannot serve as a substitute for a living father or husband. But it can remind them of what was best, best for them and best simply, in the one who is gone.

In short, it is more reasonable to understand the dying person as "seeking authority over everything"—not because he faces death in a selfish and cringing manner—but because he loves others, and has so much more that he would like to do for them. That love, and the limitation put upon its expression by death, explains too why the dying person so easily becomes angry. If he had no one to live for, what sense would it make for him to become angry at dying?

Finally, such love explains why, precisely in the face of these desires, the dying person—or at least the aged lawgiver Kleinias—accedes to the stranger's stern proposal. If the dying person sought only to benefit himself through his will, then it is hard to imagine that he would ever obey a law that put such limitations upon his legacy. But the stranger makes clear that he and the dying person have the same goal: to benefit the dying person's friends—his family and his city. The stranger kindly but firmly shows the dying person the likelihood that he will make mistakes in pursuing this paramount goal. Because he respects and shares the dying person's desire, the stranger can turn the testator away from reliance upon his own (perhaps flawed) judgment to obedience to the dictates of the lawgiver and law. And because the dying person never truly, in his heart of hearts, saw his testament as a way to benefit himself, he will agree to abandon the claim to follow his own judgments in such matters and instead obey a wise and beneficent law.

Divine Madness?

Clearly, then, the stranger has a very broad notion of "business transactions," the subject of Book Eleven. As seen, he offers preludes and laws concerning how wills should be written, about how guardians should be assigned, and about orphans should be cared for. That is, he carefully considers what should happen when parents die.

He also goes on to consider other sad possibilities in this book. For example, he utters laws and preludes about how to disown children, about how to get parents declared insane, about how divorces and remarriages should be conducted, and what to do with children produced from the unions of slave and free citizens. At the conclusion of this long discussion of "dysfunctional families," as they might be called today, he offers a substantial prelude and law that commands children to respect their parents, to respect them as though they are "holy statues" (931a5) in the house (930e-932d). This law would surely be pleasing to parents. But it seems an odd conclusion to this discussion of familial matters.

For one thing, it is odd given the subject that has just been discussed—parents and property. As seen, the stranger knows that old people, people who are about to die, usually rebel against death. They seek authority over everything. They know that they cannot have that total authority. So they get angry. The stranger puts strict limits upon what the dying may do in their wills. It is clear from his words that he does not think they are god-like, and that if they do so, he thinks they are deluding themselves. And yet here, a few pages later, he sings a prelude that parents—especially old and dying parents—are close to the gods and that the gods hearken especially to their aged prayers.

True, this prelude makes some sense if we remember that old and dying parents often do act like beneficent gods in their desire to continue to benefit their loved ones even after their death. Still, the stranger's prelude praising parents as close to the gods also surprises readers because of the familial discord that he has just discussed and legislated about in Book Eleven. Fathers get very angry with their sons and seek to disown them. Parents, especially aged ones, go insane. Spouses may be angry and cruel to each other and need to be divorced. And fathers in particular may commit adultery with other women, even slave women, and sire illegitimate children. Are these the people the stranger calls "statues of the gods," to be respected only second to the gods themselves?

As if to drive home this very problem, in his prelude about respecting parents the stranger mentions three examples of fathers who cursed their sons and whose curses the gods seem to have heard. These examples are no doubt meant to strike fear in the hearts of wayward children. But the examples—Oedipus, Amyntor, and Theseus—are very questionable ones (931b). Oedipus cursed his sons after having killed his own father and slept with his mother. Amyntor cursed his son after his son caught him cheating on his mother with a slave-woman. And Theseus, the legendary founder of Athens, cursed his son after his much younger second wife deceitfully slandered his son to him. In other words, all three of these aged fathers acted out of lust and rage, sometimes throughout their entire lives, and definitely in their curses. No doubt, the stranger's point here is that if the gods listen to these malefactors, then they will listen to any parent. But that observation begs the question. Why should parents, including stupid, angry parents, be respected as though images of the gods?

Old-Timers

Perhaps, in calling for children to respect their parents as god-like, the stranger is thinking exactly of these cases of familial discord. Families are fragile constructions. They are ready to fall apart for all sorts of reasons. There are tensions in them that can break out in awful violence. This is all regrettable. If people are to avoid such violence, there have to be some firm limits. So, the stranger commands, children, respect your parents, no matter what. That way order, at least, will be preserved.

This is one possible reason for this odd prelude and law. But it is not particularly satisfying. After all that the stranger has done to weaken private families, why deify parents now? The stranger is without a doubt an imaginative would-be legislator. If he thought families were accidents waiting to happen, would he not try to modify them in some way in order to lessen the danger? He is certainly no traditionalist. Yet the commandment "honor thy mother and father" is about as traditional as one can get.

To begin to answer these questions, one must look at the stranger's prelude, which is meant to persuade children to honor their parents as part of their honoring the gods. The stranger begins the prelude by distinguishing two types of gods. He explains, "Some of the gods, seeing them clearly, we honor; of the others, we set up images to worship, which delight us even though they lack souls" (930e7-931a2). Who are these two types of gods? The first type, the gods people see clearly, are clearly beings such as the sun, the moon, the stars, and the earth. Their divinity is what one senses when looking upon the vastness of the heavens or the immensity of the Grand Canyon or the power of the oceans. These gods show themselves to human beings all the time or at regular intervals. The sun rises, runs his course, and then returns, at night, in a golden chariot to his golden palace. The next day he does the same exact thing.

The habit of the Greek philosophers was to call these first gods the cosmic gods. The other gods, the second type, are then the more personal gods that people can see only in images, whether those images take the form of paintings or of statues. These are gods such as Christ, or Zeus, or Odin, or Krishna. These gods do not show themselves or their power always or at regular intervals, the way that the sun or the moon or the oceans do. These more personal gods show themselves or their power only when they will, for brief and surprising moments, that human beings then call miracles. They are mysterious, unpredictable deities. By making images of them, people hope to dispel some of the mystery. They hope to fix some connection between these gods and themselves, and perhaps even gain some favor from the gods to themselves.

Now, the stranger says, people honor that first type of gods, the cosmic gods. But, he adds, they seek goodwill from the second type, the personal gods. And it is those personal gods, not the cosmic gods, to whom the stranger says parents are closest. The reason he says this lies in part in the difference between the two types of gods. The cosmic gods are honored because they give people good things: the sun gives light, the earth and ocean give food. But the cosmic gods give these good things to all people. The sun shines every day on both the wicked man and the righteous man. The earth sends up crops every summer to the vicious and the virtuous alike. The ocean yields fish to both the evil and the good. These cosmic gods do seem to care for human beings, in their way. But they do not seem to care about the distinction between justice and injustice, which is so important to human life.

That is exactly what the more personal deities, the type represented in pictures or in statues, do care about. Christ, Zeus, Odin, and Krishna do not treat the wrongdoers the same as those who do good. The personal gods do not reward everyone or punish everyone alike. They reward the virtuous and punish the vicious. They care about the things that human beings specially care about; they care about justice. That is why people almost always imagine them as looking like human beings. And that is why the stranger could, with some plausibility, sing that these gods do listen to the prayers of human beings.

But the stranger does not simply say that this second type of gods listens to the prayers of human beings; he says that they listen especially to the prayers of parents. He links parents, above all, to these gods. He says they are even closer to these gods than those images of the gods that people make and worship. Why are parents so special?

Here one must notice that the stranger stresses that it is the prayers of old parents that the gods especially listen to. The obvious fact that parents are always older than their offspring seems to be of particular importance. Parents are not closer to the gods by being wiser or smarter; after all, many parents—such as Oedipus or Theseus—do not behave in especially wise ways. Rather, their age seems to be the most direct connection between them and the divine.

But what does age have to do with it? Why is age so important? The stranger seems to be initiating a thought of this sort: Parents are old. So they must be respected. After all, the gods are the oldest of all beings. And they are the most worthy of the greatest respect. In other words, just as the oldest beings—the gods—deserve the greatest respect, so too parents, who are older, deserve considerable respect. This idea seems to be what his prelude tries to persuade us. But this merely pushes the question about age to the level of the gods. Why should it matter that parents or gods are very old? What does age have to do with respect?

Here we travelers must set sail on our own, with our own thoughts. But even our own religious tradition helps us to some degree. If one looks closely at chapter five of the book of Genesis, what is very striking and peculiar about the perhaps boring list of fathers and sons found there is that as the reader goes back in time, in this list, the life spans get longer. The increase is almost completely uniform. As one approaches the beginning of time, the life spans are the longest. Or, conversely, as one approaches the historical times, the lives get shorter and shorter. This striking characteristic of this chapter of Genesis teaches that the closer human beings are to the source of human being—God Himself—the more they partake in God's greatness, in particular, in His longevity. God is the oldest and longest-lived of all things. The human beings close to Him resemble Him more closely in their long lives. And, as humanity moves in time further and further from its source, God, human lives lose more and more of this divine longevity. They become shorter and death comes all the more quickly.

The general lesson taught by this chapter of Genesis is the same as that taught by the stranger's prelude. The lesson is that the closer one approaches to the "old times," the better things were. Lives were longer then. People were happier then. People were better then. Today human life is short and miserable. But our parents are a bit closer to those old times than we are. So our parents must partake of their goodness a bit—maybe a lot—more than we do. And so as we revere the oldest and best of all beings, the gods, so we will respect our parents.

In other words, the nearly universal human practice of honoring mothers and fathers—which the contemporary West holds on to even in this secular age (with a good deal of relaxation, to be sure)—is based on a deep belief that the oldest times were the best times, that the oldest beings were the best beings. But who can be older and better than the god or gods who sit at the beginning of all things?

Still, one can and should wonder, why this nearly universal identification of oldest with best, especially when there are everywhere examples of older people who do very bad things? Why should age or antiquity—by itself—be a badge of honor?

To understand this identification of age with goodness one needs to return to the distinction between cosmic and personal gods. The personal gods speak or respond to the human concern for justice in a way that the cosmic gods, as good as they are, do not. Human beings want the gods to be just and to care about our justice or injustice. In other words, they want the oldest beings to be most just beings. That, above all, is what saying that the oldest is best means: the oldest is the most just. But why should people insist that the oldest beings also be most just? Why should they insist that justice sit at the beginning of things?

To see why this is the case, one should consider the alternative. The alternative would be that the oldest thing or oldest things do not care about justice. They are indifferent to justice. Justice is an entity or concern that arises only late, after the primary things are already established. The gods who care about justice are secondary beings or even secondary creations. What would be the result of this hypothesis? The result is that no one could be sure that justice could ever, finally, be done. People do not want justice to end, forever, in misery or for injustice, forever, to rejoice. But if justice is not primary, if there is something prior to a just god, then no one can be sure that these hopes will be fulfilled. If something else comes before the just god, then that something else may limit the power of the just god to enact justice. That something else may be indifferent power, dumb matter, some malevolent demon, or mindless chaos. Whatever it is it would limit that just god and may frustrate that god's desire that justice be done. This is the result, if justice and a god who cares about justice are not first and oldest.

There are several other serious results of this view—results for how people view themselves, their free will, or their ability to do what is right and wrong. But this one result, concerning god and god's power, is enough to show how important the belief about the oldest things is. People's belief about the oldest things—are they just or indifferent to justice?—shapes the way they live. It shapes things as seemingly mundane as whether or not they respect their parents, even when their parents do stupid things.

Also, this belief about the oldest things is not something to which one can be indifferent. It is bound together with all of one's other thoughts and actions concerning oneself and others by iron bonds of logic. If one honors one's mother and father, if one is concerned with justice, then one must be led—if one thinks about it—to this view about the beginnings. Likewise, only this view of the beginnings supports true respect for parents or true concern for justice. The parts must all go together as one whole. Of course, many people do not think things out so fully. But just because they do not think things through, does not mean that the logic of the human heart does not hold them fast.

Winged Love

We observed earlier in this chapter that the stranger had turned from an initial discussion of property to his treatment of the gods and then back again. We asked why property should remind him of the gods. This analysis of the central passages of Book Eleven suggests that parents serve as the middle term between property and the divine. Parents seek property and seek to use it, while alive and at their deaths, in order to benefit not themselves but their children. In this manner—though the parental judgment may, naturally, fail at times—parents imitate God, who also does all good for the world he has made and who, in his primacy, stands as the ultimate guarantor of goodness and justice. In the end, these parents are no more selfish in loving their children than is God for loving the world.

This interpretation of the stranger's account reminds one of a tale ascribed to Jewish folklore, but hardly sectarian in its applicability. There once was a father swallow and his three children who, in their migrations, had to cross an enormous river. The young birds were too weak to attempt the crossing on their own; the father was strong enough to carry only one at a time. He took the first and, midway through, asked him, "Young swallow, when I am old and weak, will you do the same for me?" The child happily answered, "Of course," and the father immediately shook him off his back and into the murderous waves. He returned and fetched his second child. Again he asked the same question and, when he received the same answer, threw his second child into the deep. Finally he took the third. Halfway across the river he asked him, "Young swallow, when I am old and weak, will you do the same for me?" The child responded, respectfully but firmly, "No, Father, but I will for my children."

Notes

[1] For a short discussion of the changes in inheritance law in Athens from the 5th to 4th centuries, see Morrow (110).

[2] The stranger's Greek literally reads that the dying man seeks to be a "lord" or "master," a *kurios*, over everything.

Chapter Twelve:
Point of Departure

Guarding the Laws

After all our traveling through Plato's *Laws*, we now come to its conclusion, Book Twelve. Like the other eleven books, Book Twelve rambles through many curious topics. But the most curious of them all, and the one most worth our inspection, is certainly the strange institution of the nocturnal council.

First, however, we should observe that Book Twelve has a rather odd beginning. The beginning of this book does not hint that it is going to introduce any new topic whatsoever. It appears rather to be a seamless continuation of Book Eleven. There is no "And next..." or "After these things..." that would signal to the reader that the stranger is embarking on something new. Instead it seems as though the stranger says that the things he discusses here in Book Twelve—embassies, theft from public goods, and military discipline, to begin with—are still part of his discussion of "business transactions."

However, as we survey Book Twelve we can see that its own theme or unifying topic does gradually emerge: the theme of safeguarding the law. The theme of Book Twelve is in fact the final theme that the stranger announced back in Book One when he described to Kleinias how Kleinias should praise a good law-code. At the end of all his praise, the stranger says, Kleinias should talk about how the good lawgiver sets up certain "guards" so that "intelligence may tie together" the whole law-code (see 632c4-7). This, the safeguarding of the law, is the theme of Book Twelve. In a way it is the highest theme of all, for without guarding, the rest of the laws will become worthless.

But, one could ask, why do the laws need safeguarding? What is the problem that this discussion is meant to address? The problem is at least this: this city, which the stranger has been describing, is supposed to be a city of laws. In this city, laws are supposed to rule, rule both by persuasion and by force. This city of laws is supposed to be unlike many other cities, where angry or lustful men rule and use their power, in factions, to oppress other citizens (recall 712e-713a). This sounds good. After all, Americans and many other people say such things about their own nations: that they are nations ruled by laws, not men.

However, this description—of a city ruled by law and not by men—faces a basic problem: if the laws protect the citizens, who protects the laws? Who, or what, safeguards them? For, as experience teaches, the laws do face certain threats. For example, they face the threat of manipulation at the hands of angry or greedy people. They face repeal or disregard in the face of popular discontent. They face the fluctuations of time, when external changes may make a long-standing law suddenly irrelevant or even harmful. They face the problem that there may be imperfections in their original setting-forth, imperfections that need correction sooner or later. And they face the danger of being interpreted or rather misinterpreted by simply stupid men. These are all real dangers that face the laws. Who or what protects them from these dangers?

The topics discussed in Book Twelve build toward a solution of these difficulties. Certainly there must be honesty among the citizens and their officials if they are to protect the laws. There must also be widespread respect for the public good among all the citizens in order to maintain the sanctity of the laws. And the citizens, all of them, must feel great loyalty and subservience to the public order. The stranger begins Book Twelve by stressing this honesty, this respect, and this loyalty (941b-945a). These are all certain habits that help protect the laws.

But in addition to these habits, the city needs men, human beings, whose main concern is to protect the laws. So, for instance, the stranger describes the office of public auditors (945b-948a). These are not like present-day auditors, public servants who check the books every few years or so and make sure public institutions are not wasting money. Rather, these are highly honored older statesmen who inquire into all the activities, public and private, of public officials and make sure they account for every part of their lives. They have great powers to discipline officials and hence to protect the laws. They are so important to the safeguarding of the regime that the stranger describes these sought-for auditors as "divine" (945c2).

But above all, even above the auditors, the city needs the human beings that make up that mysterious "nocturnal council" (951d and see 908a4). The nocturnal council emerges as the true safeguard of the laws. That means, for instance, that the nocturnal council will be the highest and final interpreters of the law. And hence, in a city ruled by law, this makes the nocturnal council the highest rulers in the city. For, one could say, and one must say, the human beings that make up the nocturnal council are higher than the law. Obviously they are not "above the law" in the sense of being able to murder or pillage whomever they like. Clearly they must be law-abiding. But they are above the law since they may interpret the law and even change it. In the end, it seems, no law can stand alone. In the end, even in this most lawful city, men rule, not the laws. Plato's broader lesson is that this will always be the case: no matter how good a city's laws (or how bad), in the end men must rule, not laws. Of course, the questions then always are, "Which men will rule? What sort of men will rule?" Now the stranger faces the answer to that question, for this city.

It may have seemed that the *Laws* was going end quietly, just tying up a few loose ends or the like. Instead, here in the last book, in Book Twelve, the stranger brings out into the daylight, so to speak, the greatest and most important innovation of them all. Book Twelve is the summit, as well as the conclusion, of Plato's *Laws*.

The Stranger's Think Tank

As one might expect, the nocturnal council emerges in a shadowy, piecemeal fashion. The stranger does not bring attention to it until the end of the *Laws*. He certainly does not blow horns or put spotlights upon it. Because of the way he proceeds, this piecemeal way, in order to understand the nocturnal council, one must observe its growth within the conversation of the *Laws*.

The stranger discusses this council in three separate places. The first time he brings it up is at the end of Book Ten. He then brings it up twice more in Book Twelve. In each place Kleinias, Megillus, and the readers of this dialogue learn something new about its purpose and its activities.

At the end of Book Ten, the book about impiety and the gods, the stranger refers to the nocturnal council only in passing (see 908a and 908e-909a). He says very little about it, and instead leaves it shrouded in mystery. For example, he does not say anything about who makes up this council. What he does say, of course, is the council meets at night. He also says a bit about its purpose, or at least one of its purposes. The nocturnal council, he says, is supposed to "be with" (909a3) people who are in prison for speaking impiously, but only with people of a certain sort: those who have spoken impiously out of a lack of intelligence rather than out of anger or greed.

These are the basically just people who have been put in prison for five years for their impiety. The members of the nocturnal council are the only citizens whom these prisoners are allowed to associate with during that time. And the nocturnal council associates with them in order "to admonish them and to save their souls" (909a4-5). So, the first job of the nocturnal council is to persuade these impious people that gods exist, that they care for us, and that they cannot be appeased. In other words, the nocturnal council first comes to light as a defender of the city's faith, or a defender of the city's belief. Of course, that means that the nocturnal councilors must get to know all the possible forms of impiety or impious beliefs. Still, their primary task seems to be to safeguard the city's orthodoxy about the gods.

The nocturnal council finds its way into the discussion a second time in the middle of Book Twelve (951c-953d). Here it comes up, again, in a seemingly indirect or even accidental manner. The stranger is talking about who among the citizens gets to travel abroad (949e ff.). In fact, very few citizens will be allowed to leave the city on trips. No vacations to other parts of the world for most of them. Why not? Because the stranger is worried that visiting other cities—worse cities—and then coming home will lead to corruption and innovation within this city. So most people cannot travel abroad.

There are, however, two exceptions. One exception is that the city will send embassies of very good citizens to the holy games or to the holy shrines around Greece. Not much chance of corruption there, it seems. The other exception is that a few very mature, excellent people may be sent abroad as general observers. These observers are to travel to other cities and to see whether or not they can learn any good things from these other cities or from wise people living in these other cities. Why do this? Because then these observers can come back to the stranger's city and use their learning to help improve it. As the stranger says, "The wise people in other cities the observer, if he's incorruptible, must always track down, going out on sea and land, in order to more firmly establish those laws that are nobly laid down, but to correct others, if they are lack something. For without this observational mission and search no city will ever remain perfect." (951b6-c4) So again, the goal of these observational missions is to keep this city as good as possible. The stranger's law acknowledges that the city they are discussing may be able to learn from other cities or from foreigners. This only makes sense. This is an Athenian stranger teaching in Crete, after all.

These details relate to the nocturnal council because, when the observer returns to the Cretan city, he is to report to this council. It is at this point that the stranger reveals something more about the purpose of the nocturnal council. That purpose, it turns out, is much broader than what was allowed in Book Ten. Now he says that this is the council of those who "oversee the laws" (951d4-5). It will meet every day, from dawn until the full rising of the sun, and it will spend its time in dialogue "about laws and their own city" (952a1).

This is obviously a very large topic, as the heft of the *Laws* itself attests. And it is a topic that may require studying other related fields as well. Thus the stranger adds that the nocturnal councilors will talk "always about laws and their own city, and...should, from any source, learn about such things, especially those subjects whose inquiry benefits the learners by making these matters clearer..." (952a1-4). These other "subjects" may be very broad. And, one should recall, the observers of other cities come to this council to tell if they have learned or thought up anything good for the city. Thus it is through this council that innovations will be introduced, innovations used to keep the city "perfect" (951c4). So this council or its members must have ultimate authority over keeping or changing the laws themselves. This is an extremely large power, the largest, politically speaking. But they are to use this power to safeguard the whole city's goodness.

Still, the nocturnal council itself is not described as a legislative body. Its members may be able to change the laws. Its deliberations may guide them in their innovations. But legislation is not the activity of this council. Legislation, after all, is a sort of doing, an action, with a product—laws. The nocturnal council is not described as doing anything. Rather, it is consistently described as a place of talking. The nocturnal councilors are not primarily doers, but talkers and thinkers. Their main business, on this council, is to talk and think about laws and related matters. As seen before, this includes talking with atheists and thinking about god. Now their mandate also turns out to include talking and thinking about laws and the common good. Their main business is studying and conversing about political things, of the very highest order. In other words, in a good city, according to the stranger's proposal, the highest political activity turns out not to be warfare, or business, or legislation, or even ruling in any direct sense; rather the highest political activity turns out to be talking and thinking.

In his third and last discussion of the nocturnal council, the stranger tries to prove to Kleinias that the nocturnal council is the "savior" or "salvation" of the city (see 962a1). This is quite an amazing claim. And it is astounding that the stranger should try to prove it to Kleinias. Kleinias is, after all, a hard-bitten old Cretan. He is provincial. He is law-bred. He knows nothing or next to nothing about philosophers or other thinkers. Above all, he began the whole conversation by thinking that the best activity that a city could engage in is war and victory in war. Now the stranger has led him to the point of entertaining the idea that a council composed of old and young thinkers is absolutely necessary for the existence of a good city. And not just that such a "think-tank" is necessary, but that this institution and no other is the "salvation" of the whole city.

The stranger has not tricked Kleinias. He has not led Kleinias by the nose to a conclusion that Kleinias detests. Instead he has developed Kleinias' serious political concerns so that Kleinias sees that his own concerns demand this body of thinkers as absolutely necessary.

Getting Inside the City's Head

But how could this ever be? How could a body of old and young people who think and talk together about political things be the necessary "savior" of a city? How is that at all possible? Only by facing these questions can one understand the stranger's surprising argument and Kleinias' surprising response (see 960b-969c).

To approach these questions, one should consider the image that the stranger uses to describe the nocturnal council to Kleinias: he says that the nocturnal council is like the head of the city (see 961d-e and 964e-965a). The rest of the city, then, is the body. The stranger fleshes out the image further in this way. The nocturnal council has two parts. Half of it is composed of older men—the ten oldest of the Guardians of the Laws, the living Supervisors of Education, and the priests who have won prizes for excellence. These older members then each pick one younger person, between the ages of 30 and 40, to join the council. The stranger explains the image by likening the younger people to the senses of this head. They are the eyes and ears, so to speak, of the council. The old councilors, conversely, are like the intelligence. They receive the images passed to them by the senses and they think these things over. The human head does both of these things. And, one could say, anyone who altogether lacked sense or lacked intelligence would be severely deficient and imperfect. So, just as an individual human being cannot do well without a head, so, the stranger argues, a good city needs such a council.

This image—comparing the nocturnal council to a head—is quite pleasing. It gives the listener or the reader the sense that this city has some direction, some thought guiding it. It is not just a headless body blindly stumbling about. But the image also raises an important question. The excellence possessed by the human head is not simple. For example, the human head is excellent in the sense that it is the primary location of the senses, especially the most important sense, the sense of sight. It is the head—with its eyes—that observes all around a person; one cannot do that with one's elbow. But the head also possesses the excellence of deciding what to do and giving commands—whether to the rest of the body or to other people, through the mouth. Bodies without heads not only do not see; they also do not move or speak. Finally, the head also houses the excellence of simply thinking and understanding—whether that thinking results in commands or not. One cannot understand the truth of the Pythagorean Theorem without a head.

So, within the human head there seems to be housed at least three possible forms of excellence: sensation, judgment, and contemplation. The nocturnal council seems to partake in all three forms. But the diversity among them does leave one wondering what exactly the "intelligence" of this council will consist in. What will these wise old men (and young men, possibly) be wise in? This question is critical, since otherwise one cannot see fully the need for the nocturnal council to "save" this city and make it good. To better understand the intelligence of this council, one must look at its education.

The Everest of Education

The stranger says at this point that the nocturnal council will need a "more precise" nurture and education than the rest of the citizens (965a6-7, 965b1-2). The intelligence these councilors possess is of a different and higher form than that imparted by the rest of the civic education. Thus here in Book Twelve, at the very end of the *Laws*, the stranger introduces one more step in the ladder of education.

As has been seen, the *Laws* raises from the very start the question, "What is a good education?" Several answers are proposed. The first answer is that a good education consists in learning justice and perfect citizenship. The second answer is that a good education trains the passions so that they will be "consonant" with prudence, if prudence ever comes to you. The third view is that a good education "drags" children to obedience to the law, to lawfulness.

In Book Seven, where education is discussed most extensively, and Book Eight, with its civic festivals, it seems as though the city adopts this last view of education: children are nudged, pushed, or even dragged to an "education" that teaches obedience to the law and a preparation for defending the city. Sure, some of them may study seemingly "higher" subjects, such as arithmetic, geometry and astronomy. But even these subjects are defended simply as helping them better protect the city from danger. The last word in Book Seven, the book on education is that the most important learning the citizen acquires is by hunting.

But here, in Book Twelve, we travelers suddenly stumble on one last ascent, an unseen higher ground in education. It as though we have hiked high into a mountain range. As we hike we think we see many high peaks in front of us. But once we climb one of those peaks, suddenly from behind the others one final summit appears that was hidden before but now towers above the rest. This final summit beckons.

This last peak is the education of the nocturnal councilors themselves. This education is not overseen by any other institution. It is an education that the councilors pursue on their own and in their discussions with each other. It is the content of this education that will reveal the "intelligence" of the nocturnal council.

So what does their self-directed education cover? It seems, from the stranger's description to Kleinias, to have three parts. The first subject that they are said to discuss is virtue (962a-964d and 965b-e). Virtue is, after all, the goal that city's law, as a whole, aims at. As has been seen many times, the stranger says that a good law should aim at those four divine goods—those four virtues—courage, moderation, prudence and justice—above all else. But if the law is to do that, then the leaders in the city—the people who have the final say over the meaning of the law—must understand and know what virtue is. No city is going to hit upon virtue by stumbling around in the dark. So these nocturnal councilors are to discuss the four virtues, to try to get to know these divine goods better.

In particular, they are to ask these very sensible questions: What is each virtue? That is, what makes each virtue one? For example, people may say that a soldier is courageous in battle or that a doctor is courageous in treating a patient or that a little boy is courageous in telling the truth. What makes all these separate instances "courageous"? What is the "courage" that shines forth in each one? Conversely, the councilors must ask this question too: what is virtue itself? That is, what unites all four virtues as one whole? Courage is a virtue and moderation is a virtue and prudence is a virtue and justice is a virtue. They all seem different. But they are addressed by this same name, "virtue." What does that word mean? These questions or this subject forms the first part of the nocturnal councilors' education.

Second, they discuss things that are said to be "beautiful and good" (966a-b). The Greek word for "beautiful" can also be translated as "noble" (see 966a5). So their subject of inquiry could also be called the "noble and good" things (cf. *Apology* 22). Just as with virtue, the stranger says that the councilors should try to understand what is "the beautiful" and "the good" that shines forth in the many beautiful and good things.

As the *Apology* reveals, this is a subject that is very dear to Socrates' own heart. He spent his whole life, he says, in this inquiry, the inquiry into the question, "Is there anything that is both noble/beautiful and good?" One might ask, "Who cares? What does it matter?" This inquiry matters for these two reasons: First, virtue itself would seem to be the preeminent example of something both beautiful and good. Does not each virtuous act shine forth both as noble and as beneficial? Second, the stranger says that the noble and good things encompass all "serious" things

(966b4). If one comes to understand the "noble and good," one comes to understand seriousness itself and what is serious in human life. So this second subject of education is closely related to the first and highly important.

Finally, the nocturnal councilors converse with each other about "one of the noblest things" (or most beautiful things), as the stranger puts it: the gods (966c1-2). They study all the proofs that can be devised concerning the divine things. And they study all the counter-proofs. (Their conversations with impious people would obviously help these researches.) Above all, they try to know what can be known about the divine. And, the stranger emphasizes, they focus on two points in particular: They focus on the claim that soul is the oldest of all things and on the seemingly orderly motion of the stars (966e). These are, if one remembers, the main props of the stranger's proof that the gods exist. To put it a slightly different way, these nocturnal councilors closely study physics (the study of motion) and astronomy (the study of the stars). So, as was emphasized in Book Ten, they will be firm defenders of the city's faith. But, beyond that, they will know as much as humans can know about the gods. To put it most succinctly: divine science is at the peak of the education pursued and promoted by this city.

Bon Voyage

To study each one of these topics—virtue, the noble and good things, divine science—even a little bit, would require many years of thinking. That is the task that the rest of Plato's works, or the rest of classical philosophy, or even much of modern philosophy, points us towards. These moral, political, and theological questions are always at the heart of true philosophy and true science. And to see how these three seemingly separate inquires relate to one another is another grand inquiry. It is good for travellers such as ourselves just to see that this question exists, even if we cannot explore it fully at the moment.

To raise these very questions, to remind us of our ignorance, is the true task of political philosophy. The raising of these questions—the seeing of them—justifies the existence of political philosophy. As the stranger says, the nocturnal council "saves" the city. This does not mean that the nocturnal council will always keep the laws good or that it will always get the city out of every jam. The stranger himself emphasizes that all cities—good and bad—come into being and must pass away some day.

So the nocturnal council does not save the city by keeping it good or keeping it in existence forever. It "saves" it in a much deeper sense. What the stranger means is that the existence of the nocturnal council, the existence of the education that this council pursues, by itself justifies the existence of the city. Or, to put it as strongly as possible, only the existence of a nocturnal council or that special kind of education justifies political life. What Kleinias—who is a very serious political man—has come to conclude is that without the existence of such an education, a city is nothing more than a camp of very well-trained, well-habituated soldiers. And that is a good scenario. Cities could be much worse: they could be nothing more than hives of busy slaves.

The serious political man in the *Laws* comes to conclude, then, through this conversation, that only such an education as the nocturnal council pursues would make all the trouble and turmoil of civic life worthwhile. And so, depicted in the *Laws*, is Plato's defense of politics. The final teaching of the *Laws* is this: that politics is, in the final analysis, and above all, worthwhile only insofar as political life points to the questions pursued by human beings such as these nocturnal councilors. In the end, only from this highest and most frigid vantage point—which reveals that the *Laws* subjugates all political life to a few scholars' pursuit of divine science—can we truthfully judge the goodness of that city and the way of life it promotes, as compared with our nation and its way of life.

Conclusion

In his *Discourse on Method*, Rene Descartes deprecates ancient cities for their disorder. True, one may find in them many individual buildings of great beauty. But, on the whole, having grown in most cases from little villages to large towns through a long and slow process of accretion, and having never enjoyed the supervision of one mind during that growth, they present a scene of winding streets, crooked alleys, houses jostling one another for space—an arrangement that seems utterly due to chance rather than thought.

Perhaps the experience of modern architecture and "urban renewal" has taught us in the present, to a degree unanticipated even by Descartes, the frightful sterility of buildings owing their form to one "reasoned" vision or of entire cities planned by the rational mind of an engineer. Or perhaps so few of us know ancient cities in the way Descartes did that we find them, with all their inconveniences, charming. In any event, many people do find pleasure in the very disorder of old cities, a disorder obviously lacking geometric justification, yet possessing its own finesse. In them one finds warmth in the layers of history, the competing claims of beauty and right, and the comedy of cross-purposes. The human soul is not only a thinking thing; it is not composed of reason alone. Thus it responds gamely to the richness found in a multiplicity of conflicting plans, to the depth of generational struggles embodied in stone, rather than to the inevitably shallow constructions of a single, though gifted, vision.

Leaving aside flickering controversies over its authorship, Plato's *Laws* presents itself as the construction of one mind. It cannot be described in the way ancient cities can, as the product of slow accretion, of the work of many competing hands. It is a book, which is to say that one vision governs its whole, and every part of that whole appears there for a reason.

Nonetheless, we must distinguish between the book as a whole, which is Plato's work, and the conversation it records. The conversation arises from the mixture and conflict of three personalities, three points of view. It is not a unified whole. Further, one must distinguish both of these, the book and the conversation, from the city that the stranger proposes. This city in speech grows out of his own vision, but he proposes it in the face of two other men's desires, prejudices, assumptions, agreements, and rejections. Finally, even if we ignore the conditions placed upon this proposal by the two other interlocutors, even if we took the stranger's vision all by itself, still he makes clear that the vision of a new city must shape itself to the rocky soil of human nature—never a perfectly level or levellable surface.

Thus the *Laws* is a tale of human reason's inability to subsume politics. We have learned this lesson at every point in our journey through the text. We saw it in the conflicting aims of the types of education offered. We saw it in the realization that most people do not even recognize their need for education. We saw it in the dialogue's analysis of the legislator's complex views of the past. We saw it in its argument that human beings cannot hope for justice on earth. This lesson appears forcefully in the problems of political union and of popular rule. It appears in the surprising combination of radicality and conservatism the stranger espouses. It prepares us for the role that habit must play in all governance. We learn it even from the wonderful teaching of parental love. We see it in the service that myth does to argument and in the aporetic efforts of the mysterious Nocturnal Council. In all these observations and arguments do the stranger and his creator teach us to respect the limits of reason in governing human life.

But this lesson should not lead students of philosophy to despair. For its recognition also issues philosophy a strong but sober call to interest itself in what might be called politics, in the largest sense of that word. Reason's recognition of its own limits goes hand in hand with the reasoner's recognition of his need for and love of others. As this dialogue reveals in its arguments, its scene, its characters, the philosophic life revolves incessantly between the attempts to better oneself and the attempts to better others—between the sun and the cave. Socratic philosophizing is neither simply pedagogic nor simply contemplative. The philosopher—if he finds the opportunity—is at once a thinker, teacher, and commander.

The crisis of our times, the crisis of faith, has led many people to put politics and the struggle for human power above all else, even thinking. It has also led some thinkers to repudiate politics and advocate a selfish retreat into contemplation—a repudiation that in its way also seeks purely human power, but which, like Peter Goldthwaite's search, often results in self-destruction.

The *Laws* offers an antidote to both maladies and perhaps a way of beginning to address the underlying crisis. It shows the interest the thinker should take in others, especially in establishing a sober political life. But it also shows how the sobriety of that politics derives from our seeing that there is more to life than the struggle for power—from the friendships and loves of other men and women, to the love and care of a power that surpasses all human things.

Appendix One—Study Questions

Chapter One

Read *Laws* Book One.
Focus on the beginning of the dialogue and 630a-632d.
Why does the stranger begin the dialogue with this question?
What are the "divine goods" according to the stranger?
What makes these things good? What makes them divine?
What are some possible reasons that Plato wrote in the dialogue form?

Chapter Two

Read *Laws* Book Two.
Re-read Book One, 643a-645c.
Focus also on 644b-647b, 654c-670e.
How do the three definitions of education in these sections compare with each other?
How does the stranger's definition of "liberal education" compare to its definition today?
Does a good education have any place for drinking or lies?
Why does the stranger think that censorship of music is necessary and good?
Are you getting a good education in college? Explain your judgment.

Chapter Three

Read *Laws* Book Three.
Focus on 677a-683b and 690a-e.
Does history, in the stranger's view, progress or regress?
What does it matter whether the world has gotten better or worse over time?
What makes "the seven worthy titles to rule" worthy?
Is the stranger's list of "worthy titles to rule" complete and self-consistent?

Do the stranger's criticisms of democracy apply to modern democracy too?

Chapter Four

Read *Laws* Book Four.
Focus on 712b-718a and 719e-720e.
What is the good of tyranny?
What is the good of theocracy?
What does the stranger's myth teach about justice?
How does the stranger define law?
What is wrong with saying that law is simply force?
What is wrong with saying that law is simply the distribution of the intellect?

Chapter Five

Read *Laws* Book Five.
Focus on 726a-734d and 739a-e.
What does the good citizen of the *Laws* look like?
What does he or she do most of all? Or never do?
How does this good citizen compare with the contemporary ideal of a good citizen?
What are the first laws of the *Laws*?
What is the "first and best" political regime, according to the stranger?
How does this regime differ from the one he is creating?
How does this regime differ from our own?

Chapter Six

Read *Laws* Book Six.
Focus on 756b-758a and 771e-776b. (Compare Book Four 721a-e.)
What is the ideal criterion for choosing rulers in this city?
How does is the Council chosen?
Why does the stranger propose using a lottery for important offices?
How does the prelude to the marriage law in Book Six differ from the one in Book Four?
Does either book offer good reasons for marrying?

Chapter Seven

Read *Laws* Book Seven.

Focus on 797a-799e, 788a-c, 793b-d, and 806d-809a
Why is the stranger opposed to "change"?
What does he propose to do about it?
What is "puzzling" about his proposal?
How do the citizens of the proposed city spend their nights and days?
What do they do together at home?
How does their private life compare to that of modern people?

Chapter Eight

Read *Laws* Book Eight.
Focus on 828a-835b; Book Seven, 803a-804b; 837d; and 838e-842a.
Why will this city have so many festivals?
What does the stranger think is serious in life? What is just play?
Does erotic desire have a "natural" direction, in the stranger's view?
Where does the stranger try to direct it? Why? How?
Why does he speak mainly to men about sex?

Chapter Nine

Read *Laws* Book Nine.
Focus on 857c-e; 853a-864c; and re-read Book Five, 731b-d.
How does the free doctor differ from the slave doctor?
How does the philosopher differ from the legislator?
Why should philosophy appear first in a discussion of punishment?
What is punishment for?
How does voluntary action differ from what's involuntary?
Why difference does it make?

Chapter Ten

Read *Laws* Book Ten
Focus on 891c-907b
What is the stranger's argument that gods exist?
What is his argument that gods care about human beings?
What is his argument that the gods are just?
What are the premises of each argument?
Are all three arguments equally good?
If you do not accept their results, what criticisms of them do you have?

Chapter Eleven

Read *Laws* Book Eleven
Focus on 922a-923c, 918a-920e, and 930e-932d
Why does the stranger think dying people become "difficult"?
What would his laws tell dying people?
Is the message comforting?
What laws would the stranger make concerning retail trade?
Why can't a businessman be a good citizen or a good man?
Why should the law hold that parents are "living statues of the gods"?
What are some reasons for respecting parents and other ancestors?

Chapter Twelve

Read *Laws* Book Twelve
Focus on 949e-953e, 960b-968e (recall 908a-909a)
Who makes up the Nocturnal Council?
What is its purpose or purposes?
How might its existence help or harm the city?
What kind of "education" do the nocturnal councilors get?
What do they study about virtue?
What do they study about the gods?

Appendix Two—Related Readings

Chapter Two

Allan Bloom. *Closing*. "Liberal Education," 336-347. "Music," 68-81.
Plato. *Republic*. 514a-519b (on education).

Chapter Three

On the human beginnings:

Genesis. Chapters 2-4.
Homer. *Odyssey*. Book Nine.
Lucretius. *On the Nature of Things*. Book Five.
Hobbes. *Leviathan*. Chapter Thirteen.
Rousseau. *Discourse on the Origin of Inequality*. Part One.

On the fundamental political dilemma:

Aristotle. *Politics*. Book Three.

On the stranger's criticism of democracy:

Plato. *Republic*. Book Eight.
The Federalist Papers. 10.
Lincoln. "On the Perpetuation of our Political Institutions." January 27, 1838.

Chapter Four

Plato. *Republic*. Book Five, 459d-460d (on marriage)
Aristotle. *Politics*. Book I, chapters 3-7 (on household management)
Bloom. *Closing*. "Eros," 132-137.

Chapter Nine

Aristotle. *Nicomachean Ethics*. Book III, chapter 5.
Roger Scruton. *Untimely Tracts*. "The Supreme Punishment."
The Catechism of the Catholic Church. Part Three: Life in Christ. "Legitimate Defense." Sections 2263-2267.

Chapter Ten

Thomas Jefferson. "Letter to the Danbury Baptists." January 1, 1802.
Pope Pius IX. *Syllabus of Errors*. 1864. Sections VI, 39-55; Section X, 77-80.
Second Vatican Council. *Gaudium et Spes*. Section 76.

Chapter Eleven

Genesis 4:17-5:32.
Alexis de Tocqueville. *Democracy in America*. Volume II, Second Book, Chapter XIX. "What Causes Almost All Americans to Follow Industrial Callings."
Second Vatican Council. *Gaudium et Spes*. Chapter III, "Economic and Social Life."

Chapter Twelve

Plato. *Apology of Socrates*. 20c-23a.
Aristotle. *Nicomachean Ethics*. III.6-VI.

Appendix Three—Map of Plato's *Laws*

Initial Overall Plan (see 631b-632c)

Book One-Book Four	Prudence is highest of divine goods
Book Five-Book Six, 771a	Human goods
Book Six, 771a-end	Marriage and birth
Book Seven	Nurture
Book Eight, beginning-842b	Erotic longings
Book Eight, 842c-Book Ten, 885a	"Disturbances"
[Book Ten, 885b-end	Impiety][1]
Book Eleven-Book Twelve, 956b	Acquisitions and associations
Book Twelve, 956b-958c	Judicial honors and penalties
Book Twelve, 958d-960b	Burial honors
Book Twelve, 960b-end	Safeguarding the laws

Outlines of Individual Books

Book One

Pages	Description
624a-625c	What is the proper source of your laws? Gods.
625d-	What is the goal(s) of your laws' institutions?
625d-632d	War vs. Peace
632e-635e	Courage
635e-	Moderation
637c-II.674c	"Athenian" Drinking Parties
637c-641a	Inquiry
641a-II.674c	Their good
641b-644b	Education
643a-d	Nurturing love for an occupation
643d-644b	Perfect citizen citizenship
644c-650b	Testing one's ability to rule oneself
644c-645c	Divine puppets

Book Two

Book III

Book Four

Book Six

Book Seven

Book Eight

<u>Book Nine</u>

Book Eleven

Book Twelve

Note

[1] Book Ten is the only book whose subject matter is not foretold by this outline in Book One.

Bibliography

Aristotle. *Nicomachean Ethics*. Trans. Joseph Sachs. Newburyport, MA: Focus Press, 2002.

_____. *Politics*. Trans. Carnes Lord. Chicago: University of Chicago Press, 1985.

Ast, Friedrich. *Platons Leben und Schriften*. Leipzig: Weidmannishen Buchhandlung, 1816.

Barker, Ernest. *Greek Political Theory: Plato and his Predecessors*. 1918. New York: Barnes and Noble, 1960.

Barnes, Jonathan. Rev. of *Plato's Cretan City*, by Glenn R. Morrow. *Review of Metaphysics* 14 (March 1961): 570-571.

Bloom, Allan. *The Closing of the American Mind*. New York: Free Press, 1988.

_____. *The Republic of Plato*. New York: Basic Books, 1968.

Bluestone, Natalie Harris. *Women and the Ideal Society: Plato's Republic and Modern Myths of Gender*. Amherst, Mass.: University of Massachusetts Press, 1987.

Blundell, Sue. *Women in Ancient Greece*. Cambridge, MA.: Harvard University Press, 1995.

Brochard, Victor C.L. *Etudes de philosophie ancienne et de philosophie moderne*. 1912. Paris: J. Vrin, 1966.

Burke, Edmund. *Reflections on the Revolution in France*. New Rochelle, NY: Arlington House. [N.D.]

Burnet, John. *Greek Philosophy: Thales to Plato*. 1914. New York: St. Martin's Press, 1964.

Lord Charnwood. *Abraham Lincoln*. New York: Madison Books, 1996.

Chatters, James C. *Ancient Encounters: Kennewick Man and the First Americans*. New York: Simon and Schuster, 2001.

Cherniss, Harold. Rev. of *Studien zu den platonischen Nomoi*, by Gerhard Mueller. *Gnomon* 25 (1953): 367-389.

_____. *Selected Papers*. Ed. Leonardo Taran. Leiden: E.J. Brill, 1977.

Clark, Randall Baldwin. "The Healer's Word: Medicine, Magic, and Rhetoric in Plato's *Laws*." Diss. U of Chicago, 1997.

Cohen, David. "Law, Autonomy and Community in Plato's *Laws*." *Classical Philology* 88 (October 1993): 301-317.

_____. *Law, Violence and Community in Classical Athens.* New York: Cambridge University Press, 1995.

_____. "The Political and Legal Status of Women in Plato's *Laws.*" *Revue Internationale des Droits de l'Antiquite* 34 (1987): 27-40.

_____. "Seclusion, Separation and the Status of Women in Classical Athens." *Greece and Rome* 36 (April 1989): 3-15.

_____. *Sexuality and Society: the Enforcement of Morals in Classical Athens.* New York: Cambridge University Press, 1991.

Crombie, I.M. Rev. of *Plato's Cretan City*, by Glenn R. Morrow. *Philosophical Review* 75 (January 1966): 104-107.

Davis, Morris. "On the Imputed Possibilities of Callipolis and Magnesia." *American Journal of Philology* 85 (1964): 394-411.

Descartes, Rene. *Discourse on Method and Meditations on First Philosophy.* Trans. Donald A. Cress. New York: Hackett Publishing, 1998.

des Places, Edouard. Rev. of *Studien zu den platonischen Nomoi*, by Gerhard Mueller (2nd edition). *Revue Belge de Philologie* 48 (1970): 119-120.

Diamodopoulos, Peter. Rev. of *Plato's Cretan City*, by Glenn R. Morrow. In *Philosophy and Phenomenological Research* 24 (December 1963): 278-280.

Dies, Auguste. "Introduction." *Platon: Oeuvres Completes.* 1951. Vol. 11, first part, *Les Lois.* Paris: Societe d'Edition "Les Belles Lettres," 1976.

Diogenes Laertius. *Lives, Teachings, and Sayings of Famous Philosophers.* Trans. R.D. Hicks. Cambridge, MA: Harvard University Press, 1991.

Duering and Owen, eds. *Aristotle and Plato in the mid-Fourth Century.* Goeteborg: Studia Graeca et Latin Gothoburgensia, 1960.

Elshtain, Jean B., ed. *The Family in Political Thought.* Amherst, Mass.: University of Massachusetts Press, 1982.

_____. *Public Man, Private Woman.* Princeton: Princeton University Press, 1981.

England, Edward B., ed. *Plato's Laws.* 1921. New York: Arno Press, 1975.

Ewins, Ursula. Rev. of *Plato's Cretan City*, by Glenn R. Morrow. *Philosophical Quarterly* 13 (April 1963): 171-172.

Feder-Mareus, Maureen. "Gendered Origins: Some Reflections." Rev. of *Fear of Diversity*, by Arlene W. Saxonhouse. *Interpretation* 23 (Fall 1995): 101-110.

FitzGibbon, Scott. "Marriage and the Good of Obligation." *The American Journal of Jurisprudence* 47 (2002): 41-69.

Foley, Helen P. "Conception of Women in Athenian Drama." In *Reflections of Women in Antiquity*, 127-168. New York: Gordon and Breach Science Publishers, 1981.

Fortenbaugh, W.W. "On Plato's Feminism in Republic V." *Apeiron* 9 (1975): 1-4.

Foxhall, Lin. "Household, Gender and Property in Classical Athens." *Classical Quarterly* 39 (1989): 22-44.

Friedlaender, Paul. *Plato: the Dialogues*. 1958. Trans. Hans Meyerhoff. Bollingen Series LIX. Princeton: Princeton University Press, 1969.

Fustel de Coulanges, Numa Denis. *The Ancient City*. Baltimore: Johns Hopkins University Press, 1980.

Glotz, Gustave. *The Greek City and its Institutions*. Trans. N. Mallinson. New York: A.A. Knopf, 1929.

Goergemanns, Henwig. *Beitraege zur Interpretation von Platons Nomoi*. Munich: C.H. Beck, 1960.

Gomperz, Theodor. *Greek Thinkers*. Trans. G.G. Berry. London: John Murray, 1905.

Greene, Jack P., ed. *Colonies to Nation, 1763-1789: A Documentary History of the American Revolution*. New York: W.W. Norton, 1975.

Grote, George. *Plato and the Other Companions of Sokrates*. 1888. New York: Burt Franklin Press, 1973.

Grube, G.M. Rev. of *Plato's Cretan City*, by Glenn R. Morrow. *Phoenix* 16 (Winter 1962): 281-283.

Guthrie, W.K.C. *History of Greek Philosophy*. Vol. 5. Cambridge: Cambridge University Press, 1978.

Harrison, A.R.W. *The Law of Athens, Part One: Law of the Family*. Oxford: Oxford University Press, 1968.

Hawley, Richard and Levick, Barbara. *Women in Antiquity: New Assessments*. New York: Routledge and Kegan Paul, 1995.

Hawthorne, Nathaniel. *Tales and Sketches*. New York: Library of America, 1982.

Hobbes, Thomas. *Leviathan*. Ed. Edwin Curley. Indianapolis, IN: Hackett Publishing. 1994.

Homer. *The Odyssey*. Trans. Robert Fagles. New York: Penguin Books, 1999.

Howland, Jacob. "Re-reading Plato: the Problem of Platonic Chronology." *Phoenix* 45 (Autumn 1991): 189-214.

Huby, Pamela. *Plato and Modern Morality*. New York: Macmillan Press, 1972.

Humphreys, Sarah C. *Anthropology and the Greeks.* Boston: Routledge and Kegan Paul, 1978.

_____. *The Family, Women and Death: Comparative Studies.* 1983. London: Routledge and Kegan Paul, 1993.

Kahn, Charles H. Rev. of *Plato's Cretan City*, by Glenn R. Morrow. *Journal of the History of Ideas* 22 (1961): 418-242.

Kant, Immanuel. *Groundwork of the Metaphysic of Morals.* Trans. H.J. Paton. New York: Harper and Row, 1964.

_____. *Prolegomena to Any Future Metaphysics.* Trans. James W. Ellington. New York: Hackett Publishing, 2001.

Klosko, George. *Development of Plato's Political Theory.* New York: Methuen, 1986.

Kofou, Anna. *Crete: All the Museums and Archeological Sites.* Athens: Ekdotike Athenon, 1990.

Kraut, Richard, ed. *Cambridge Companion to Plato.* New York: Cambridge University Press, 1992.

Kreeft, Peter, ed. *Summa of the Summa.* San Francisco: Ignatius Press, 1990.

Lacey, W. K. *The Family in Classical Greece.* Ithaca: Cornell University Press, 1968.

Lachterman, David R. *The Ethics of Geometry: A Genealogy of Modernity.* New York: Routledge University Press, 1989.

Laks, Andre. "Legislation and Demiurgy: On the Relationship Between Plato's *Republic* and *Laws*." *Classical Antiquity* 9 (October 1990): 209-229.

Levinson, Ronald B. Rev. of *Plato's Cretan City*, by Glenn R. Morrow. *Classical Philology* 57 (January 1962): 132-137.

Locke, John. *A Letter Concerning Toleration.* New York: Hackett Publishing, 1983.

_____. *Second Treatise of Government.* Ed. C.B. Macpherson. New York: Hackett Publishing, 1980.

Lucretius. *On the Nature of Things.* Trans. Walter Englert. Newburyport, MA: Focus Press, 2003.

MacDowell, Douglas M. "The *oikos* in Athenian Law." *Classical Quarterly* 39 (1989): 10-20.

Machiavelli, Niccolo. *The Prince.* Trans. Harvey Mansfield. Chicago: University of Chicago Press, 1998.

Madison, James et al. *The Federalist Papers.* New Rochelle, NY: Arlington House. [N.D.]

Mahdi, Muhsin. *Alfarabi and the Foundation of Islamic Political Philosophy.* Chicago: University of Chicago Press, 2001.

Morrow, Glenn R. "Aristotle's Comments on Plato's *Laws*." Duering and Owen 145-162.

_____. *Plato's Cretan City*. Princeton: Princeton University Press, 1960.

Mueller, Gerhard. *Studien zu den platonischen Nomoi*. Munich: Zetemata 3, 1951; 2nd ed. revised with an additional chapter, 1968.

Nichols, Mary. Rev. of *The Laws of Plato: Translated with Notes and an Interpretive Essay*, by Thomas Pangle. *Ancient Philosophy* 4 (1984): 237-239.

Nietzsche, Friedrich. *Beyond Good and Evil*. Trans. Walter Kaufmann. New York: Random House, 1989.

Nightingale, Andrea. "Writing/Reading a Sacred Text: A Literary Interpretation of Plato's *Laws*." *Classical Philology* 88 (October 1993): 279-300.

North, Helen, ed. *Interpretations of Plato*. Leiden: E.J. Brill, 1977.

_____. Rev. of *Plato's Cretan City*, by Glenn R. Morrow. *Classical World* 54 (February 1961): 185-186.

Okin, Susan Moller. "Philosopher Queens and Private Wives: Plato on Women and the Family." *Philosophy and Public Affairs* 6 (Summer 1977): 345-369. Reprinted in Elshtain (1982) 31-50.

_____. *Women in Western Political Thought*. Princeton: Princeton University Press, 1979.

Oliver, James H. Rev. of *Plato's Cretan City*, by Glenn R. Morrow. *American Journal of Philology* 83 (October 1962): 447-449.

O'Neill, W. Rev. of *Plato's Cretan City*, by Glenn R. Morrow. *The Personalist* 45 (July 1964): 416-417.

P.J.W.N. Rev. of *Plato's Cretan City*, by Glenn R. Morrow. *The Personalist* 42 (October 1961): 581-582.

Pangle, Thomas. *The Laws of Plato: Translated with Notes and an Interpretive Essay*. Chicago: University of Chicago Press, 1980.

Plato. *Dialogues*. Vol. 5. Trans. Benjamin Jowett. Oxford: Clarendon Press, 1892. 5 vols.

_____. *The Laws*. 1926. Trans. R.G. Bury. Cambridge, Mass.: Harvard University Press, 1961.

_____. *The Laws*. Trans. Trevor Saunders. New York: Penguin Press, 1970.

_____. *Opera*. Vol. 5. Ed. John Burnet. Oxford: Oxford University Press, 1987. 5 vols.

Plotinus. *The Enneads*. Trans. Stephen MacKenna. New York: Penguin Books, 1991.

Plutarch. *Lives*. Trans. Dryden and Clough. New York: Modern Library, 1992.

_____. *Moral Essays*. Trans. Rex Warner. London: Penguin Books, 1971.

Pomeroy, Sarah B.. *Families in Classical and Hellenistic Greece.* London: Oxford University Press, 1997.

_____. "Feminism in Book V of Plato's *Republic*." *Apeiron* 8 (1974): 33-35.

_____. *Goddesses, Wives, Whores and Slaves: Women in Classical Antiquity.* New York: Shocken Books, 1975.

_____. "Women's Identity and the Family in the Classical *Polis*." Hawley and Levick 111-121.

Popper, Karl R. *The Open Society and its Enemies.* 1945. New York: Harper and Row, 1962.

Raeder, Hans Henning. *Platons philosophische Entwicklung.* 1905. New York: Arno Press, 1976.

Rider, Bertha Carr. *Ancient Greek Houses.* 1915. Chicago: Argonaut Press, 1964.

Rousseau, Jean-Jacques. *Emile or On Education.* Trans. Allan Bloom. New York: Basic Books, 1979.

_____. *First and Second Discourses.* Trans. Victor Gourevitch. New York: Harper and Row, 1986.

Russell, D.A. Rev. of *Plato's Cretan City*, by Glenn R. Morrow. *Classical Review* 12 (March 1962): 40-42.

Sabine, George H. *History of Political Theory.* 1959. Hinsdale, Ill.: Dryden Press, 1973.

Saunders, Trevor. "Plato's Later Political Thought." Kraut 464-492.

_____. Rev. of *Plato's Cretan City*, by Glenn R. Morrow. *Journal of Hellenic Studies* 82 (1962): 181-182.

Saxonhouse, Arlene W. *Fear of Diversity: the Birth of Political Science in Ancient Greek Thought.* Chicago: University of Chicago Press, 1992.

Scarrow, David S. Rev. of *Plato's Cretan City*, by Glenn R. Morrow. *Ethics: an International Journal of Social, Political and Legal Philosophy* 72 (April 1962): 216-217.

Scruton, Roger. *Reflections on the Revolutions in Eastern Europe.* Boston, MA: Boston University Press, 1991.

_____. *Untimely Tracts.* New York: St. Martins Press, 1987.

Seabury, Paul and Codevilla, Angelo. *War: Ends and Means.* New York: Basic Books, 1989.

Shiell, Timothy C. "The Unity of Plato's Political Thought." *History of Political Thought* 12 (Autumn 1991): 377-390.

Shorey, Paul. "Plato's *Laws* and the Unity of Plato's Thought." *Classical Philology* 9 (1914): 345-369.

_____. Rev. of *Plato's Laws*, edited and translated by R.G. Bury. *Classical Philology* 23 (1928): 403-405.

_____. Rev. of *Plato's Laws*, edited by E.B. England. *Classical Philology* 17 (1922): 153-155.

_____. *The Unity of Plato's Thought*. 1903. Chicago: Archon Books, 1968.

_____. *What Plato Said*. 1933. Chicago: University of Chicago Press, 1968.

Sinclair, T.A. Rev. of *Plato's Cretan City*, by Glenn R. Morrow. *Political Science Quarterly* 76 (September 1961): 439-441.

Skemp, J.B. Rev. of *Plato's Cretan City*, by Glenn R. Morrow. *University of Toronto Quarterly* 31 (April 1962): 394-396.

Slater, Philip E. *The Glory of Hera: Greek Mythology and the Greek Family*. Boston: Beacon Press, 1968.

_____. "The Greek Family in History and Myth." *Arethusa* 7 (1974): 9-44.

Spalding, Matthew, ed. *The Founders' Almanac*. Washington, D.C.: Heritage Foundation, 2001.

Stalley, R.F. *Introduction to Plato's Laws*. Oxford: Basil Blackwell, 1983.

_____. "Persuasion in Plato's *Laws*." *History of Political Thought* 25 (Summer 1994): 157-177.

Stern, Phillip van Doren. *The Life and Writings of Abraham Lincoln*. 1940. New York: Modern Library, 2000.

Strauss, Barry S. *Fathers and Sons in Athens: Ideology and Society in the Era of the Peloponnesian War*. Princeton: Princeton University Press, 1993.

Strauss, Leo. *Argument and Action of Plato's Laws*. Chicago: University of Chicago Press, 1975.

_____. *The City and Man*. Chicago: University of Chicago Press, 1964.

_____. *Natural Right and History*. Chicago: Chicago University Press, 1953.

_____. *What is Political Philosophy?* Chicago: University of Chicago Press, 1959.

Taran, Leonardo. *Academica: Plato, Philip of Opus and the pseudo-Platonic Epinomis*. Memoirs of the American Philosophical Society, volume 107. Philadelphia, Pa.: American Philosophical Society, 1975.

Taylor, A.E. *Plato: the Man and his Work*. New York: Methuen Press, 1949.

Vanhoutte, M. Rev. of *Plato's Cretan City*, by Glenn R. Morrow. *Revue Philosophique de Louvain* 61 (February 1963): 144-146.

Versenyi, Laszlo. "The Cretan Plato." Rev. of *Plato's Cretan City*, by Glenn R. Morrow. *Review of Metaphysics* 15 (September 1961): 67-80.

Vlastos, Gregory. "The Theory of Social Justice in the *Polis* in Plato's *Republic*." North 1-40.

Weil, R. Rev. of *Plato's Cretan City*, by Glenn R. Morrow. *Revue des Etudes Grecques* 74 (1961): 499-503.

Welles, C. Bradford. Rev. of *Plato's Cretan City*, by Glenn Morrow. *American Historical Review* 66 (April 1961): 708-709.

Wender, Dorethea. "Plato: Misogynist, Paedophile and Feminist." *Arethusa* 6 (Spring 1973): 75-90.

Willetts, R.F. *Cretan Cults and Festivals*. New York: Barnes and Noble, 1962.

Woodhouse, C.M. *George Gemistos Plethon: The Last of the Hellenes*. Oxford: Clarendon Press, 1986.

Wycherly, R.E. *Stones of Athens*. Princeton: Princeton University Press, 1978.

_____. *Philosophie der Greichen in ihrer geschichtlichen Entwicklung*. Leipzig: Fues' Verlag, 1875.

Zeller, Eduard. *Platonische Studien*. Tubingen: C.F. Osiander, 1839.

Zimmern, Sir Alfred E. *The Greek Commonwealth: Politics and Economics in Fifth-Century Athens*. 1911. London: Oxford University Press, 1947.

Index